CUS

21 Marke

Assets

5 Habits

D1199981

How Good Attorneys Become Great Rainmakers:

A Breakthrough Referral Marketing Process

Mark Powers and Shawn McNalis

How Good Attorneys Become Great Rainmakers:
A Breakthrough Referral Marketing Process

Publisher: Atticus Ink
345 S. Highland St.
Mount Dora, FL 32726 USA
www.atticusonline.com
www.atticusrainmakers.com

Portions of this document have been previously published in *Lawyers Weekly, Lawyers USA* and in a syndicated series of articles entitled, "Rainmaking Lessons."

Cover design by Leanne Thomas

Page layout by Creative Business Design, LLC

ISBN: **978-1-61584-081-6**

12 11 10 09 08 5 4 3 2 1

Table Of Contents

About The Authors

Mark Powers, president of Atticus, has been coaching attorneys on practice management and marketing for nearly 20 years. An international speaker, Mark has coached thousands of attorneys in his work with the Law Society of Scotland, the American Bar Association, and Bar Associations in Arizona, Florida, Massachusetts, Mississippi, New York, Connecticut, South Carolina, Texas, and the Midwest. Mark also conducts a program titled "Rainmakers" for attorneys across the country who wish to build client-development skills, and a boot camp–style program called the "Practice Builder" for solo, small, and mid-size firm practitioners. In addition, he leads troubleshooting retreats that deal with partnership issues, difficult retirement scenarios, client development, and productivity problems. Mark is known for his expert advice on legal marketing, and in 1995 he co-authored *The Making of a Rainmaker: An Ethical Approach to Marketing for Solo and Small Firm Practitioners,* published by the Florida Bar. He has been featured in publications such as *Lawyers Weekly USA, Money Magazine, Journal of the American Bar Association, Journal of the Law Society of Scotland, Florida Bar News,* and *Massachusetts Bar Association Lawyers Journal,* among many others. Prior to beginning work with the legal profession, Mark served as the chief executive officer and president of a multimillion-dollar, privately held company, and as a corporate manager in a Fortune 500 company based in Connecticut. A native of Massachusetts, he has a master's degree from Northeastern University. His undergraduate studies include bachelor's degrees in economics and criminal justice.

Shawn McNalis is a former Imagineer with the Walt Disney Company and credits her 15-year career with Disney for her creative, collaborative approach to advising attorneys. In partnership with Mark Powers for 12 years, Shawn is a senior practice advisor, director of curriculum and trainer for Atticus. With Mark she co-authored *The Making of a Rainmaker,* commissioned and published by the Florida Bar in 1995, and *Time Management for Attorneys: A Lawyer's Guide to Decreasing Stress, Eliminating Interruptions & Getting Home on Time,* published in conjunction with the ABA in 2008.

Currently a columnist for *Lawyer's USA,* Shawn has authored and co-authored numerous articles on law practice management that have appeared in the ABA's *Law Practice Management Magazine, Journal of the Association of Legal Administrators, ABA Family Law Section Magazine, The Florida Bar News, The Lawyer's Competitive Edge, The Florida Bar Workers Compensation Section Journal,* and *Massachusetts Bar Journal,* among many others. A faculty member of the Massachusetts Bar Association Institute in 1998 and past coach for the *Orlando Sentinel's* "Career Makeover" column, she was a contributing author for the *Association of Legal Administrators Online Encyclopedia,* published in 2002. Shawn has been a featured speaker at meetings of the Law Society of Scotland, the New York State Bar Association, the Florida Bar Association, the Massachusetts Bar Association, the South Carolina Bar, and the 2003 Coaching Convention in Tokyo.

Acknowledgments

We gratefully acknowledge each and every Atticus client who allowed us to use their marketing experiences and client development lessons as inspirational anecdotes and cautionary tales. Without their input, feedback and in-the-trenches perspective, this book would not be grounded in reality. We thank them for sharing their experiences, both good and bad.

Thanks also to Carole Warshaw and Jane Trimble of Creative Business Design for their excellent proofreading, page design and layout skills. We appreciate their efforts to make this book more visually interesting and easy to navigate. Medea Minnich deserves our thanks for her indexing skills.

We'd also like to acknowledge the copy editing, fact-checking, and research provided by Molly McCormick. Kelly McCormick we thank for giving us the idea of breaking down our Rainmaking approach into a collection of Assets and Habits that could be 'acquired' by our clients and readers. The concept of this book and the Rainmakers program grew from that kernel of an idea.

Also appreciated are the many contributions of the Rainmakers Resource Assistants who work one-on-one with our Rainmakers to provide them with access to all the materials and support they need in their quest to better their client development skills: Chris Lee, Heather Harris and Cindy Moore.

A special thanks is owed to Henry Harlow for authoring Asset #6, and to our Atticus Practice Advisors: Patrick Wilson, Glenn Gutek, Glenn Finch, Cammie Hauser, Nora Bergman, Gary Holstein, and Vinnie Bonazzoli who lead seminars, conduct firm retreats and dole out great advice to Atticus clients across the nation.

INTRODUCTION

The Most Important Marketing Lesson
Go where the fish are, not the fishermen.

The most important marketing lesson I ever received came, not from a marketing guru, but from a professional fisherman named Dave Harper. One day, Dave shared with me how his father had taught him to fish. When he was a little boy of eight or nine, his father would take him to the lake, but he wouldn't let him fish. Instead, his dad gave him an assignment. His father told Dave that he had to follow the bank of the lake and study the other fishermen. "Watch what they do and report back to me with the lessons you've learned," he said to Dave. As you might imagine, Dave didn't care for the assignment; he was eager and wanted to fish. But he dutifully took on the task. Over a three month period, each time Dave and his father went fishing, young Dave would study the others and share his observations with his father. Dave noticed that the other fishermen tended to fish in the same areas. He also noticed the differences in their behaviors and personalities: some took the activity very seriously; some others came for a good time with their buddies, drinking for a bit, then fishing for a bit. He discovered that most of the men fished from the shoreline.

Finally, Dave's father decided that he had learned enough from the other fishermen, and proceeded to give him the most important lesson: "Dave," he said, "if you want to be a great fisherman, I don't want you to bother with the other fishermen anymore. From this point on, I want you to go where the fish are and study them."

Dave then proceeded to make this his mission. He read books, experimented with what bait to use for different types of fish, where to cast the lines, at what time of day, for how long, in what parts of the lake, and, most importantly, what activities caught the fish he was targeting.

From a marketing perspective, this lesson is profound. Most attorneys spend very little time truly understanding a client's mindset or perspective. They mostly watch what other attorneys are doing, and emulate them. As Dave put it, they "go where the other fishermen go." If the other attorneys are listed in the *Yellow Pages,* so are they. If the other attorneys attend Bar meetings or Rotary or Kiwanis meetings, so do they.

While observing the behavior of other colleagues is no doubt important, it is also important for an attorney to understand how a prospective client behaves. The average attorney rarely studies the prospective client; he does not identify the type of client that would best suit his practice, nor does he understand what the client's key frustrations are. Attorneys do not study the demographics or psychographics of their clients. They market out of necessity or desperation, and there is little mastery or strategy behind their efforts.

Dave Harper is a professional. When he throws his fishing line into the water, he has a very high probability of not only catching a fish, but the exact type he is fishing for. If he is fishing for trout, he uses special bait, goes out into the habitat the trout occupy, drops the line at the most appropriate depth, and moves the bait in a way that the trout will recognize as food.

The difference in Dave's approach to fishing and most attorneys' approach to marketing is that most attorneys are sitting behind their desks waiting for the clients to come to them. This would be like Dave standing on shore, expecting the fish to jump into his arms!

This book approaches marketing as a process of mastery and will help you with one of the most important marketing lessons you'll ever get: Go where the clients are, not the other attorneys. This book is about mastery and how good attorneys become great marketers.

The Vicious Cycle

You wouldn't be reading this book if you didn't think marketing was important to your practice. But most attorneys have no idea just how critical marketing is to their personal success. You understand that without retaining good clients or originating new clients, you won't have a practice, and that Rainmakers hold the proverbial cards in the law firm. But the real cost of not mastering how to attract new clients on a predictable basis is the accompanying stress and 'survival mentality' that develops.

This is the ongoing stress that comes from not knowing where your next client is coming from, having to negotiate fees, or working with clients that are not the right fit for your practice. The result is too many low value cases, and the inability to produce profitable work. It's a prescription for extreme stress and ensures that the most valuable resource in the firm – you, the attorney – are too busy with C and D level cases to market for better paying clients. Poor decisions around client selection account for the vast majority of frustrations that attorneys experience on a daily basis.

Becoming selective about the clients you accept into your practice is one of the most important practice management lessons you will learn in this book. Very few practice management issues have such an important impact on your cash flow, stress, or quality of life. We know it's difficult to deal with management issues, constant staff interruptions, and demanding clients. These issues alone leave little time to actually get production done, let alone find time to effectively market for better cases. Unfortunately, if prospective clients are not knocking at your front door in great enough numbers, it's impossible to be selective. This problem feeds upon itself and becomes a vicious cycle, with you working harder and longer for clients that don't appreciate your services. You end up living in hope: hope that someday it will all work out. It won't. Not unless you change something. But what?

The Four Levels Of Competency

At some time in your life you didn't know what you didn't know about how to practice law. It may sound odd, so read that sentence again. It means that you were, at one time, unaware of what it would take to become a practicing attorney. You didn't know what it would take and you probably didn't much care. You were *unconsciously incompetent.*

The day you decided to become a lawyer, however, something changed – you still didn't know how to practice law, but you were now invested in the idea and very aware of what you didn't know. At that moment you became *consciously incompetent.*

So you decided to enroll in law school to learn what you didn't know. You concentrated your efforts and developed a game plan. The school of your choosing had a curriculum for you to follow and sold you books – lots of books. You went to class, listened to the instructors and took the exams. You developed your knowledge over those years until you graduated. Perhaps you worked as an intern during your school years to develop additional experience. At some point you took the bar exam and passed. The state then agreed that you were *consciously competent* to practice law. You knew that you knew how to practice law. You just had to prove it to everyone else.

Over the years, as you practiced your profession and gained experience, it became less necessary to refer to your law books or senior attorneys for the answers. Soon others were turning to you. As the years went on you developed *unconscious competency:* meaning that your mental database of substantive, legal knowledge, combined with your experience, was so highly developed that you knew the answers to many legal questions almost without thinking. In your pursuit of legal knowledge, you've passed through the four levels of competency:

- Unconscious incompetence
- Conscious incompetence
- Conscious competence
- Unconscious competency

All disciplines offer a similar route to knowledge. Marketing is no different. Doesn't it make sense that you would apply the same logical progression to developing your marketing skills? That is what this book is about: helping you work through all the levels of competency to ultimately become a highly conscious and very competent Rainmaker.

Marketing Wealth

In your personal life you build financial wealth by acquiring assets: your home, 401K, investment property, stocks and bonds. And, if you've done well, you've developed a few good habits along the way: saving more than you spend, paying down debt, and balancing your checkbook. In the same way, good Rainmakers build marketing wealth by acquiring marketing Assets and Habits. Atticus has identified 21 Marketing Assets and Five Marketing Habits that are the foundation of every successful Rainmaker. With this book you have the opportunity to develop and acquire these Assets and Habits to become an extraordinary Rainmaker yourself.

Each of the 21 Marketing Assets represents some aspect of client development. These are the most leveraged marketing activities, tools, or methods employed by great Rainmakers. The Five Marketing Habits are activities that accelerate your ability to attract new clients. Each marketing Asset and Habit requires individual attention to achieve, and, like building financial wealth, it may take years to fully realize them. Ultimately you will create a pace that works for you.

Asset #1, for example, *The Top Twenty,* may only take a little research and a few hours to put together. However, Asset #3, *The Marketing Assistant,* could take several months to put in place if you don't have anyone on staff appropriate for the position. Here's our advice: if you hit a road-block while trying to acquire an Asset or Habit, see if you can delegate the remaining Asset-related tasks to someone else in the office. Sometimes it helps to enlist the assistance of others to move beyond obstacles. If that fails, enroll an Accountability Partner from among your team. Many of our clients work on several Assets at once — or even a combination of Assets and Habits — as there will be lag time in the achievement of some and a few will require work to be done by others. To make this process work for you, focus first on those Assets that will have the biggest impact on your ability to earn referrals, and set a pace for yourself that's slightly challenging.

Your Rainmaker Profile

I magine for a moment that you want to get into better physical shape. You might join a gym, and if it's a good gym the first thing they'll do is establish your baseline biometric. This means they'll check your weight, body fat, waist measurement and height to establish your base-line. In this program, your Rainmaker Profile establishes your baseline marketing metrics. In addition to providing you with a baseline market-ing score, it ranks you in one of the following categories:

- Mistmaker
- Rainmaker Level I
- Rainmaker Level II
- Rainmaker Level III
- Master Rainmaker

There are two ways of determining your baseline score. First, in Appendix #2 of this book, there is a hardcopy version of the Rainmaker Profile for self-scoring purposes. It only takes a few minutes to fill in and will give you your starting rank. Second, you can call Atticus at 888-644-0022 for a full Rainmaker Diagnostic. No matter how you do it, prior to starting the Atticus Rainmaker process, it is a good idea to get your baseline score. From there the game consists of adding Assets and Habits to your profile, increasing your score and becoming a great Rainmaker.

To further help you in this quest, we've included a series of audio files that you can access on our Web site with the purchase of this book. These recordings feature discussions, interviews and accounts of other attorneys working through each of the Assets and Habits. To take advantage of these additional resources, go to **www.atticusrainmakers. com**, click on the image of this book and follow the prompts to download the audio files. For access, you will need your e-mail address and the code **RM521**. You can download the recordings to your MP3 player or computer and listen to them at your convenience – or whenever you need a little more motivation.

Throughout the book, we will plant "hints" which offer additional information or support on each discussion. At the end of each chapter we have provided clear-cut instructions on how to successfully acquire and incorporate each Asset, and forms that you can use to develop your Rainmaking abilities.

The Pathway To Becoming A Rainmaker

Throughout the last 20 years of working with attorneys, Atticus has proven that there is a simple and direct path to becoming a successful Rainmaker and attracting new clients on a predictable basis.

> • First, as our professional fisherman pointed out, you must understand who your prospective clients are and who surrounds them as Referral Sources. As you answer the basic question of who your target client is, and identify the relevant Referral Sources, you'll find your marketing activities begin to make sense. And these ef-

forts will become much more successful as you leverage your time by spending it with those who are most likely to send referrals.

- Second, it's important to be clear about what you can say to a Referral Source or prospective client that will best attract them to your practice. There are a series of strategic conversations that are important for you to learn, given that you don't want to sound desperate or like an insincere salesperson.
- Third, you need to develop a basic action plan, congruent with your individual personality and style that lays out how and when you will connect with your Referral Sources on a consistent basis.
- Fourth, it's imperative you track your results so you can determine which of your efforts are working and which need to be adjusted. As with any process, as you learn what is most effective, you'll do more of what works and discard what does not.
- The final step is to create an Accountability Partner who will support and motivate you in your marketing efforts and commitments – especially for those moments when you'd prefer to do anything other than marketing.

This book will walk you through this process by outlining, step-by-step, the 21 Marketing Assets and the Five Marketing Habits that Rainmakers acquire on their way to becoming successful. Each Asset is broken down into digestible, easy-to-follow concepts offering you the chance to learn and assimilate the information even when you lead a very busy life. With the Rainmaker Profile, you'll have a way of measuring your ability as a Rainmaker and can put together a practical action plan to achieve the results you want.

We can tell you from years of experience and working with thousands of Rainmakers that every attorney reading this book has the ability to become a successful Rainmaker. When you apply the principles and methodologies in this book, you will be able to bring clients in your door on a predictable basis – and have a practice that serves you instead of enslaves you.

How Good Attorneys Become Great Rainmakers

A Breakthrough Referral
Marketing Process

THE FIVE MARKETING HABITS

Habits are first cobwebs, then cables.
~ Spanish Proverb

Embracing Practice-Building Habits

If *you want to learn how successful people became successful, examine their habits. Habits consistently adhered to are the underpinnings of how successful you are. The successful Rainmaker, for example, routinely thanks Referral Sources for the clients they send. If they fail to send a thank you card or express their gratitude upon receiving a referral, it would bother them the same way that failing to brush their teeth would bother them. Once powerful habits are in place, they compel the person that elected to cultivate them into action.*

What can you do to become a successful Rainmaker? Adopt new habits. Embrace new routines and change your customary way of approaching client development. Each of the Five Marketing Habits described below was selected because it will accelerate your ability to generate referrals and new clients.

Habit 1: Three Marketing Contacts A Week

In Atticus' early years, as we studied Rainmakers, we noticed that successful ones averaged three contacts with Referral Sources on a weekly basis, while those who struggled to bring in new clients averaged one marketing contact. And that was in a good week!

The first Marketing Habit, Three Marketing Contacts a Week, is probably the best example of how adopting a new habit can dramatically alter your effectiveness as a marketer. This level of focused client development activity will be effective even for a novice. Since marketing is primarily a numbers game, the volume of people you interact with counts. Once employed, this new habit delivers on its promise and is one of the most powerful new routines you can adopt.

In order for a marketing contact to be considered substantial, it must be long enough – 20 minutes to 1 hour - to allow you to connect with the person and develop further rapport. Generally, lunches, dinners, longer phone calls, and face-to-face meetings fall into this category.

Three contacts a week is a marketing plan in a nutshell. You have very limited time, so be sure to focus your attention on your Top Twenty Referral Source List (Asset #1) first, and then those on your Farm Team (Asset #14). If you do nothing more than this, by the end of a year you'll have 150 marketing contacts to your credit.

When you begin to recognize that you don't want to be taking the same five or six people to lunch week after week, you have to meet new people to put on your list of contacts and then into the rotation. So, just setting this standard and attempting to stick with it forces you to be very proactive in seeking new contacts. All of a sudden, your monthly Bar meeting, for example, begins to look less like a boring luncheon and more like a good place to meet new people. And, if you are invited to sit on a committee or a board – it may have added appeal due to the pressing need to meet more people to feed into your lunch rotation.

Research on building intimacy indicates that after 12 minutes of personal conversation, the two conversing begin to feel a connection. Double that and you start to build the foundation for a real relationship. This Habit is the part of marketing that requires an investment of your time – there are no shortcuts when it comes to building rapport with another human being.

Conversations between two relative strangers develop fairly predictably at the beginning, with each person presenting their best side for evaluation by the other. To begin the process, a friendly exchange of information is necessary to give a potential Referral Source an adequate chance to assess you and begin to establish your trustworthiness. Typically, the conversation will center first on the people, school or firm experiences that the two of you might have in common.

Perhaps it will be the person who introduced you that is discussed at first with questions such as, "How do you know so-and-so?" From there it will branch off in tangents to cover new subjects as you search for further areas of commonality. Questions such as, "Where did you go to law school?" might arise if your lunch companion is an attorney. Or, "Knowing I was going to meet you today, I looked at your firm's Web site. I was impressed. How long have you worked there?" might come up (by the way, researching the person you are to meet, ahead of time, is generally perceived as flatter-

TIP

A conversation with a contact should last a minimum of 12 minutes and longer whenever possible. More time spent in conversation allows you to develop a sense of what we call, "know, like and trust," with the other person.

ing). Each of you will talk about yourselves, ask questions about each other and search for common ground.

It's helpful to remember that nearly all of your marketing activities involve engaging and interacting with other human beings. The only solitary activities associated with marketing are the planning and scheduling you or your Marketing Assistant must do to coordinate the rest of your efforts. During each of your three weekly contacts, you'll be exercising different conversational strategies which are associated with different Assets:

• Ask questions that show an interest in a potential Referral Source's life. As you are getting to know them, do 30% of the talking and 70% of the listening. After you know them well, and they've sent you referrals, interview them about the level of service you provide (Asset #8).

• Tell stories that illustrate how you work and how you've helped clients in the past (Asset #5).

• Be straightforward about what you do and the benefits of working with you. Use your Laser Talk (Asset #4), or laser phrases, frequently.

• Talk to media contacts and comment on hot topics (Asset #7).

To embrace the Three Contacts a Week Habit is to just get out there and do it. You'll see this Habit referred to over and over in everything we write about marketing. Why do we emphasize it so much? We find that setting and following a standard such as having three marketing contacts a week is not only a powerful predictor of success, but many other Rainmaking habits fall into place when you commit to this level of activity.

To help you maintain a minimum of three purposeful marketing contacts per week with a network of Referral Sources, you'll likely need a Marketing Assistant (Asset #3) to support your efforts. Your assistant will schedule

TIP

Make at least three marketing contacts a week to increase your odds of establishing good Referral Sources. Try weaving personal questions into conversations with Referral Sources and clients in order to deepen your connections.

lunches, dinners and catered events, plan office parties, gather intelligence on your referrer's preferences, and purchase gifts for acknowledging referrals. Most of the attorneys we know say that the cost of an assistant has paid for itself in increased business.

Habit 2: Asking For Referrals

It is important to regularly let clients know, either at the conclusion of a case or somewhere in the middle, that your practice thrives on referrals from people like them. Ask and you shall receive. There is a direct correlation between the number of times one asks for referrals and the directness with which they make the request to the number of referrals one receives.

Simply asking clients to remember you can also be a very effective avenue for increasing your client referrals. Certainly, delivering a high level of service to clients will earn a high percentage of referrals: people who like you will tell others. But what about those who use you, like you, then forget about you when their grandmother slips or the neighbor is bitten by a dog? While you're working with clients, plant a few seeds to let them know you're open to referrals, and you will see a difference.

An attorney in the Atticus Rainmaker

TIP

Build rapport with your potential referral sources by asking how you can help develop new business for them – this should inspire them to ask the same of you.

Program started using a new verbal strategy when talking with clients: he began mentioning, a few times each day, that his firm was built on referrals, and asked clients to send their friends and family. As a result, he's seen his referrals from clients jump dramatically. Afraid that people would find it offensive, he was initially reluctant to try this approach. But once he found a comfortable way to mention that he was open to referrals, no one seemed turned off. This was an easy way for him to tap a market that existed just beyond his reach: the family and friends of his past and present clients.

What about your own friends, family and Referral Sources – people you

TIP Don't be aggressive when looking for referrals. Instead of asking for a referral directly, let your client know you are open to building a business relationship.

Can you send me some clients?" lacks finesse. The best referral requests start out as compliments or expressions of gratitude – this is the secret – and are said in a way that is friendly and service-oriented.

To show you what we mean, we've gathered examples used by successful Rainmakers when they want to request referrals. Some of their language may sound too formal to you, some too familiar, but all of it conveys the right message and does so without sounding pushy. To begin to adopt this powerful Habit, take a look at what other attorneys say, and then modify the phrases to fit your situation and specific way of speaking.

This first group of statements is intended for use with your clients. Most Rainmakers use them at the conclusion of a case, though there might be points during a case when comments like these are appropriate. The better marketers make it a point to take well-connected clients out to lunch and conduct informal exit surveys. Before they finish lunch, they deliver their version of the statements listed below:

• Steve, we've really enjoyed working with you on this matter. Our practice has been built on referrals from satisfied (or good, or great) clients like you. Please don't hesitate to mention our name to others we might be able to help.

• Pat, I really enjoy working with cli-

have an existing personal relationship with and hope will send you business on a regular basis? Is it appropriate to come right out and ask them for referrals? For some attorneys, the answer is no. They find it uncomfortable to ask clients, existing Referral Sources, family and friends for referrals. They don't want to sound desperate or too aggressive. They don't want to sound like they're soliciting business.

But you don't have to sound desperate to market yourself. The key to developing this small but powerful Rainmaking Habit lies in the ability to ask the question in a way that doesn't come across as overly aggressive. The language you use makes all the difference, not only in your own comfort level, but also in how the message is received.

Blurting out, "I need business," or

ents like you and I'd appreciate it if you would mention our firm to anyone else who could use our assistance.

• Grace, I thank you for your business and would appreciate it if you passed my name on to anyone you think I could help.

• Referrals from good clients like you, Carole, are the foundation of my practice. Thank you for your business and feel free to recommend us to others.

• Ben, I built my practice by working with great clients like you; please let us know if we can be of further help to you or assist your friends or family in any way.

• Judy, if you feel we served you well, please let others know what we can do for them.

TIP

Remember: the best referral requests start out as compliments or expressions of thanks.

• Rachel, it was a pleasure getting to know you. Please keep in mind we'd be happy to help any family or friends of yours who need legal services in the future.

You can take a similar tack when talking with your Referral Sources. Create the opportunity by asking them out to lunch to thank them for a client they've recently referred, or, if you haven't been good at thanking your Referral Sources along the way, all the clients they've referred in the past:

• Thank you for thinking of us with your many referrals, Tom. Though we're not good at saying it, we really appreciate the clients you send and make every attempt to take great care of them.

• I've enjoyed working with all the clients you've sent, Chris. Please don't hesitate to send anyone else you work with who could use our services.

• Pam, thanks for sending Hugh over to see me. I really enjoyed working with him and would certainly do my best to help any of your other clients.

• Please don't hesitate to send us clients – we're never too busy to take care of anyone you might refer, Larry. In fact, my receptionist has special instructions to interrupt me immediately whenever one of your referrals calls.

If you've briefly met a potential Referral Source and want to cultivate them, but don't quite know what to say to initiate the relationship, use the following script to get you over the hump:

• Why don't we get together and go out to lunch next week? I'd enjoy learning more about your practice and could tell you a little bit about mine…

• I'd like to invite you over to my of-

TIP

Taking Referral Sources out to lunch doesn't cost much and is a good way to show your appreciation for their efforts. Select a restaurant convenient to your Referral Sources to reduce their travel time.

fice to learn more about what you do and see if there's a way we can network in the future…

Yet another situation in which having a few simple scripts can be helpful: you have a friend who has the ability to send you clients, but, for some reason, never has. First, make sure they know what you do. You'd be surprised how many of your friends and acquaintances don't know exactly what you do. Once they understand (see Asset# 4, *The Laser Talk*), use one of the following scripts to take the relationship to the next level:

• John, I'd enjoy building more of a business relationship with you to see if I can be of some service to your clients in the future. Why don't we meet for lunch next week and talk about it?

• Jason, I've built my practice on referrals from a lot of people in this community and it would be a privilege to work with anyone you think could use my services. Why don't we get together next week and talk about it?

These brief, scripted phrases and statements are not aggressive, but have the power to produce significant results for your practice. Whether that means you motivate your clients to send referrals or you turn a casual friend into a friendly Referral Source, you possess the power to make these changes by uttering the right words at the right time. This is the beauty of a word-of-mouth marketing approach.

Don't rely upon the client, friends or potential Referral Sources to automatically know you welcome referrals. Many professionals are savvy about this, but many of the other people you work with or meet may not be. It is up to you to educate them. Don't rely on the Blanche DuBois method of marketing: "I've always depended on the kindness of strangers." Master the power of your language to take you where you want to go.

• *Never Eat Alone* by Keith Ferrazzi

• *Personal Village* by Marvin Thomas, MSW

• *Developing Knowledge-Based Client Relationships* by Ross Dawson

• for more book recommendations, go to *www.atticusrainmkers.com*

Habit 3: Sharpening The Saw

You have done a great job up to this point of developing the mindset and perspective of a good lawyer. Now it is time to start learning to think like a Rainmaker. Reading a marketing book, article, or attending a marketing workshop once per quarter will help to keep you on top of your game. Staying current with the latest marketing ideas can help to keep you in action and motivated to promote your firm. Your habits and skills need constant reinforcement to stay sharp. You can find marketing seminars and workshops through community colleges, local business development organizations, online courses and, of course, your Bar Association.

Here is a list of suggested reading to help you sharpen your edge in your practice marketing :

Habit 4: The Thank You Habit

While Asset #21, *A Thank You System,* is designed to ensure you have all of the resources to thank your Referral Sources, this Thank You Habit represents the act of acknowledgment that is so important to your marketing efforts.

Thanking your Referral Sources each and every time they send a referral will reinforce your referral base. Even if you don't end up working with the referred client, thanking your Referral Sources is vital to maintaining your referral relationships. You must acknowledge any attempt to send you business because you want to reinforce their urge to do so. Depending on the situation, this can be done through cards, letters, phone calls, gifts, lunches, dinners, gift certificates or site visits. Asset #21 gives you a system to ensure that this process becomes ingrained in your office protocol.

Habit 5: The Adding Names Habit

Adding new names to your contact list will give you a great base to grow your practice and will support your goal of having three contacts a week.

To take on this new Habit, you will need to add at least five new contacts each month to your list.

This doesn't mean that the new name on your list is a great Referral Source, but now they are part of your referral network. If you don't have enough people in your network, you will need to make an effort to meet more through Bar Association activities, community efforts, service clubs and charitable organizations. Remember to join only those organizations in which you can be authentically interested. People will be more interested in you if you're enjoying your association and are genuinely involved in the cause. Though we suggest you keep an eye open for those charities your Referral Sources favor, don't join them if they are organizations you can't legitimately support.

The traditional way most lawyers are comfortable marketing their services – through word-of-mouth referrals – is still the best way to gain new clients. Clients referred to your practice tend to be more loyal and less price-sensitive than those who come from any other source. These are clients who have already decided they want to work with you when they walk through your door.

If your list of contacts is too small to sustain and grow your practice (we believe it takes 20 good Referral Sources to do the job), and you don't want to be taking the same five or six people to lunch week after week, you have to capitalize on every opportunity to meet new people. And not just any kind of people – you specifically want to meet people who are positioned in such a way that they have real potential to become new sources of business.

To qualify, they must see or be involved with the kinds of people who need your services on a regular ba-

> **TIP**
>
> How often have friends sent referrals to attorneys who do what you do? Don't assume that your clients, friends or family understand that you rely on referrals to build your business. It is up to you to let them know.

sis. This is why other attorneys often qualify as superior Referral Sources -- they consistently see clients who need more than they have to offer.

If, for example, you recognize that other attorneys are a good potential source of business for you, all of a sudden your monthly Bar meeting may look less like a boring luncheon and more like a good place to meet people. And, if you are invited to sit on a committee within the Bar, or on a board for an association involving attorneys – it may have added appeal due to the pressing need to meet more people to add to your list. Make it a point to initiate conversation with everyone in the group and invite select members to lunch or to see your office.

A technique that works for almost every practice area is this: when seeking new referral relationships, ask your existing Referral Sources for introductions to others they think would be good potential Referral Sources for you. You may be surprised by how willing your current Referral Sources are to help you network with people they know.

If no introductions are possible, or if asking for them would be awkward in your particular situation, join trade organizations that are likely to be made up of your targeted Referral Sources. Write articles for their journals. Attend their conferences and speak at their meetings. By making your expertise known among your target influencers, you will position yourself to start receiving more of the referrals you seek.

Raising funds for charitable organizations is a great way to not only fund worthy causes, but to meet new people. Likewise with board memberships: initiate lunch with everyone on the board who looks like a good prospect as a Referral Source.

The opportunities to meet new people – the kinds of people who are well-positioned to send good clients – are all around you. Marketing your services one-on-one through word-of-mouth referrals is still the best way to gain new clients.

Growing a practice requires that you market yourself. Your willingness to grow as a professional and push beyond your comfort zone drives the growth of your practice. Growth means survival, and Rainmaking is one of those activities you learn by doing. All it takes is a willingness to see your practice as a client-centered, service-driven business. This approach has proven to be an effective solution to help reluctant marketers become more successful Rainmakers.

In the rest of this book we'll explore the 21 Rainmaking Assets, discussing each one in depth. These are all the attributes you need to acquire in order to graduate from a mist-maker to a Rainmaker. The different sections are loaded with tips, techniques, examples and new perspectives to help you step beyond the client development efforts you've tried in the past. With continued attention to adopting and integrating the 5 Habits and the 21 Assets to come, you'll learn the skills and discipline necessary to successfully market your practice. The sky's the limit!

ASSET #1

THE TOP TWENTY

Friendship, 'the wine of life,'" said Boswell, "should, like a well-stocked cellar, be thus continually renewed." And Dr. Johnson added to this "A man, Sir, should keep his friendships in constant repair. ~ Samuel Johnson

Cultivating Your Referral Sources

Figuring out who sends you your best business is the first step in building your Rainmaking skills and acquiring your first Asset. It's no accident that the Top Twenty is the first Rainmaking Asset on the list. Identifying and cultivating those people who send you your best business is the most important thing you can do to build your practice, and lays the groundwork for most of your future client development efforts.

If all of your Referral Sources were created equal, you wouldn't have to think about this too much. They'd all send you a steady stream of high quality work and just the kind of clients with whom you enjoy working. Unfortunately, that's not the way it usually works. We know from working with thousands of attorneys in several countries that there's typically a wide variation in the quality of your Referral Sources and the cases they send. Some are far from equal in terms of the amount and quality of work that they refer. To be a successful Rainmaker, it's important to know who these people are and what kind of referrals they send.

Many attorneys affect an all-too-casual attitude toward their Referral Sources. During a recent consultation, a civil trial attorney commented to us, "I've never written down who my best Referral Sources are." He came to us interested in expanding his firm and was exploring what he needed to focus on first. "Don't misunderstand me." He continued, "I basically know who refers to me – I just keep track of them in my head."

Unfortunately, your head is not the best place to keep such important information. We hear things like this all the time and it usually indicates the attorney isn't really keeping track of the people who have sent business over the years. Further discussion with this attorney revealed, not surprisingly, that he's been lax about acknowledg-ing people who send clients, and consequently doesn't retain Referral Sources long-term – other than a core group of colleagues with whom he attended law school.

The dangerously casual attitude typified by this client and other novice Rainmakers indicates they dramatically undervalue the contribution made by their best Referral Sources, and do so at their own peril. Your Referral Sources are a group of individuals who have kept your practice alive and deserve to be treated with great respect.

Your Top Twenty

As we said before, however, not all of your Referral Sources are created equal. To help you distinguish the best Referral Sources from those less desirable, imagine for a moment that there are two tiers of Referral Sources. The top tier, the Top Twenty, was originally referred to by Dan Sullivan, the Strategic Coach, as your Top Twenty Percent. His theory may have been based on the Pareto Principle, a scientific phenomenon first observed by the Italian economist Vilfredo Pareto.

While working in his professional capacity as an economist, Pareto observed that 80 percent of the property in London, where he was residing at the time, was owned by only 20 percent of the people. Apparently fascinated by the idea that a small part of a whole is more powerful or productive or significant than the whole itself, Pareto began to wonder if this ratio was a recurring theme in other areas of the natural world. Upon observing that in his garden 80 percent of his peas came from only 20 percent of his plants, he furthered his research and discovered this ratio occurred in almost every aspect of the natural world as well as in human society.

Interestingly enough, as Dan Sullivan observed, it applies to your Referral Sources as well. If you look at the group of people who send you business, you'll likely find that 80 percent of your referrals come from about 20 percent of the group. We've done this exercise repeatedly with our clients over the years and have never been disappointed by its accuracy. Your

Top Twenty are those Referral Sources who are the most active and send you your highest quality business: the kind of matters you most prefer and the types of clients you most enjoy. In this productive group are the Referral Sources that consistently send potential clients with significant cases and send them most frequently.

So what does this mean to you? Most of you will have acquired a small group of referrers who fit within this category. Since you don't have a lot of time to spend in your client development activities and should prioritize your efforts, targeting this group of people is critical to your growth. These Referral Sources have probably kept you in business over the years because their good referrals have resulted in money in your pocket; often, very substantial amounts of money. It's important to know who they are.

What's The Value Of Your Referral Sources?

With 42,000 new attorneys graduating from law school every year, competition is on the rise. If you haven't thought about your Referral Sources as the valuable assets they are – take a moment to calculate their worth. Not just over the course of a year, but over the lifetime of your

TIP

If you have a casual attitude toward those who send you business, and take their referrals for granted, they may disappear one day.

practice. One good Referral Source can send thousands of dollars worth of business every year, and hundreds of thousands over the life of your practice.

This is important. It's likely your firm owes its existence to a handful of people who know you, like you, and have faithfully sent clients over the years. Since most attorneys don't depend entirely on advertising, the very survival of your firm is tied to the continuing good will of these people.

Calculated or not, you've done something to impress them and they demonstrate their trust and confidence in your abilities by continually sending new clients.

Take a moment to think about what you've done to cultivate the relation-

ship you have with each of them. Have you invested time and energy in getting to know them as human beings, over and above the relationship you have with them as colleagues or people with whom you network? Have you befriended their staff? Do you know their spouse or family? This will be discussed in depth later, but for now, keep in mind that the best marketers regard their Referral Sources as friends and make a serious effort to sustain and deepen the relationships over time. Most of the Rainmaking Assets contain activities, ideas, tools or concepts to do just that.

The people in your social and family networks, your colleagues, clients, other professionals and assorted business people in the community make up the bulk of your Referral Sources. Your Web site and any advertising you do also serve as marketing channels which direct business to you, but aren't considered Referral Sources. If you don't have a Top Twenty list and aren't sure exactly who is sending you business, here's how to find out, using the form Discovering Prominent Referral Sources in the back of this Asset:

• Look at all the files on your desk to begin the process. If there are a great many open and active files that aren't on your desk, or your secretary's, but are scattered around the firm, then you should generate a report of all cases, files or clients – ranked by fees – for the last year or two from your bookkeeping software program.

• Go through the list and transfer the names to the Discovering Prominent Referral Sources form. Rank the clients A, B, C or D. An A ranking indicates a great case (profitable to do and the type of work you enjoy) and a great client to work with (cooperative, low-maintenance, possesses reasonable expectations). A case marked D means the exact opposite. Within the limitations of your memory, try to place each case somewhere on this spectrum.

• Finally, using the form, list the Referral Source for each client by searching your memory banks, the intake sheet in the file, or the Referral Source listing in your client database or case management software, if you have it. Then list the type of Referral Source that is responsible, whether it be the *Yellow Pages* or another attorney.

Why would we ask you to rank your clients as A, B, C or D level clients? We will go into this in more depth in Asset #13, but for now, we want to highlight the aforementioned correlation between types of clients and the referrers who send them. Some Referral Sources are connected to lower level referrals because their business, social circle, circumstance or community puts them in contact with more of these kinds of clients. Other Referral Sources are plugged into social groups and situations out of which come great referrals.

To properly focus your marketing efforts on the right Referral Sourc-

> **TIP**
>
> Since most of you don't depend on advertising to acquire clients, the positive word-of-mouth generated by your Referral Sources and clients is, in effect, your advertising campaign. Keep the buzz positive.

es, we recommend you identify the characteristics of your best and most profitable clients, then establish who influences this type of client, and finally, market yourself to these Referral Sources.

In this process, it may help to think of actual clients, or combinations of them, who in your mind exemplify the ideal client for that practice area. Think in terms of their personality, their level of cooperation with you and the type of case they presented.

Maybe they were a small business owner who needed help defending their intellectual property. Perhaps they were an institutional client who needed the kind of work for which you have great systems. Maybe they came with a case that you have a lot of experience with and enjoy doing. Research with our attorney clients has shown us that almost without exception your A and B clients generate 60 to 80 percent of your revenues and only take up 20 to 40 percent of your time. They pay their bills on time, cooperate with you and send referrals. This is a group you want to replicate. Study these individuals and target their peers as primary clients.

Who Influences These A and B Clients?

In the early days of your firm's development, it's appropriate to have slightly lower standards and to do much of the work that comes your way. But given the high emotional and financial toll C and D level clients can exact, and the high burn-out rates associated with attorneys, it's not the kind of long-term strategy which leads to a profitable and well run firm.

It's not a good use of your time to cultivate those Referral Sources who send clients who can't or won't pay, clients with unreasonable expecta-

> **TIP**
>
> Not all potential Referral Sources are created equal — cultivate those who have the greatest potential to send A level work and the type of clients you most prefer to serve.

tions, or clients who need the kind of help you can't provide. To help you separate the best Referral Sources from those less desirable, consider that there are two tiers of Referral Sources.

Analyze Your Top Twenty List

For an eye-opening experiment, analyze your Referral Sources using the Top Twenty Referral Sources form at the end of this chapter. In the left-hand column under "Name," write in each of their names. Hopefully, you've followed our directions on how to discover your Referral Sources mentioned earlier in this chapter (the Discovering Prominent Referral Sources form) – you can use that information for this exercise.

Next, list the type of Referral Source they are, such as Attorney or CPA or Former Client. Then, in the columns marked "Level of Rapport" enter A for high, B for medium or C for low. (You have high rapport with the person if you are very friendly, enjoy each other's company and talk about more than business when you get together.)

Finally, in the far right column, list the amount of revenue that their referrals adds up to on a yearly basis. If you don't know the exact total, have your bookkeeper research these figures or estimate them yourself. When the exercise is complete, you'll have a chart that clearly illustrates your most valuable relationships – both in terms of high rapport and high income. These are the people you should spend most of your time cultivating.

Those Referral Sources with whom you already have high rapport should be put into a maintenance rotation – that is, you should continue to contact them at a rate appropriate for the relationship. For some relationships, this will be two or three times a month; for others, two or three times a quarter. Continue to build upon the rapport that already exists.

Now, take another look at your chart and notice that contained in this analysis is the basis for an additional action plan: For those relationships marked "Low Rapport," if a different level of activity is appropriate. Cultivate these people a little more aggressively based on their receptivity, their availability and their ability to send you more work. Not everyone with whom you have low rapport has equal ability to send future clients, but, with a little thought, you should be able to identify those who can. Invest time and energy into developing your relation-

TIP

When cultivating new referral relationships, focus on the passions, hobbies and interests of the Referral Source. If the Referral Source happens to love the same things you do, your relationship will thrive on your shared passions.

Rainmakers we work with go to great extremes to cultivate their top referral relationships – and do so in a way that connects squarely with that person's hobbies, passions or interests (more on this can be found in Assets #2 and #21).

ship with these people. Add them to the list of people you lunch with on a regular basis.

Caring For Your Top Twenty

The people that make up your Top Twenty list deserve to be recognized as a big part of your marketing plan and treated as such. To be effective in your dealings with them, you must nurture the relationships and build on whatever level of trust and rapport exists between you. This book is dedicated to making you aware of this very important connection, because, without fail, the most successful

A Wise Investment

Take John, an attorney in Texas, who recently discovered that his most significant Referral Source, who seemed to be faltering in his referrals of late, loved single malt Scotch. As luck would have it, John's brother-in-law was a liquor distributor who was happy to recommend a truly impressive bottle of Scotch. John initially balked at taking the time and spending the money, but remembered the nearly $300,000 in business revenue the Referral Source had sent over the last five or six years. Ultimately, it was a small investment for John to do something this man would really appreciate.

In the end, John's Referral Source was impressed that his attorney would go to so much trouble to get him something he loved. Because John went out of his way to buy something so specifically favored by his Referral Source, this small act further cemented their relationship and ensured future referrals. Without fail, the Referral Source always mentions the gift whenever he and John get together.

Ed's Story

When an estate planning attorney in Massachusetts realized he'd never taken a methodical approach to cultivating Referral Sources, he sought our advice. His unscientific marketing approach had served him to a point, but he was ready to take his practice to the next level in terms of developing higher quality clients. Ed already subscribed to the notion of befriending Referral Sources, and made new friends readily, so we didn't have to convince him to adopt a new philosophy, but we did have to teach him to be more strategic. To better assess his situation, we took a look at where his business was currently coming from. Consistent with every other estate planner we've worked with, his typical A clients were high net worth individuals, typically highly paid corporate executives, investors, residential and commercial real estate developers, owners of small and mid-sized businesses, plus a couple of clients who had inherited their wealth. His better B clients were those in the process of building their assets and had great potential for future business. Unfortunately, these A and B level clients only made up a small part of his practice.

Much publicized market research has shown high net worth individuals typically confide in and trust their CPAs more than any other professional. Because of this extraordinary position, CPAs are unsurpassed in their ability to influence clients. Some large CPA firms are capitalizing on this trust by employing attorneys to provide services in-house, but a great many CPAs in small firms still send their clients to independent estate planning attorneys whom they know and trust (this is one referral relationship in which reciprocity is important, so Ed must consider this fact when cultivating CPAs). Ed should continue to target CPAs in small firms who, his research showed, had been good Referral Sources for him.

Ed also discovered that many of his best referrals came from his better A and B level clients – some had recurring work to send and those who didn't were often well-connected and would send their friends. Further research revealed that insurance agents sent him a fair amount of business as well.

After putting all of this together, the game plan for Ed was clear-cut: we recommended he focus on cultivating a few new CPAs, but, more importantly, take very good care of the ones who already sent him business – with a special focus on those CPAs who fed several other attorneys. Since the CPAs' methodology for picking who got their referrals is often discretionary, the idea was to capture more of the business they have to send. Next, we recommended he put new energy into caring for his existing A and B clients in the hope of earning further work and referrals. Last, but not least, we told him to spend more time with the insurance agents on his list. All of these efforts were specifically aimed at producing more A clients by working through those who knew and could refer them. By working backward from the desired result – increasing A and B level clients, and figuring out who influenced them – it wasn't hard to arrive at a targeted plan.

Like Ed's practice, once you've determined who your better clients are, work backward to determine who sends them. You don't want to end up in a situation like the attorney in this next story.

A Rising Tide

There's a saying, "A rising tide lifts all boats." Conversely, when that tide goes out, a lot of people are swept out to sea.

One of our clients, a real estate attorney whom we'll call James, was almost one of them. He came to us a very worried man: his current group of Referral Sources had stopped sending work due to the dramatic decline in housing sales. For the last couple of years, he'd benefited from the stream of real estate work which had flowed to him almost effortlessly and had become dependent on a small handful of Referral Sources – mostly developers. The decline in the developers' business meant a dramatic drop in his revenues. At the edge of panic by the

time he called us, he had downsized his firm and was facing an uncertain future. He'd gotten out of the habit of cultivating the larger pool of his Top Twenty list and had ridden the wave of business that came his way from two or three people.

After hearing his story and assessing what could be done to turn his practice around, we realized that he previously had received referrals from a wide range of sources. His files were rife with old referrals from high end realtors, commercial real estate brokers, past clients and bank vice-presidents. Reconnecting with those referrers whose high end residential and/or commercial clients were still buying, despite the downturn in new developments, looked like the best way to shore up his practice.

For his first assignment we asked him to formally list all of his past Referral Sources. Once this was complete, we discussed each one and ranked them according to their viability. Many of the relationships, though they had grown cold, appeared to be worth reviving.

In addition to the bank of referrers James had cultivated in the past, we also recognized he had a naturally friendly personality. This asset had served him well with the small group of developers he had focused on in the last several years and with his prior Referral Sources. It was still an important asset. His second assignment was to use his outgoing personality to reconnect with old friends (again, the best marketers authentically view their referrers as friends) and make a few new ones.

A motivated man, James soon settled into a routine of attending at least three, and usually many more, marketing events a week. Since he didn't have a lot of legal work to keep him in the office, client development became his top priority. He sometimes met one person for breakfast, another for lunch and yet another for dinner. We encouraged him to keep working through his list as he traveled from one end of town to the other, catching up with people, obtaining introductions and meeting new contacts.

Several months after he had begun this effort, business had picked up, but not enough to match the level of effort he was exerting. To discover the problem we delved a little deeper. James would show up at his various events, have enjoyable conversations and start to rekindle his relationships. He did this part very well. Unfortunately, however, he was not diligent in following up with anyone after meeting them. Attempting to cover a lot of ground, he turned his attention instead to the next meeting or lunch he had scheduled. Though we had emphasized the importance of writing notes (Asset #21) and making follow-up phone calls, James had ignored that aspect of his marketing, hoping it wouldn't actually make much of a difference.

But it does make a difference. Given that James was attempting to warm up old relationships, his need for follow-up was even more critical than someone who had consistently stayed in touch. He was operating in a highly competitive environment where the number of potential clients had shrunk to an alarmingly small number. Since James was trying to reestablish himself with the people who influenced those few clients, his ability to demonstrate his reliability and thoughtfulness would distinguish him among the field of hungry real estate

> **TIP**
>
> Begin your new referral relationships by listening closely to what is being shared in the conversation. Don't dominate the conversation – let the Referral Source tell you about their lives, their families, their hobbies and interests. Listen for common interests.

attorneys. James is not alone in his disregard for following up with Referral Sources after he's made contact. Not following up is one of the most common mistakes made in referral marketing and we see it all the time. Like many of his colleagues, James felt a large percentage of his marketing impact occurred when he was face-to-face with his contact – and he's right. However, referral relationships are built on trust and trust is built by one conversation or lunch or phone call leading to the next, and then the next conversation or lunch or phone call leading to the one after that in an unbroken string of contacts.

By not cultivating these particular friends and Referral Sources for awhile, James had violated the traditional order of things and had the difficult task of warming up relationships that had grown cold from lack of attention.

ing events armed with business cards, notes scrawled on scraps of paper and phone numbers. They make it a ritual to collect information during their meetings so they have reasons to call in the future. They give these notes to their secretaries or Marketing Assistants to post in their client database, knowing they won't remember details for very long. Asset #2 describes how to use a database to maximize your marketing efforts.

Follow-Up Phone Calls And Notes

The impression you make during the first 10 seconds of your call is the most critical. After a day or two has passed, pick up the phone and thank whomever you went to lunch with for taking the time to meet with you. You might start the conversation with something like this:

Build Follow-Up Time Into Your Schedule

Your follow-up plan should be built right into your schedule. Some attorneys book an additional 15 minutes after each marketing event they attend so they can immediately pen a handwritten note to the person with whom they've just met. Keeping a box of note cards within reach of your desk will make this easy. Other attorneys come home from market-

- "Hi, Judy. I'm calling to say thank you for taking the time to meet with me yesterday for lunch. I know you're a busy person and it's not easy for you to break away."

- "Hi, Ben. It was great spending time with you and catching up. Let's do it again sometime soon..."

If you prefer to send a handwritten note, do it! We highly recommend them – especially since so few people write anything by hand anymore. We recommend our clients get blank, fold-over cards with their firm's name and/or logo imprinted on the front. When using them as a thank you card, you might express a sentiment similar to the previous phone conversation prompts:

> • Thanks for meeting me yesterday for lunch. I know how busy you are and I appreciate that you could take the time to catch up. It was great to see you again, and I hope we can do it again before too long.

Feel free to add a personal touch by referring to something that was mentioned, such as:

> • Good luck with your upcoming trial.
>
> Or,
> • I hope your daughter does well in her soccer tournament on Saturday.
>
> Or,
> • Give my regards to your wife, Susan.

Just listening to what people talk about, then referring to it later, is very important. You'll find lots of reasons to initiate another contact with a Referral Source by listening to the problems they are having, by hearing what they are currently frustrated about and by paying attention to any mention of their families, upcoming plans, hobbies, passions or interests. Simple comments will reveal ample information for customizing your handwritten notes or initiating informal follow-up calls – if you are attuned to them.

As mentioned in Habit 1, in the normal course of a conversation it is not unusual to begin by discussing whatever you have in common, such as the person who introduced you, mutual friends, or a common interest you both might share. Then, most conversations move from topic to topic, following tangents as they present themselves. Many would-be Rainmakers start relationships with new potential Referral Sources, but after a while feel they have no basis on which to continue calling or initiating contact. This often happens because they aren't listening closely enough to their contact and lack creativity when it comes to this aspect of marketing. We have one thing to say in response to this dilemma: listen. In marketing situations, do 30 percent of the talking and 70 percent of the listening. Your contacts are giving you plenty of clues – if you will take the time to hear them.

When your potential Referral Source or new contact mentions a book they are reading, a problem with their staff, a love of fine wine or an interest in music, they are giving you clues to what they're interested in. Marketing is not unlike a courtship. Acting on the conversational tidbits revealed gives you perfectly legitimate reasons to pick up the phone and call them, thus adding to the string of ongoing contacts you have with them. String enough of these kinds of conversations together and a relationship will develop.

The Basketball Tickets

Years ago another one of our clients received a small piece of business from a potential Referral Source who was testing the waters; in other words, giving the attorney a try to see how well she handled his referrals. During a phone conversation with the Referral Source, who happened to be a physician, the attorney listened carefully for insight into what his interests were. The doctor happened to mention that his son loved basketball. Luckily, our client happened to jointly own season tickets for the local basketball team. Before the next game, she sent the physician an envelope containing two tickets, accompanied by a note indicating that the tickets were for the doctor and his son. This is another great strategy that anyone can adopt as a means of

getting to know someone better. Physicians are especially difficult to cultivate, but Susan's thoughtful gesture won her a great deal of good will with this particular one.

Here are some samples of informal follow-up conversation starters that are built upon listening carefully to conversations, then finding a reason to follow up:

- By the way, yesterday you mentioned a client who had some zoning questions. When I came back to the office, I did a little research and found some information...

- Yesterday at lunch you mentioned you were looking for a new secretary. One of my staff members knows of a potential candidate...

- Last week at lunch you happened to mention you're interested in photography. I just noticed in the newspaper that there's an exhibit of black and white photography opening on Friday...

- At the Bar meeting two weeks ago you mentioned an interest in the Stearn method of litigation. I happen to have one of his books and thought you might want to read it...

- I found that article we discussed last week after the board meeting. If you are still interested in it, I'll send it over...

- Here's the name of that Web site we were talking about yesterday at lunch...

They will most likely appreciate the information. More important is that the additional interest and effort you've shown will transmit that you were listening and paying attention to them as a person.

Is This A Good Time?

Is your Referral Source interested in talking a little once you get them on the phone? If so, it's a good indication that they are interested in what you're saying. Listen for any cues they might offer. If, when you make your call, the person sounds distracted, rushed or annoyed, pay attention. Don't come across as inconsiderate; acknowledge the importance of their time by saying something like:

> • I'll let you go — you sound busy. I'll call you soon and perhaps we can get together to talk at another time.

The Rule Of Seven

In the world of commercial sales, studies show that 81 percent of sales happen on the fifth contact or later. No statistics exist to show how many times an attorney must be in the presence of a Referral Source for trust to develop and for that trust to translate into business, but, generally speaking, once is not enough. Marvin Thomas refers to this need for consistent cultivation in building relationships, naming it the *Rule of Seven* in his book *Personal Village.* According to the *Rule of Seven,* a person attempting to build relationships in any given group or community must be seen seven times to be considered an "insider."

For Referral Sources to trust you, you must show up inside their world consistently. The lesson for James, and anyone else who struggles to develop and cultivate their Top Twenty, is this: consistent follow-up demonstrates your determination to build relationships with Referral Sources, new or old. As an added incentive, cultivating those you know is more cost-effective than chasing and developing new contacts, once the initial investment of time and energy is made.

To earn Rainmaking Asset #1, The Top Twenty, complete the Discovering Prominent Referral Sources and the Top Twenty form to construct a list of your most productive Referral Sources. Begin to cultivate and deepen your relationships with the people on the list by taking them to lunch, meeting with them or inviting them to join you in other activities. Post this list

**somewhere you can easily access it
and refer to it often when planning
your client development activities.**

Invest in your Top Twenty and you'll
be rewarded with an abundance of
referrals. This list of people is the
foundation needed for future effective marketing efforts.

To help support you in building on
this foundation, there are 20 more
Rainmaking Assets to read, learn
from and incorporate into your client development efforts. Asset #14
Your Farm Team discusses the level of
Referral Sources just below your Top
Twenty list and is an important companion to this chapter.

Coming up in the next section is a discussion of how to remember all the
details about the clients and Referral
Sources you'll be cultivating. When
your memory banks are full, Contact
Management Software saves you the
embarrassment of forgetting all the
little things that go into building rapport and relationships, like names and
dates and details.

Discovering Prominent Referral Sources

Directions: To fill out this form, go through the files on your desk, recording the client's name, the level of client they are, and finally the name and type of Referral Source. Do this with all the open and active matters currently in your inventory.

File Name	Level of Client	Name of Referral	Type
Andrews, Ryan	A	Joseph Smith	CPA

Top Twenty Referral Sources

Exercise: Fill in the blanks below with the names of the Referral Sources who send your best referrals most frequently. Use A for high, B for medium, C for low.

Name of Referral Source & Profession	Potential to Send Clients	Actual Level Clients Sent	Level of Relationship	Days since Last Contact
Andrews, Ryan CPA	A	C	C	60

ASSET #2

CONTACT MANAGEMENT SOFTWARE

I only wish I could find an institution that teaches people how to listen. Business people need to listen at least as much as they need to talk. ~ Lee Iacocca

Technical Support Can Help To Streamline And Organize Your Office

Have you ever answered the telephone and had no idea who you were talking to — even after the callers identified themselves? This happens to the best of us and is a painful experience as your mind races to connect the dots. But let's face it: it's impossible to remember the name of everyone you meet in the course of a busy social and professional life.

Yet building referral relationships requires you to remember a lot of detail. And referral marketing is all about developing and maintaining rapport with a large number of people. Contact Management Software helps you remember names and maintain up-to-date information on prospective clients, present clients and Referral Sources. This software allows you to create instant rapport during every phone conversation because you have pertinent facts about your client and their case at your fingertips. You will be able to track your last conversation or commitment as well as record the next time you will be in communication with clients. On a broader scale, you can track trends and commonalities among your various clients, prospects, and influencers, thereby refining your demographic data.

If you don't currently have a client list, create one by collecting names from your billing system, mailing lists, personal checks you have received, client files and client intake or information sheets.

As a general rule, you should strive to be as personable as you can be in conversations with potential clients, past clients and Referral Sources. Each client wants to feel that their case is important to the attorney; each Referral Source wants to think they and their clients are receiving your best attention. Remembering who they are is imperative. Contact Management Software allows you to be on top of the case and demonstrate care for the client as a person. The kind of instant access provided by the software helps your firm give a little extra touch of personal service.

There are different approaches to doing this, both high and low tech; Contact Management Software is high tech and replaces the scraps of paper, index card file and lost notes that were the traditional method.

Many Atticus Rainmakers make gathering information on their Referral Sources an important part of their marketing efforts. Upon returning from marketing events, they hand the notes to their secretary or Marketing Assistant. They are then posted in the notes section of that person's record and are available for future reference. They make it a point to update the person's notes after every meeting or lengthy phone call in which they learned something new about their contact. For real marketing success, stop relying on your memory alone, and automate the process.

Contact Management Software Provides Solutions

Problem: You've just heard a Referral Source has had a new baby and you

> **TIP**
>
> Generate a client list by collecting names from your billing system, mailing lists, personal checks or client files.

want to call to congratulate him and his wife – but you can't remember her name.

Solution: Fortunately, you remembered to jot down his wife's name when you first met at a social function two years ago. You gave the note to your Marketing Assistant and she entered it into the Referral Source's contact sheet. You can easily retrieve the information before you pick up the phone.

Problem: You want to send an announcement to all of your Referral Sources and clients regarding a new partner who has joined your firm.

Solution: Your Marketing Assistant has kept track of the names and addresses of all clients and Referral Sources in your database, making this an easy thing to do.

Problem: You want to forward an informative e-mail attachment to a certain segment of your Referral Sources – the CPAs – whom you think will find it valuable.

Solution: You and your Marketing Assistant have noted the profession of each of your Referral Sources in searchable fields. You have also recorded their e-mail addresses. Consequently, you can run a report on this group and quickly generate a list of their names and e-mail addresses.

Problem: A Referral Source has a son who just graduated from college, but you don't want to call with congratulations because you can't remember the son's name.

Solution: You didn't note the information in the Referral Source's notes so you have your Marketing Assistant call, speak to the man's secretary, then report back with the name, after putting it into the database for future use.

Problem: You've just heard from the staff member of another attorney that her boss, a good Referral Source for you, is celebrating her 10th wedding anniversary. You want to send her a bottle of wine, because she is passionate about the subject, but can't remember her favorites.

Solution: Since you noted the wine the attorney likes in the database after your last lunch together, it is easy to send something appropriate .

Problem: A Referral Source just sent you a case that will generate a large fee. You want to send her and her husband to their favorite restaurant for dinner, but you can't remember which one they like.

Solution: At a lunch meeting with the Referral Source some time ago, you discussed local restaurants and she mentioned where she likes to go for special occasions. Since you have the information at hand, you instruct your Marketing Assistant to search the notes and buy a gift certificate to a listed restaurant as a thank you gift.

Types Of Information To Collect

Following are the types of information you will want to collect on clients, future clients and Referral Sources in your target market. Basic information should include the following:

• name, title, address (work or home, whichever is more pertinent)

• telephone numbers (work, cell, home and fax number)

• secretary's name (if applicable)

• status (prospect, Referral Source, client)

• last activity (i.e., met for lunch or visited office); next activity (i.e., call in December or attend upcoming dinner), if known

TIP

Use your Contact Management Software to recall important details about clients and Referral Sources. This will help you communicate with them in a more personal way.

- income range

- occupation

- marital status

- spouse's name; children and/or parents' names/ages

- date of birth

- hobbies or passions

- legal services they desire, types of clients they seek and/or send

- who or how they were referred to your office

- A, B, C, or D client rating (if a client)

Maintaining Your Files

The database should be maintained on your computer. *Act*, *Goldmine* and *Outlook* are some of the most popular database managers, but many case management software programs such as *Amicus, TimeMatters,* and *Needles* have an adequate contact management function and can also be used. Make sure whatever you use links to your PDA if you use one. If you are just getting started you can temporarily maintain your contact information in a file or notebook until you purchase software.

The importance of maintaining an up-to-date database should not be underestimated. Most of your new business will be referrals from the people whose names are in this file. Treasure and cultivate this cache of information and treat it like the gold mine it is.

Marketing is very much a numbers game. Simply put, the more people you meet and can develop a relationship with, the more referrals you can generate.

As we've said before, 80% of your referrals will probably originate from only 20% to 40% of your referral base. The goal is to always be meeting new prospects which add to the quality of your base. You will find yourself rotating new and better Referral Sources into your Top Twenty as you increase and maintain information on your network. Give your Referral Sources some designation in the database so you can tell who is in your

TIP

Making a client or Referral Source feel valued is essential; they will remember your civility and appreciate your firm's attention to personal service.

TIP

Choose a Contact Management Software that will help you keep pace with an ever-changing business climate, and will benefit your firm's marketing efforts.

Contact Management Software

If you've been accustomed to keeping your referral database in your memory, you've no doubt seen the limitations of that method. Even if you are very successful in remembering facts about your clients and influencers as you visit with them face to face, you cannot perform from memory many of the advanced marketing functions made so easy with a computer. Finding software that is a good fit to your existing storage and record-keeping systems need not be intimidating. Your needs will be industry specific and vary also with regard to your individual preference.

Software for contact management allows you to perform the following high-leverage functions with more ease, speed and in greater numbers:

• Track data (such as the list of clients each Referral Source has sent, the type of clients they'd be interested in, etc.) on all of your Referral Sources, other marketing contacts and activities.

• Generate reports on all legal services performed for a past client and identify future legal needs.

• Send mailings to groups of existing clients and influencers informing them of events in your office.

• Send periodic mailings to invite cli-

Top Twenty and who is not. Some attorneys give their Referral Sources a "T20" notation; some use an A, B, C and D ranking system. Since you always want to concentrate your best efforts with your Top Twenty group, it will help to identify those who are in this group. Choose a database that allows you to put a rank or code into a searchable field so you can easily generate a list of your current Top Twenty. Also, make it a point to update the notes on each person in your database as soon as possible, either by doing it yourself or delegating it to a secretary, or better yet, *The Marketing Assistant* (Asset #3). This will reduce not only the amount of clutter (notes, business cards, etc.) you have floating around on your desk or in your pockets, but also the chance that the information will be lost.

TIP

Networking is vital in maximizing the amount of your Referral Sources. Meeting people and developing relationships with them leads to gaining Referral Sources who will benefit you in the long term.

ents to stop by and update their files in your office.

• Target groups of clients in your database who fit the criteria for other firm services, i.e., the real estate client who qualifies for estate planning services. These letters can be invitations to attend information sessions or an offer for a complimentary consultation.

• Create reports on how many referrals have been generated by existing clients through the years.

• Track the follow-ups to each meeting with a Referral Source and create

reminders to send thank you cards or make follow-up phone calls when the time is right.

Database Features

It may not be a good idea for you, the attorney, to do all of the research needed to purchase Contact Management Software. It may be wiser to assign someone in your office who is very computer literate to take this on instead. You might also find that your Case Management Software has some or all of these capabilities. If you have Case Management Software in place, look into its capabilities and see if it can perform the following functions:

Contact History

Look for software that has a clear, understandable and readable format for its contact history pages. These pages are the backbone of the system and will be referred to constantly. Features must include the ability to:

• Segment your database into different groups – having a generous number of customizable fields will allow you to do this.

• Import data from other formats.

• Merge many databases into one for the easy reconciliation of all your data.

• Auto-dial any phone number within its database for added convenience.

• Date-stamp the notes you take for each contact.

• Store an unlimited number of contacts (this will allow you to expand your efforts without adding capacity).

Integrated Scheduling

• This feature allows you or a staff person to easily manage your calendar through an integrated scheduler – unless you possess the capability in your practice or time management software already. Since so much of referral marketing is event- and activity-driven, you'll want easy access to your calendar when using this software.

• If you use a PDA, look for software that will accommodate it.

Report Generation

Choose a software that has:

• pre-defined reports that have phone lists, address books, activity and status reports, and task lists

• the ability to customize so it allows you to change fields to generate different reports such as "All past clients who own their own businesses" or "All past and present clients who are over age 65"

TIP

Consider your existing storage, your current needs, and individual preferences when researching software. These factors will help you determine the appropriate type of system for you and your firm.

Word Processing Features

Look for software that can:

• mail merge letters, envelopes, and mailing labels

• fax merge documents to multiple contacts using *WinFax PRO*

• customize templates for business letters, report forms, memos, fax cover sheets (this is a must have)

• add fonts and graphics to customize your presentation

• perform spell check (but never trust this implicitly)

Security Features

Since inter-office confidentiality is a concern, choose software with security options that suit your needs. These options can include:

• different security levels for added control

• record locking, i.e., a public/private toggle switch

• individual passwords and log-in IDs

• an advanced utility that allows you to manage user accounts and access rights

E-Mail

If you wish to take advantage of e-mail as a method for contacting clients and Referral Sources, look for software that has it integrated in the format you already use, such as Outlook. You'll want to store and track your correspondence.

Networking

If your firm's computers are networked, be sure to verify that the Contact Management Software can be shared among different users. If

TIP

Make sure all of your contact information is clear and up-to-date in your database. This way, you can ensure that the information you have is accurate when communicating with a client or Referral Source.

programs already in use? (*Word, Word Perfect,* etc.)

• What is the amount of hard disk space it consumes before data is entered?

• What is the speed of responsiveness when run on your computer's megahertz?

• How much memory (RAM) does the program require?

• Is the software compatible with your printers and printer drivers?

• Most importantly, is there reliable technical support?

Once you figure out the technical configurations to maximize the ease with which you use your Contact Management Software, it is imperative to maintain up-to-date information on past clients, present clients and Referral Sources. Remember: your database is only as good as the information you put into it.

needed, your appointments and activities can generally be kept private and accessible only by password.

Technical Considerations

Ask the following questions to help you evaluate which Contact Management Software would be most compatible from a technical point of view:

• Does it operate with your computer's existing operating system?

• Is it compatible with other software

To acquire this Asset your job is to not only put Contact Management Software in place, input all of your key Referral Sources and clients, but to set up a system to regularly capture and update the data.

As we've mentioned before, if you take notes after each meeting with a client or Referral Source, make it a habit to personally update the contact's notes or pass the information off to someone else to enter. Having information about the individuals you want to cultivate or maintain a relationship with, and being able to instantly access it when someone calls, is critical – and will make you look like someone who really pays attention to the details important to others. No one can remember everything about everyone in their universe simply by relying on their own memory. In fact, many of us can't even remember our own family members' birthdays. Acquiring this Asset sounds difficult, but it will eventually make your life easier and your practice more prosperous.

If all of this sounds like a lot of work, rest easy. The next Asset, entitled *The Marketing Assistant,* addresses your concerns about how to get it all done – and still be able to practice law.

Top Twenty Influencer Profile Sheet

Influencer Name:

Firm/Company:
Secretary/Assistant:
Dept:
Title:

Office Address:

Cell:
Phone:
Fax:
Email:

Spouse's Name:

Home Address:

Cell:
Phone:
Fax:
Email:

PERSONAL INFO

Birthday:

Favorite Restaurants:
1)
2)
3)

Hobbies/Special Interests: (Sports Teams, Favorite Wines, Food, Preferences, Etc.)

Anniversary:
Spouse Birthday:

Children:

| Name: |
| Age: |
| Birthday: |
| Name: |
| Age: |
| Birthday: |
| Name: |
| Age: |
| Birthday: |

Notes On Influencer Education & Experience:

ASSET #3

THE MARKETING ASSISTANT

If it weren't for my Marketing Assistant, it would be impossible for me to market at the level I do — it's that simple.
~ Jim Periconi

Developing Your Right-Hand Person

As marketing advisors, one question we constantly grapple with is this: how can good lawyers become great marketers? Driven to distraction by constant interruptions, difficult staffing issues and demanding clients, most attorneys don't take the time to do what it takes.

Yet many of our Rainmaker clients are very good at marketing when placed in the right situations. It's getting them there that is the problem. Making phone calls to contacts often involves a lot of phone tag; calendaring client development events takes time; planning the basic logistics of marketing is distracting. As a rule, attorneys aren't very good at the initiation phase of marketing.

At Atticus, we believe this phase is essential – without someone to initiate and organize these steps, most marketing efforts will never get off the ground.

What Can You Do?

If you aren't successful in setting up lunches, dinners and meetings with Referral Sources, your client development efforts aren't going to be very strategic. If you're not meeting with the right people, then you're relying on nothing more than happenstance to promote your practice. Happenstance will take you only so far. We advise a more proactive approach.

Large firms can rely upon marketing directors to deal with client development. But what does the small firm practitioner do? Enter the Marketing Assistant.

The Para-Marketer

A Marketing Assistant can be your secretary, a part-time or full-time employee, an intern, or even a contract part-time person who works virtually. When you think of the Marketing Assistant, think para-marketer. In your law office, a paralegal leverages your ability to get substantive legal work completed. In the marketing world, we use Marketing Assistants to leverage our marketing activities.

Hint: A marketing director is not the same as a Marketing Assistant in that a marketing director manages your overall marketing efforts and directs you on what activities to do.

Hire a Marketing Assistant to maximize your firm's marketing efforts. The ideal candidate is detail-oriented enough to handle all the logistics, but personable enough to work well with all types of people.

Marketing Assistant. Though his new assistant had little experience, Chinn immediately noticed the difference hiring a Marketing Assistant made to his practice. Every morning, armed with a list of contacts, she and Chinn would have a short meeting to strategize, set up lunches and plan client development events. They also focused on placing articles about his firm in both local and statewide newspapers.

To accomplish this last task, they compiled a list of publications and set up the list as an e-mail group in their database system. Consequently, whenever something newsworthy happened in Chinn's office – a new promotion, a new award – his Marketing Assistant could automatically distribute the news to the state or local press.

"She was so ambitious and proficient. Any assignment I gave her came back to me tenfold," Chinn explained.

With the Marketing Assistant, you delegate marketing support functions to them.

When Mark Chinn, a very good Rainmaker and an attorney from Jackson, Mississippi, had difficulty marketing himself to the level he wanted, he sought change. That change came to him in the form of a young college student studying marketing at a local junior college.

For a number of months Chinn had been listening to us promote the idea of leveraging himself by hiring a

Rick Law, an estate planning attorney in Aurora, Illinois, also found it time consuming to market his practice to prospective Referral Sources. To overcome this obstacle, he hired a Marketing Assistant, Jonathan Johnson, who instantly impressed Law with his initiative and drive. Formerly a manager at a title-insurance company, Johnson used his background in sales to assist Law in his marketing efforts.

Since hiring Johnson, Law's marketing efforts have been revitalized. "Attorneys can tend to be a little…

> **TIP**
>
> Make sure you or your assistant has an accurate and ongoing record of your firm's marketing efforts so you can follow up on new leads and past contacts.

the idea was received quite well. We limited it to our top Referral Sources, which fit perfectly with our clientele – mostly caregivers and nursing home professionals. Without my Marketing Assistant, this event would never have gotten off the ground," Law said.

To leverage your marketing efforts by working with a Marketing Assistant, consider delegating a number of different client development activities:

• Schedule lunch/breakfast marketing meetings.

• Manage your database of clients and Referral Sources.

• Plan and manage parties, seminars and other group events.

• Build and manage Top Of Mind Awareness (TOMA) programs – newsletter, e-mail, birthday list.

• Assist in preparation for speaking engagements.

• Write thank you notes.

• Deliver gifts and buy tickets for your Referral Sources

prickly in our attitudes," Law admits. "With my Marketing Assistant, there was a complete lack of that. It was very refreshing to me to see this outsider help implement some of my ideas, but also bring fresh new ideas for marketing my practice."

The Tapas Dinner

Recently, Johnson created an event for Rick Law's top Referral Sources. Similar to a Spanish tapas dinner, the evening's menu featured many small dishes instead of one main course. "It was different, but

There are several different ways for small firms to employ a Marketing Assistant. For $8 to $15 per hour, depending on your location, you can hire someone to work for you part time, such as Mark Chinn's college student. If you require more support, hire someone full-time, as Rick Law did, or draft one of your existing staff members to help. This last option is the most popular among our Rainmaker clients, but I'm particularly fond of contracting with virtual Marketing Assistants.

Consider this option if you have limited office space or are not interested in hiring another employee. Since virtual Marketing Assistants work from their homes or remote office locations, a law firm doesn't have to free up office space or include them on the payroll. The firm can specify how much time they need on a weekly, monthly, or per project basis. Virtual Marketing Assistants are used on a project basis for the most part and paid between $20 to $45 per hour, depending on their qualifications. At Atticus, we currently work with several virtual assistants who will work as little as 10 hours per month, or upwards of 80 hours per month, depending on our need for their services.

No matter how you set it up, this is an idea that works. We have identified the 21 most important marketing Assets that a Rainmaker must acquire to be successful, and rate having a Marketing Assistant third overall in effectiveness.

If you work with your Marketing Assistant to plan two or three marketing contacts a week, by the end of a year you'll have made 100 to 150 marketing contacts. If that many market-

ing contacts a year won't stimulate new business, nothing will. If you are too busy to initiate client development activities, don't despair – delegate.

Low on office space? Consider hiring a virtual Marketing Assistant. There are several great Web sites that offer virtual marketing services, including:

- Susan Schmidt, Virtual Marketing Assistants
virtualmarketingassistants.com

- Virtual Assistance Online
virtualassistanceonline.com

- Your Virtual Resource
yourvirtualresource.com

Quick Tips

• Hire a young intern – preferably a college student with some experience in marketing – to re-energize your marketing.

• Meet with your new assistant frequently with several projects – it will be their job to "lighten your load" and help you market your practice.

• Newspapers are the single greatest source of Public Relations. Study the content filling the pages of your local newspaper. Make contacts with the staff of the local papers, and have your Marketing Assistant regularly submit newsworthy articles to them.

• Have your Marketing Assistant organize an event for your top Referral Sources.

• Determine your top Referral Sources by listing all of your files ranked by fees – from highest to lowest – for the last year. Read through the list and attribute each case to a Referral Source. This exercise will point you to your top referrers.

• When appropriate, have your Marketing Assistant cultivate relationships with your Referral Source's staff members.

TIP

When hiring Marketing Assistants, it's important to take a broad view. Specific experience does not always apply. Often, if the candidate is personable or has a demonstrated interest in event planning, this person may prove to be an excellent fit for you and your firm.

Tips On Hiring Marketing Assistants

A person with experience or training in marketing, sales or Public Relations is usually well suited for this role. An individual with an active interest in the community and experience in volunteerism may also be a good fit. Even without specific experience, someone who is personable, has good phone skills and likes to plan events may be capable. Additional traits to look for: someone who is good at follow-through, calendaring and database management. A person who possesses the ability to write well can be extremely helpful to firms that depend upon written materials for promotion, such as articles and newsletters.

Scripts For Marketing Assistants

At the end of this chapter you'll find a script for your Marketing Assistant to use when scheduling appointments for you. We have also included a script for your Marketing Assistant to use when setting up a meeting between themselves and other staff members. We encourage you to have your Marketing Assistants be very proactive on your behalf when scheduling lunches, dinners and other marketing activities because most of you will not stop and take the time to do it yourself.

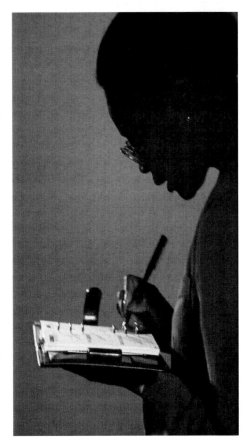

Keeping Track

You must keep track of the marketing efforts that are being made on behalf of the firm. Whether the attorney is taking action, or the assistant has sent out thank you notes, it should be recorded in order to provide a historical account of your marketing. This is especially valuable when follow-up actions are required

and the firm does not have Contact Management Software or other mechanisms to prompt appropriately timed contacts.

To help you, we have developed a variety of forms which follow the scripts at the end of this chapter. The first is the Marketing Dashboard, that, when maintained, will tell you at a glance what client development efforts are taking place. It is a report form that the Marketing Assistant can fill out to help the attorney track what the assistant is doing. We recommend that the attorney and Marketing Assistant meet once a week to discuss client development plans. Using this dashboard as a discussion aid and

TIP

A Marketing Assistant should devote time each week to scheduling marketing events, working on Public Relations activities, and supporting firm communication efforts with clients and Referral Sources.

planning tool can help you and your assistant stay in action.

The Marketing Matrix form is designed to give you plenty of good ideas for giving small, token gifts tied to the interests of your Referral Sources. Once you've sent handwritten notes for the sixth or seventh time, or when a Referral Source has sent you a particularly large client, you might want to express your appreciation in a different way. We believe that the more personal your gestures of appreciation are, the more meaningful they are to those who send you business. You don't have to buy elaborate and expensive gifts to make an impression. So many attorneys, though, run out of ideas quickly when it comes to this kind of thing.

The Marketing Matrix form, which can be a tool for the attorney or the Marketing Assistant, is set up with hobbies, passions and interests of typical Referral Sources listed in the far left column. Reading down from the top, they are: History Buff, Wine, Reading, Travel, Football Fan, Golf Fan, Amateur Chef, Theater Fan, Single Malt Scotch Fan and Likes Dogs or Cats.

Reading across from each category on the left are related gift ideas. In the first row, for example, next to History Buff, we have Book on Period, Print of a Period Map, Tour of Historical Location and Give Tickets to Museum – all things you or your Marketing Assistant could purchase or arrange for a Referral Source who loves history. Countless clients have told us they get business from colleagues who are interested in the Civil War or World War II.

These attorneys are often quite busy and don't have a great deal of time to pursue their interests. Buying them a book or giving them tickets to an exhibition demonstrates you know what's important to them and gives them an unexpected opportunity to indulge their interests.

The next form, Top Twenty Referral Sources, is a duplicate of the form found in Asset #1, *The Top Twenty.* It is an extra form which can be used by your Marketing Assistant, who should make copies of it and keep it updated. To refresh your memory on how to fill it out, details can be found in Asset #1.

If you aren't able to hire a Marketing Assistant, delegate the tasks to an existing employee and allocate time in their schedule to perform the functions. Acquiring this Asset by putting a Marketing Assistant in place will focus your Rainmaking efforts on just what you do best: showing up at the lunch or dinner or Bar event and developing relationships with existing and potential Referral Sources who can send referrals in the future.

To claim The Marketing Assistant as an Asset, you must have someone full- or part-time in this position. He or she must devote time each week to scheduling marketing events such as lunches and meetings; work on Public Relations activities; and support firm communication efforts with clients and Referral Sources.

Now that you know who is on your Top Twenty list, have begun a database to keep track of them, and are on your way to enlisting a Marketing Assistant, you'll need to know what to talk about when faced with a potential Referral Source. In the next section, we introduce you to the first conversational strategy, *The Laser Talk*. Read on to learn how to describe your services in a compelling manner.

Top Twenty Appointment Setting Script

This script is for a staff person or Marketing Assistant when setting up a Top Twenty Appointment on behalf of the attorney.

Hi! This is _____ with _____.

May I speak with Mr./Mrs. _____'s Assistant please?

Hi, _____ (Assistant's Name)!

This is _____ with _____.

Mr./Mrs. _____ asked me to give you a call.

He/She would like to meet with Mr./Mrs. _____. . .

OPTION #1
Just to thank him or her for sending so much business our way!

OPTION #2
He/She hasn't seen him/her in some time and would like to catch-up!

Mr./Mrs. _____ is available on

_____, _____ and _____.

Which day works best for Mr./Mrs. _____?

Perfect! I'll let Mr./Mrs. _____ know.

Does Mr./Mrs. _____ have a favorite restaurant?

Great! I'll look into that and be back in touch shortly with details.

Thanks again. I appreciate your help! Good bye.

~ IF DATES DO NOT WORK ~
When IS Mr./Mrs. available for lunch?

I'll review Mr./Mrs. _____ 's calendar and see if there is an open time slot. There is....I'll put this on the calendar now and get back to you if there is any problem. Does Mr./Mrs. _____ have a favorite restaurant? Great! I'll look into that and be back in touch shortly with details. Thanks again. I appreciate your help! Goodbye.

Top Twenty Appointment Setting Script

Use this script when a staff person, or your Marketing Assistant, initiates a call with a Referral Sources's staff member to schedule a lunch.

Hi! This is _____ with Attorney _____ office.

May I speak with Mr./Mrs. _____ Assistant please?

How are you doing? (Chit chat, if appropriate)

Well, the reason I'm calling is that

I would really like to take you to lunch.

We've had a chance to chat briefly in the past

but I would love to spend some time with you

in order to get to know you better.

CONTINUE, IF YOU FEEL COMFORTABLE...

I'm anxious to hear more about what you do at _____.

Who knows? We may be able to send some business your way

in the future... or vice versa...

If you're interested, I'm available on

_____ and _____ at noon.

Does either one of those days work for you?

(If those dates don't work, find one that does)

Perfect! I marked my calendar so it's official.

Do you have a favorite restaurant or type of food you like to eat?

IF YES -- Excellent! I'll try to make arrangements for us there.

IF NO -- OK, I'll choose and get back in touch with details.

Thanks again, _____!

I look forward to it.

Good bye.

Marketing Dashboard

Month:_____

Referral Source Cultivation:
Lunches Scheduled: (Top Twenty Influencers and Farm Team)

_____
_____
_____
_____
_____
_____
_____
_____
_____

Client Appreciation Efforts: (Notes sent, gift certificates, gifts, lunches, etc)

_____
_____
_____
_____
_____
_____
_____
_____
_____
_____

Public Relations Efforts: (Press, Articles, TV, Newsletters)

_____
_____
_____
_____
_____
_____

Number of New Client Inquiries: _____
Number of New Clients Signed: _____

Marketing Matrix

Passion/ Interest	Related Book	Related Product	In-Person Activity	Ticketed Activity	Food/ Meal	Event/ Party
History	Book on Period	Print of Period Map	Tour historical locations	Museum		
Wine	Book on Wine	Fave/new wine/cheese Basket	Wine-tasting	Wine-tasting	Meal at upscale bistro	
Reading	Hard-bound favorite book	Book stand, book light or marker	Book lecture	Breakfast with the author		
Travel	Book on Travel	Passport Holder	Travel Together	Tickets for a trip		
Football	Book on Team	Team merchandise	Go to game together	Tickets to game/ skybox		Super Bowl Party
Golf	Book on Golf	Golf merchandise	Twosome or foursome	Gift certificate to course	Dinner at Golf Club	Masters Party
Amateur Chef	Book of Recipes	Pots, pans, special oils, vinegars, herbs, apron	Take cooking class together	Cooking course gift certificate	Fix a meal at home	
Theater	Book on Theater	Posters or memorabilia	Go to a play together	Tickets to a play	Pre-show dinner	Back-stage access
Single Malt Scotch	Book on Scotch	Glasses or Favorite Scotch	Go to a Scotch Tasting		Visit bar that has specialty Scotch	
Dogs/ Cats	Book on Breed	Toy for pet, Pet bed, gift cert. for grooming		Tickets to a dog or cat show		
Tennis	Book on Tennis	Racket, racket cover tennis balls	Play together	Tickets to a tournament	Eat at Tennis Club	

Top Twenty Referral Sources

Exercise: Fill in the blanks below with the names of the Referral Sources who send your best referrals most frequently. Use A for high, B for medium, C for low.

Name of Referral Source & Profession	Potential to Send Clients	Actual Level Clients Sent	Level of Relationship	Days since Last Contact
Andrews, Ryan CPA	A	C	C	60

ASSET #4

THE LASER TALK

*Speech is power: speech is to persuade,
to convert, to compel. ~ Ralph Waldo Emerson*

How To Be Remembered

Relax. This is not about speaking at the speed of light. Rather, this is a conversational strategy every good marketer should be familiar with: the Laser Talk. Similar to the movie and book industries' "Elevator Pitch" — so named because a writer must be able to 'pitch' an idea and engage an agent in the time it takes for a quick elevator ride — an attorney's Laser Talk must convey engaging information in one to two well-rehearsed sentences.

At first glance, the Laser Talk is nothing more than a brief description of what a lawyer does for a living – a response to the question, "What do you do?" that is asked hundreds of times in any attorney's lifetime of social, personal and business encounters. Interestingly, when asked this question, most answer by telling the listener "who" they are, not "what" they do. The common reply is, "I'm an attorney." Or, "I'm an estate planning attorney." Or, "I'm a matrimonial attorney." You fill in the blank. Usually, the listener replies, "That's interesting," and heads off to the cheese dip. You end the conversation thinking they know what you do. In reality, they have no real idea of what you do or who you help.

While social encounters about what you do may seem like casual inquiries, the savvy marketer recognizes such questions as true marketing opportunities – and the chance to deliver an answer that goes beyond the typical, uninformative, "I'm an attorney" response. A particularly frustrating experience, not uncommon among lawyers, occurs when a friend, family member or colleague refers a potential client to a competitor. They don't do this because they think the other attorney is better, but because they don't really know what you do. This happens to some of you with alarming frequency. It is our responsibility to educate our Referral Sources.

The Formula

An effective Laser Talk has the ability to both communicate a message and brand an attorney. While referrals are the goal, an even more important aspect of the Laser Talk is the thought process that must precede its creation. To successfully follow the Laser Talk formula, you will need to answer the following questions:

1 Whom do you work with? (This is your target market.)

2 What problems do you resolve and how do your clients benefit?

3 How do you resolve their problem or frustration? (This is the feature.)

> **TIP**
> Draft a few versions of your script, then listen to how you say it out loud. You will automatically give voice to a version that's more comfortable for you.

ries of catch phrases. It is like a miniature marketing plan, as it forces you to identify your target market, articulate the service you provide, and highlight what makes you unique among your peers. Deceptively simple in appearance, these are the basic elements of a successful marketing plan. Very few attorneys, unless they are working with an advisor, ever attempt to create a marketing plan, let alone boil it down to a brief, concise description intended to be spoken in a variety of different social and business situations.

4 What makes you uniquely qualified to do so? (This is your USP or Unique Selling Position.)

The Laser Talk is more than just a se-

Building Your Laser Talk

Once you've finished reading this chapter, take a moment to complete your draft Laser Talk. Your Laser Talk may take several drafts before

Your Laser Talk, at least in its initial phases, will follow this basic script:

I work with _____
(specific description of client)

in their desire to _____
(benefit statement)

by means of _____
(how one gets the benefit)

What's unique about my practice is _____
(this is your USP or Unique Selling Position)

it is complete. A word of advice: the Laser Talk is a script that helps you understand, educate, and relate to your target market and it will rarely be used just the way it is scripted. A properly crafted Laser Talk will answer the question, "What do you do?" from the client's perspective, not the attorney's. Often, you will just use pieces of it in your daily interactions with Referral Sources. That being said, it is important to outline the draft just as it is laid out in the example. In truth, if prepared properly, it is the seed of all your marketing efforts.

Step One:
Whom Do You Work With?

For now, let's break the Laser Talk into its various segments and give you samples of how others handle it. The question, "Whom do you work with?" is an opportunity to identify or speak to your target market. It might read as follows:

• I work with individuals who have been injured....

• I work with good, honest people who find themselves in the wrong place at the wrong time and on the wrong side of the law....

• I work with employers when their employees go bad....

• I work with couples who are growing their family through adoption....

• I work with professionals who find themselves in a relationship that no longer serves them....

• I work with high net worth individuals....

• I work with business owners who have been sued....

Ideally, you want to describe the client in terms they would use to describe themselves. Also, a common error in crafting a Laser Talk is describing the institution you work with instead of the person who truly works with you. For example, a business attorney doesn't work with "banks," he works with "bank presidents" or "bank managers." While this first step is relatively simple, it will be refined as you better understand your target market.

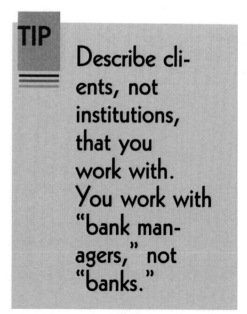

TIP

Describe clients, not institutions, that you work with. You work with "bank managers," not "banks."

Over time you will want to develop a better understanding of your clients' demographics (age, gender, income levels, educational background, where they live, where they socialize, where they work, etc.), and psychographics (key frustrations, wants, needs, etc.). The better you research and understand your ideal clients, the better you will be in describing them.

Step Two:

"In their desire to…" What Problems Do You Resolve And How Do Your Clients Benefit?

If we have properly described our target client in Step One, our next step is to identify the benefit they seek in working with you. So, what's a benefit? Most people would say quality work is the benefit of working with them, and while it is obviously important to the process and "a" benefit, it's not what the client would describe as their driving benefit. If you want to get to the heart of your client's desired benefit, every time you think you have landed on the answer, ask this question:

• If the client had _____ (fill in the blank – "quality work"– for example), what would that mean to them?

Let me give a product example. When I say Volvo, what do you think of? Most people say, "safety" or "protecting my family in an accident." Volvo is selling safety and protection. That's the benefit of buying the car. The steel reinforced frame or numerous airbags are the features that deliver on the benefit. So, if the customer, in Volvo's case, had steel reinforced frames in their car, what would that mean to them? Safety. That's the benefit. In a matrimonial practice, individuals don't perceive the divorce as

TIP

Identify how your clients can benefit from you. Communicate your services to them in more emotionally-oriented language such as, "We give our clients peace of mind," instead of emphasizing the substantive, technical aspects of what you do.

a benefit; a divorce is what they need to get out of a bad relationship or get on with their lives, with as little financial damage as possible.

Great Rainmakers know that attracting clients starts with this kind of analysis – identifying those you want to work with and figuring out how they benefit from your services – then crafting language that communicates the message with great clarity. Most of the samples we give use simple language purposefully stripped of any legalese. When you are speaking to another attorney, feel free to ratchet up your language, secure in the knowledge he or she will understand you. Our examples, though, are designed for use with non-lawyers.

TIP

Stand out! Include some component of your background in your Laser Talk that distinguishes you from your peers.

Below are a few examples of how some attorneys sum up who they are and what they do in a single sentence – you'll notice that many of the phrases leave the listener wanting more. Building on the first question, the Laser Talk may read as follows:

• I work with individuals who have been injured and want to be fairly compensated for their injuries…

• I work with good, honest people who find themselves in the wrong place at the wrong time and on the wrong side of the law and want protection from those who would put them in jail…

• I work with couples who are growing their family through adoption and want guidance through a very complicated and sometimes difficult process…

• I work with professionals who find themselves in a relationship that no longer serves them, are ready for a divorce, and want to get on with their lives with as little financial damage as possible…

• I work with high net worth individuals who want to protect their life savings and pass it on to the people they love…

• I work with business owners who have been sued and need to stay focused on what they do best, protecting their business and making a profit…

As you begin to craft your Laser Talk in these terms, like anything new, it will sound awkward. Keep with it until it starts to sound more natural for you. This will take practice.

Step Three:
"How I Do That Is…"

Where Step Two has us focus on the benefits of what we do, this step distinguishes the features of what we do. So, if the benefit for a matrimonial client is getting a fresh start in their life with as little financial damage as possible, the feature (or how you help get them there) may be "a well crafted divorce" or "by being a powerful advocate who never loses focus of your best interests." Taking a few of our examples from Steps One and Two, the continuation of the Laser Talk may read as follows.

• I work with individuals who have been injured and want to be fairly compensated for their injuries. I do that by fighting for their rights and standing up for them against the corporate giants.

• I work with good, honest people who find themselves in the wrong place at the wrong time and on the wrong side of the law and want protection from those who would put them in jail. I do that by aggressively advocating for them and guiding them

through the criminal justice system.

• I work with high net worth individuals who want to protect their life savings and pass it on to the people they love. I do this by crafting an estate plan that is customized to their individual circumstances.

Step Four:
What Is Unique About You And/Or Our Firm?

Once you've identified the markets you serve, the benefits and the services you offer, it is important to further distinguish yourself in the eyes of a potential client or Referral Source. How do you do this? By including in your Laser Talk some aspect of your personal history, training, family background, life experience or special interest that differentiates you from your peers, and, if possible, allows the client to relate better to you.

For example, the criminal attorney who mentions that he is passionate about criminal law because of his own missteps as a teenager, or the family lawyer who mentions that her own divorce left her with great compassion for those going through the process, leaves a more meaningful and empathetic impression. Sometimes, what you would consider a weakness or flaw in your background is what makes you more authentic and appealing to a potential client.

• What's unique about me is that as a divorce attorney I've been through a divorce: I understand how difficult and expensive the process can be.

• We have 120 years of combined experience to draw upon and have been in existence as a firm longer than any other firm in this area.

• We are one of the oldest firms in the vicinity; we grew up with this town and know every judge and attorney in the area.

• What's unique about me is that I'm a business owner just like most of my clients.

• What's unique about me is that I am the attorney's attorney. When my colleagues need help, they turn to me.

• What's unique about me is that when I was a young boy, I got into trouble – I have a lot of insight into how kids can get on the wrong track – and that's why I turned to the practice of law.

• We are attorneys and educators: we pride ourselves on providing a lot of education about the legal process so our clients feel informed every step of the way.

Once you can identify your clients, your services, how you help people and what makes you unique, put your own spin on the phrases and tie them together in a natural sounding talk

that takes no more than 30 seconds. After the Laser Talk is first constructed, don't worry about making it conform exactly to the formula. You can shift the statements or combine them in a way that sounds better or more appropriate. You must always, however, be comfortable with the language you use. Not only should it fit your audience, but you have to be at ease in saying the phrases. They must sound natural and appropriate for your personality. Read the following two samples to see what we mean:

•I'm a recovering litigator who now

TIP

Increase Top Of Mind Awareness (TOMA) by opening your Laser Talk with a powerful statement to compel your audience to ask clarifying questions like, "What's a Hardhat Lawyer?"

practices collaborative law. I help people who want to get divorced in a way that shields their children and minimizes the financial and emotional damage they have to endure. Even though I have 20 years of experience in court, I find I can save people time, money and emotional grief by achieving the results they want outside of the courtroom.

• I help people who want peace of mind in knowing they won't outlive their money. Our law firm takes the team approach: Crafting individual solutions, keeping clients informed, with an emphasis on education and information and allowing clients to make their own decisions.

Be Memorable

In the current climate of increased competition, being memorable should not be underestimated. Not unlike products that rely on branding to communicate their message and attract their market, successful attorneys rely heavily on referrals, which means people must remember them, want to use their services and/ or tell others about their services. A verbal form of branding, the Laser Talk is an important part of a word-of-mouth marketing program that depends upon relationship building and Top Of Mind Awareness for its success. No one comes to an attorney for documents, though documents may

be the only tangible product to be had when a case is complete. People go to attorneys to have problems resolved – usually the kind of problems that affect them deeply or weigh them down with worry. In most transactional practices, the work product is ancillary to the emotional satisfaction clients receive. Smart attorneys recognize the real wishes of their clients and design their laser phrases to speak to these needs.

Whether you recognize it or not, you are part of the vast marketplace competing for business and you want your message to stand out.

To do this, you may experiment by leading off with an interesting opening such as, "I practice preventative law," or, "I'm the business owner's best friend," to engage your listener. When you launch your Laser Talk this way, you can then fill in the rest of the information as the listener asks questions, proceeding to say more about whom you help, how you help and what makes you unique.

One of my all-time favorite opening lines comes from a construction lawyer who targeted builders, architects and developers. When someone asked him what he did, he said, "I'm a Hardhat Lawyer." He even gave out hardhats with the firm's name on it as part of his marketing campaign. When introduced, anyone within the construction industry was moved to say, "Hardhat Lawyer – what's that?" This is exactly the response you want.

It gives you permission to jump into the education process. We had a real estate attorney describe himself as a "Dirt Lawyer" when asked what he did.

Why would a lawyer want to describe his or her practice this way? To increase what we call Top Of Mind Awareness. An engaging, well-spoken Laser Talk – and by this we mean a Laser Talk that doesn't sound phony or canned – allows you to speak powerfully, passionately, even humorously about what you do. "I'm a Dirt Lawyer," tends to provoke greater interest than "I'm an attorney." Likewise, responses from a collaborative law attorney who opens with "I'm a recovering litigator," or the estate planning attorney who responds with, "I help people who don't want to outlive their money," tend to be much more memorable. Being memorable – and being specific about what you do – is important when you are marketing.

Narrowing your focus to a particular practice area helps to foster the idea that you are unique and an expert in your field. Except for small-town general practitioners, narrowing your practice to a couple of complementary areas allows you to market it more powerfully.

Different Laser Talks are created for each practice area and delivered to suit different audiences. For example, a real estate attorney who also offers estate planning services; he would have two Laser Talks: one to describe his real estate services and another to describe his estate planning services. Then he'd modify the delivery depending on whether he was speaking to a colleague or a potential client.

Pulling It All Together

One of our Atticus Practice Advisors worked with a real property attorney in Bushnell, Florida who represents entrepreneurs and real estate developers. With her help he has found a clever way to brand himself, tying both his Signature Event (more about this in Asset #12) and a key phrase from his Laser Talk: "Overcoming the hurdles of life."

Here's what he does: every year he invites select clients and Referral Sources to an annual local steeplechase. He rents several tents – capable of seating 24 people – right on the infield close to the finish line of the race. He invites a mix of clients, realtors and developers who send him business on a regular basis. Along with a buffet of smoked salmon, Swedish meatballs, shrimp and a variety of other hors d'oeuvres, he provides an open bar and encourages his guests to mingle and network with one another. Featured in the tents are tastefully done posters – actually blown-up copies of his marketing material – which show a horse jumping over a hurdle underscored with the phrase: "Overcoming the hurdles of life."

As a parting gift, he gives each guest a tumbler monogrammed with the name of his law firm, his laser phrase and phone number.

His phrase, "Overcoming the hurdles of life," is a good example of how attorneys can address the emotional needs of their clients which underlie their stated goals when coming to an attorney for help.

A Miniature Marketing Plan

Begin to experiment with your Laser Talk on family members, people you meet in the courthouse, at social gatherings or business meetings.

To claim this Asset you will need to complete a draft version of your Laser Talk and use it at least 10 times in various social situations where it is applicable: in social situations when meeting potential clients and when you are introduced to potential Referral Sources or fellow attorneys.

In actuality, any time someone asks the question, "What do you do?" some version of your Laser Talk – or phrases from it – should be employed. With practice, it will become an automatic response. Be creative, be humorous, but be clear: the Laser Talk is a powerful tool in cultivating clients. When finished, your Laser Talk should reflect a statement that you can speak with ease, comfort and confidence. Choose your words carefully. Finally, before you experiment fully with your Laser Talk, be sure to review the ABA and your State Bar advertising guidelines to ensure that it conforms to ethical standards.

In the next Asset we explore another conversational strategy which has evolved from one of our earliest forms of communication. Read on to learn how you can put the power of Storytelling to work for you.

ASSET #5

STORYTELLING

What is told into the ear of a man is often heard a hundred miles away. ~ Chinese Proverb

People Remember A Good Story

The least expensive, most ethical and effective way to market yourself and your law firm is through a well-structured word-of-mouth program. Unlike print or television advertising, it produces enough trust to generate the highest quality and least price-sensitive clients. When referred clients show up because someone said you were good at what you do, studies show they are more motivated, more likely to pay your fees and will be more loyal in the long run.

What you haven't heard us mention is that word-of-mouth marketing is effective because it taps into a very basic urge – an urge most of us find irresistible.

What is it? The urge to communicate. To talk about what's happening with the world, the workplace, and especially with our lives. Consequently, the river of information flowing through everyday communications is enormous.

And on close examination, the narrative device used to convey much of that information will be a story.

TIP

Stories act as "verbal commercials" for you and your services, but shouldn't come across as blatant self-advertising. Don't toot your own horn too obviously.

As it turns out, this is no accident. Listening to stories is how we learn. "Stories are one of the oldest and most persistent forms of communication," explains Richard Stone of the StoryWorks Institute located in Winter Park, Florida. "In fact, they are so much a part of us that the human brain is hardwired to learn best when stories carry the message." Every culture possesses an oral Storytelling tradition that pre-dates the written word. Early cave drawings are often narratives, informing their viewers about great battles, fertile hunting grounds or dangers to avoid.

In our modern society stories are everywhere. They provide the plots for books, movies, theater, and television shows. The 24-hour news channels bring you the stories of the day. Every newspaper you pick up is full of stories. The best teachers, leaders and communicators have always recognized the importance of Storytelling and have long used anecdotes to convey lessons, messages and inspiration. A well-told story has the power to evoke images and fill the listener with emotion.

Because of this, stories of all kinds achieve what no other form of communication can. When you harness the power of Storytelling in your word-of-mouth marketing program, you capitalize on the receptivity built into those you want to educate about your service. In many ways, stories are like your *The Laser Talk* (Asset #4), only longer and more expansive. When you use stories in conversations with potential clients to demonstrate your expertise, with Referral Sources to illustrate how you can help their clients, and in social settings to educate people about your firm, you are drawing on an age-old talent.

"Look for the drama in your everyday actions to formulate your stories," says Stone. "Just as a good author can find a story where others see only the commonplace deeds of ordinary people, it's possible for each of us to frame our work in heroic terms. Stories are your narrative assets."

A well-crafted story or anecdote about why you became an attorney, why you are compelled to help people or how you fought to succeed in spite of

TIP

Humans have the built-in capacity to respond to and learn from stories. Use Storytelling in your marketing program to support the message you want to convey.

great difficulty, becomes an important conversational strategy. These narrative assets are the hidden gems of your word-of-mouth marketing program. In a word-of-mouth marketing program, the stories you tell are like verbal commercials for your firm.

In working with one of our clients to develop his Storytelling ability, we asked him to answer the question, "Why did you become an attorney?" After pondering the question for a moment, he responded with, "I guess I've always been an attorney." Surprised at this answer, we asked him to explain. "Well, when I look back on my childhood, I was the guy who everyone sought out to settle arguments on the playground. In college, I was the guy elected to be the spokesperson for my fraternity when we had to go to the dean. Even in law school, people turned to me for help and advice." We asked if there was anything more. He said, "If it is possible to have been born an attorney, I think I was." Then he added with a chuckle, "Of course, it helps to have a license."

His story, told in a humble fashion with a dash of humor, paints the picture of someone who has inspired the trust and confidence of others since he was a child. He had told bits of his history before, but recognized that this aspect of himself was something he could polish and use when building relationships with potential clients and people who might be Referral Sources. It offered insight into his character and suggested he was someone who could be trusted.

How can you harvest the wealth of experiences you've had in order to craft your own stories? Read the following prompts and write down the ideas that come to mind when you hear them:

• *"I became a lawyer because…"*

• *"I'm passionate about my area of practice because…"*

• *"The types of people I like to help are…"*

• *"The reason I like to help people is…"*

• *"I make a difference for people by…"*

• *"The most interesting problem or challenging crisis I've had is…"*

To show you some results of using

Remember: the most successful stories indirectly communicate your values and ideals to your listener.

this process, here are a few of the responses that we've received when we asked clients to finish the statement, *"I became a lawyer because… ."* While not yet full-blown stories, the responses have promise and reflect what each person values:

• My uncle had a great deal of influence over me when I was a kid. He was a lawyer and even when I was a kid I could tell he was doing something important. He was helping people and I admired that.

• I'm fascinated by the law. Before law school, I was a history major and studied American History, the Enlightenment and the philosophies upon which the United States was founded. There's a reason some of our founding fathers were attorneys. They were trained in logic and rational thought and I like to think I'm carrying their goals forward.

• Attorneys are our society's warriors. They lead the charge when it comes to making society work, protecting people, defending the defenseless. They become the senators and the congressmen who devote their lives to public service.

Here's what a finished story looks like, inspired by the statement, *"I became a lawyer because… :"*

I approach my practice as if it were my mission. My parents were educators, so for me, being a lawyer is how I contribute. I provide a defense for people who have nowhere else to turn. I used to be a public defender, but got fed up with the system. I opened my own practice years ago because the PDs don't have time to construct the proper defense for their clients. In this city, they are really overworked and the dockets are packed. Clients are moved through like cattle — no one takes time with them. I take time with people — some of whom were in the wrong place at the wrong time — and truly advocate for them. It's how I give back.

TIP

Sharing stories from your past offers a client or referral source some insight into your character. These stories can convey trustworthiness, reliability, intelligence, or any other quality you'd like to showcase.

Here's a response to the question, *"I'm passionate about my practice area because…"*

• I feel like I'm actually able to help people achieve their goals. They come to me with very complex business problems and I use my training, my education and imagination to help them get the outcomes they want.

Here's what one of our clients said in response to: *"The type of people I like to help are …"*

• People who have been taken advantage of. I like coming to their defense and helping them get what they deserve when they have been wronged…"

The following is one of the best responses we've seen to the question: *"The reason I like to help these people is…"*

• Someone helped me when I was young and got into trouble…

You have the opportunity to highlight your values and skills when you answer the question: *"I make a difference for people because…"*

• I'm a good negotiator. I won't back down when I feel my clients deserve more than what they are getting from insurance companies. I enjoy separating insurance companies from their money…

And finally, *"The most interesting problem or challenging conflict I've had to resolve is…"*

• I once represented the family of two men who were burned to death in a multiple vehicle crash. It was very difficult to determine whose fault it was…

After you jot down the ideas that occur to you based on these prompts, spend some time thinking about what you've written – it's the raw material for the stories you'll create.

Ask yourself what your motivations were as you went through the experiences you recall and which of your values the stories evoke.

The stories you tell, whether short or long, reflect your values and your ideals – and often are successful because they do this indirectly. Here at Atticus, Patrick Wilson, a Practice Advisor who has been with us from the start, calls stories the "stealth bombers" of marketing because you can convey a great deal of information about yourself and your practice and entertain your listener at the same time. Stories are powerful teaching tools and can teach people about you as a lawyer, demonstrating what you value, who you help and how you help. Stories that are humorous show that you are human. You don't have to be the hero in every story; stories that are self-deprecating can be engaging, humbling and among the most memorable.

The spirit of your legal approach and the values that form that approach are encoded in your conversations – make your powerful stories, or your "narrative assets," one of your most effective Rainmaking Assets. Beyond this, Richard Stone suggests we are each driven to create the story of our own life and practice. "Fundamentally, every business is a stage for the enactment of human myths. We found, lead, manage, nurture, serve, suffer with, and exalt our businesses not just to create wealth and financial security. At the heart of every such pursuit is

something much more essential and innate to the human spirit – the need to create a story with a satisfying ending."

To claim this Asset you must construct at least three distinct stories, then use them at least 10 times to inform and educate potential clients and Referral Sources.

In the next section, we'll discuss a marketing channel that has grown tremendously in the last decade and will become a more important form of client development than ever anticipated: your law firm's Web site. Read on to learn how to maximize its ability to brand your law firm, educate Referral Sources and attract potential clients.

ASSET #6

A PROFESSIONAL WEB SITE

An Executive Summary
By Henry Harlow

Developing A Web Presence

If you're like many of our Atticus clients, you may find the Internet marketing process confusing. But it's too important to not understand at least the basic concepts. You may have resisted (or know an attorney who resisted) getting an e-mail address when electronic mail was a radical new concept. Now, prospective clients and current clients expect you to have e-mail and a Web site, and may perceive that you are behind the times if you don't.

According to www.InternetWorld-Stats.com, in 2007, 70.9% of North Americans (in the USA and Canada) were using the Internet. Additionally, according to Reuters News Services, there were more than nine million legal services searches done on the Internet in 2007.

The importance of a Web site as part of your marketing plan should not be underestimated. A Web site that is informative, professional, and easy to navigate will serve you now and for years to come.

The elements of a professional Web site are fairly straightforward and shouldn't be difficult to create if you are working with an experienced team. Your visitor's first impression of you and your firm will be formed in large part by what they see on the opening screen.

It should be the first page designed for your Web site, as all the rest of the pages will retain many of the same design elements. It will set the "look" of the design template for the pages which follow. The look of your graphics should be consistent with any pre-existing firm logos, colors, symbols or namemarks already associated with the firm. In other words, your entire graphics package should be coordinated, including the look of your letterhead, brochure, signage, Web site, etc.

If you don't have a logo or letterhead design, you might contract with a designer who specializes in law firm graphics to create one prior to creating your Web site. It may also be possible to have the Web site designer create one if they are experienced in doing so. You want a first-time visitor to your site to be able to immediately grasp and get a clear sense of your firm's mission right away.

In addition to what you've written, the look, layout, and design of your graphics convey that message and will generate the "feel" of your Web site. To help you envision the look you want to represent you, visit the Web sites of other law firms and note what you like and what you don't. Have members of your team do the same. These examples and the notes you take will be invaluable when you give direction to your Web site designer.

The first, and indeed, all the pages in your Web site, should have a balance of text and blank space. You don't want the page to appear too cluttered. The viewer should be able to see what they are interested in quickly – or be able to navigate the site to get where they need to go easily. Clearly displayed search functions and drop-down menus that feature different options will ease this process. The look of your site sets up the initial impression a potential client perceives – don't lose your viewer's attention by making your site difficult to navigate. It must be user friendly to encourage visitors to want to contact you.

Since contacting you is the point of a good Web site, be sure your address, phone number and other relevant contact information is clearly and prominently displayed instead of buried at the bottom of your front page or on another page. This is one element you don't want to hide. There are several different approaches to enabling con-

tact. Some firms just provide their phone number. Others prompt the visitor to send an instant message to the firm (only do this if you have someone monitoring and responding to incoming messages). Other firms opt for functions that allow a visitor to send an e-mail to the firm, and some sites enable visitors to fill out a questionnaire or short intake form and submit it online. The method you chose will depend on your budget and on your client's demographics. Some types of clients are comfortable send-

TIP

Your Web site is a reflection of you and your firm. Make sure its design, navigation, and content set a professional tone, as your homepage serves as a visitor's first impression of you.

ing e-mail, while others operate with a greater sense of urgency (criminal clients, divorce clients, bankruptcy clients), and will want to pick up the phone and speak to someone immediately. Keep this in mind when enabling different forms of contact on your Web site. The least expensive, posting your phone number, is often the best for many firms.

TIP

Visit the Web sites of other law firms and compare and contrast their look and "feel." This will help you to visualize the Web site you want, and help you to clearly articulate your ideas to your Web site designer.

Use A Professional

While most attorneys should not take the time to learn the technical intricacies of Web design, it pays to know the basics so you can give informed direction to your technician and understand the parameters of what's possible.

We highly recommend that you contract with a professional to assist you in all phases of your Internet marketing – attempting to do it yourself is akin to someone going to a stationary store and buying a generic legal form to handle an important legal issue, when what they really need is a lawyer to draft the document to fit their needs.

What To Look For In A Web Consultant/Vendor

It can be difficult to find a consultant who will do what you want, communicate with you frequently (and in English) and who will finish your project on time and within budget. Building a Web site is not unlike building a house, and can be equally frustrating if you deal with the wrong people. Your consultant, who will act like a general contractor, will subcontract the services of a Webmaster, keyword researcher, html writer, Web designer, technician, and Web site copywriter.

One way to locate a reputable consultant is to ask other attorneys in your community if they can recommend someone they have used locally. Once you have three candidates, get bids from each of them and be sure to compare the services each one claims they will include in their proposal.

In advance of meeting with your candidates, ask to see other Web sites they have designed or implemented. If your candidate has designed Web sites for other attorneys or other professionals, they will have the best grasp of what you need. Also, find out if their own Web site has a good Google PageRank or an Alexa rank-

ing. How highly their own pages are ranked will give you some clue as to their expertise.

As of this writing, vendors who specialize in Web site design, hosting, content writing and Search Engine Optimization specifically for attorneys are:

• *ConsultWebs.com Inc. (www.consultwebs.com)*

• *Foster Web Marketing (www.fosterwebmarketing.com)*

• *Einstein Law (www.EinsteinLaw.com)*

They typically charge from $20,000 to $30,000 and beyond, depending on what you build. Many of their fees are negotiable, so don't hesitate to ask for a discount.

TIP

Don't bury your contact information at the bottom of your page. Make sure it is displayed in a place where users can easily view it.

Less Expensive Options

You can build a smaller Internet marketing site with just bare bones but all the foundations (so you don't have to throw it away), for about $9,000 or $10,000, but it won't be as robust as the larger sites and won't get as much traffic as the bigger option above. Later you can add pages (a must – a page per month for solo and small firms).

The under $500 option is available via www.guru.com (a virtual marketplace complete with a mediated process) where you can find cheap vendors (think India, Singapore, New Zealand, South Africa and Europeans at $12 to $50 per hour), as well as value vendors (think $50 to $135 per hour in the USA).

The last option is to do it yourself via SiteSell at http://service-selling. sitesell.com for under $300 – this is recommended only if you are in dire circumstances since your time is better spent on other referral building strategies instead of learning how to build a Web site for yourself. If you can afford to spend about $1599 plus $49 per month, this service will build a 10-page Internet marketing site for you. This is a much better option than most vendors who will charge you that much just to build a Web site with no Internet marketing abilities.

Upgrading An Existing Web Site

If you have an existing Web site and want someone to come in and play the role of Webmaster, to help you improve its design or functionality, look for someone who is SBI Certified and who will:

1 Assess your current Web site in detail.

2 Make a plan for how to improve your Web site using your current vendor.

3 Manage your current vendor so they implement that plan.

4 Make the recommendation, if needed, to leave your current vendor and find you another one.

Also be sure that whoever is hosting your Web site has placed statements in their agreement regarding what they will do should the hosting equipment go down (one option is to transfer your site to another server), and what their remedies are for interruption of service for more than short periods of time (short meaning hours, at the most). If you have been with a host for some time and encounter frequent loss of service, you should be able to leave that service with no penalties. Check your agreements carefully to be sure this point is included.

Whatever path you take, make certain that you own the copyright to your entire Web site, including the domain name, content, code, graphics, text and photographs. Also, be sure the vendor warrants that it owns or has all permissions to publish any copyrighted material they use in building your Web site.

Ethical Concerns

Concerns with respect to Bar rules and ethical considerations vary by state and can be confusing as Web sites present new challenges. Check with your Bar if the advertising rules apply to Web sites or blogs, and if there are any new rules for Web sites or blogs. Some states may require very specific disclaimers on your site, and you will want to be in compliance to avoid problems.

Funding A Web Site

As of this writing, you can expect to spend from $12,000 to $15,000 to develop a professional Web site, which should have 20 to 30 pages in total and feature "on site" SEO (Search Engine Optimization) fully in place. The consultant's fee should already include the services of a Webmaster, keyword researcher, html writer, Web designer, technician, and Web site copywriter. For a custom designed site, add up to $2,000. With video add another $2,000 to $5,000 (although sometimes college level students or trade school students, who are often very adept, will do this work for much less).

For $800 to $1,000 you can have what is commonly known as a "name-squeeze page" or an "ASK" site. Both of these options are indeed Internet marketing strategies. Another option is a "brochure" site (maybe even under $500) that is NOT an Internet marketing site (and you will likely throw it away at some point).

Having A Web Site Alone Is Not Internet Marketing

While a Web site is essential as an electronic business card, it does nothing on its own; you must be strategic in planning its usefulness as part of your overall marketing plan. A Web site can serve your marketing goals in many different ways: it can add to Top Of Mind Awareness; it can act as a brochure for your services; it can be a helpful resource for new and existing clients; it can showcase the skills of its attorneys; and it can attract new clients because it paints a picture of your firm as the one to hire for the best results.

When you integrate your Web site into your overall marketing plan, the goals you set for yourself may look something like this:

• Establish a presence on the Internet with a basic site that will serve as an electronic business card. (This is perfect for those who are just getting started, have no Internet presence whatsoever and have clients who are not technologically savvy.)

• Take our existing Web site and double the amount of content on it, from 10 pages to 20 pages, using a keyword search strategy to dictate some of the content.

• Take our existing Web site and give it a new look so that it better represents our practice.

• Contract with an SEO company to increase our rankings.

• Take an existing site and add a blog to increase our rankings due to the frequent addition of new content.

Accompanying any goal you set should be a specific, measurable result such as:

• Our firm will send out 500 announcements to clients and Referral Sources announcing our new Web site this year.

• This year we will receive 10 new clients directly attributable to the Web site.

• Our Web site will consistently rank

TIP

Hire a professional Web consultant to assist you with Web site development and Internet marketing. These trained individuals are able to take on multiple roles to deliver the type of digital product that you need.

within the top 5 on Google this year.

• The number of hits on our Web site will increase from 25 a month to 50 a month by the end of the year.

Your competitors on the Internet are those people who are trying to rank high with the search engines for the same keywords that you are using. You have a great opportunity to get out in front of the pack and stay there through Search Engine Optimization (SEO), which means your Web site is one of the first listed when a search is conducted.

Keywords

Keywords are the specific words your prospective clients are using to type into their browser to search for specific legal services. This means you must be in touch with what your targeted client is concerned about and write content that contains your top keywords. To learn more in depth about keyword optimization, visit www.Wordtracker.com for their Keyword Research Guide.

If you don't begin with keywords in the beginning and build appropriately from that point forward, you are going to have to start the process over, from the beginning. Sometimes it is better to throw it away and start over. Sometimes you can use parts of what you have, and sometimes a

lot of what you have in place now. Always you are going to need to run your keyword research first and then decide from there what needs to be done next.

Links

The difference that the amount of links you have on your site can make in increasing your ranking is this: the more the better. And those links should be to other high-ranking sites, if possible.

Search Engines

Search engines are the entities that scan all available Web sites, looking for the best keyword match once a prospective client has keyed them in. When a potential client types "divorce lawyer in Seattle," or "elder law attorney in Orlando," into their Google or MSN search function, search engines are activated, they fan out and immediately gather all the Web sites with these keywords. In a matter of seconds a page of results comes up on the screen containing a list of Web sites.

The SEO process, otherwise known as Search Engine Optimization, results in your Web site being among the first shown on the search results page. Why is this important? People are more likely to click on those Web sites that appear first, or early, on the search page. We'll go into this further, but for now, know that every law firm should be concerned about their position, otherwise known as their ranking, and try to optimize it as much as possible.

Secondary Search Engines

Never hire a company or buy software that promises to submit your site to hundreds or thousands of search engines. You may need to submit to three to five carefully selected directory search engines where a live human editor looks at your site and then lists it on the search engine site. The reason you would list on these types of directory search engines is for the links they provide to their and other sites. Here are some of these types of directories:

• *www.business.com*

• *www.avivadirectory.com*

• *www.ezilon.com*

• *http://botw.org*

• *http://dir.yahoo.com*
• *www.dmoz.org* (free but often tough to get in)

Legal directories are sites such as FindLaw.com, Lawyers.com, Justia.com, and InjuryBoard.com, which are huge sites that list hundreds of legal Web sites. In addition to being expensive, your listing is likely to get lost here – your name and Web site come up with all your competitors. We believe you are not likely to get a great return on your investment dollars using this strategy. It is far better to invest that money in your own Internet marketing that drives traffic to your own site – where the visitor sees you and only you.

Visitors: Unique Vs. Regular

Visitors are actual users who view your Web pages. Unique visitors are users who visit your Web site once during a defined time period – either a day, week or month. A unique visitor is counted by using cookies – information stored on a user's computer by a Web site so the individual's preferences are remembered for future requests. By contrast, regular visitors are users who visit your Web site more than once during a defined time period. It is valuable for attorneys to create "visitor loyalty" with regular visitors, as those who regularly view your site often mention it to friends, family and colleagues. This can easily create a "traffic virus," which is born when people mention your Web site to others, who then spread the word, and so on. This viral effect increases your number of visitors and thus drives more traffic to your Web site. It may sound strange, but word-of-mouth is the primary source of traffic for many larger sites and the reason they have become what they are today.

Bounce Rate

A bounce rate is a measurement of the number of visitors that enter your site and leave - typically within the first five seconds - without viewing another page. Web marketers use the bounce rate to measure visit quality – a high bounce rate generally indicates that site entrance pages aren't relevant to your visitors. You can reduce bounce rates by creating landing pages that are interesting to prospective visitors. The more compelling your entrance page, the more visitors are likely to stay on your site.

Offerings

These are newsletters, white papers, the first few chapters of a book you are writing, a downloadable eBook, free consultations, self tests - anything you can offer to your site visitors that enrolls them into giving you permission to market to them via their first name and e-mail address.

Pay Per Click

Pay Per Click advertising is relevant to your firm only if you are in a highly competitive practice area. Asbestos attorneys, and those firms that handle large class-action suits, generate such high returns on their cases that they pay to have their site ranked above the rest on a search page. Sometimes the Web sites are listed separately, in a box above the rest of the listings, but they are always ranked high. If you are interested in this, and have a great deal of money to spend, look for a Web site consulting company who knows your market and can guide you appropriately.

Selecting A Domain Name

Your domain name affects your page ranking to some extent. Ideally, the name should include one of your main keywords, or at least describe what you do. Contrary to what you may believe, using the name of your firm is not always wise as it may not fit what your prospective clients are keying in. Sometimes law firm names are not memorable and are often difficult to spell. Your keyword research can help you select a good domain name, as well as a review of the names your competitors are using which maintain a high ranking.

Including Audio Or Video On Your Web Site

Avisual or audio presentation connects with your visitor more intimately than simple text accompanied by a static picture. Adding audio and/or video to your site makes it more memorable because it requires more of the viewer's brain to process, and embeds your message deeper into their minds, with a greater chance of retention in the future. If the audio is running while a visitor is scanning your site, so much the better.

TIP

Be aware of your state's Bar rules and ethical considerations. Check with your Bar to see if any new rules apply to Web sites or blogs.

By including audio or video, you deliver a clear message to your visitor before they have contacted you. This aids your conversion of the client during the intake meeting because you can continue to play off of and reinforce the earlier message. Audio and video of you speaking in some capacity brings your personality forward in ways the written word cannot, and gives clients a more personal sense of who you are. As an added advantage, having audio on your site differentiates it from other attorneys.

Internet Marketing Basics

One of the most commonly accepted models of Internet marketing is CTPM, developed by Ken Evoy, M.D., in 1997. This model works because it takes into consideration the habits and tendencies of those who search the Internet, understands how to maximize the chances your Web site will be found, and recognizes what those people who are searching want to find.

C stands for Content – content that is current and relevant because it addresses the problems of your potential clients. How do you determine what is in demand? You figure this out from the keyword research that is done. If you are a family law attorney, for example, you might post articles you have published on topics such as, "How to Help Children Through the Divorce Process," or "How to Adopt Children Using an Attorney." You want to focus on topics your potential clients might be searching for as they surf the Internet.

Tstands for Traffic – you attract targeted traffic from the keywords embedded in your site. This means that clients who are searching the Internet for help and information will be drawn to your site because text is loaded with specific keywords they will use in their search.

Pis for Pre-Sell – pre-sell refers to some sort of offer that the targeted traffic, your potential clients, may be interested in, i.e., newsletters, free articles or information downloads, e-books, auto responders, audio, video, recordings of teleclasses or invitations to live conference calls, etc.

Mis Monetize – this is where you convert the prospective clients to clients.

You or your advisor will need to write "keyword optimized" content to each of your top 20 keywords; in other words, write your content in the way that search engines want to see it so they rank you higher than your competitors. Your content should fit together in a site plan (the order your pages will appear and how they link to one another) that has an appropriate pyramid-type structure. This pyramid-type structure includes your home page (the peak of the pyramid) themed keyword phrase being supported by all the tier two pages (the next layer of the pyramid) and the tier three pages (usually the base of your pyramid, although you can go deeper), resulting in higher rankings for all of the pages on your site.

You don't have to do anything to get your Web pages ranked; this happens when the search engines send out their "spiders" (mechanisms for collecting and matching data), to read your site. Google PageRank is the standard on the Internet for success, since over 50% of the people on the Internet access Google for their searching.

The Google PR system ranges from 0 to 10, with 10 being high and 0 being low. Approximately 98% of all Internet sites are ranked 0, 1, or 2. The other major search engines (Yahoo, MSN and ASK) use similar models as Google. Consequently, if you rank high at Google, you will rank high anywhere.

To check your ranking, we suggest you install the Google Toolbar. This is a very useful tool that allows you to see the Google page ranking they have given you and every other Web page you visit. It's available at: http://toolbar.google.com/T4/index_pack.html.

The Firefox Web browser has a similar extension with the "Compete" Toolbar. Compete is another great way to track a site's traffic and site history.

Marketing Your Web Site

Once your Web site is created and published on the Internet, you must drive traffic to it in order for it to be viewed by prospective clients. We've covered in detail the first method of attracting people to your site with the discussion of Search Engine Optimization. But there are other methods to get people to view your site, using both traditional means and online opportunities. Some of the major ways to do this are listed below:

Press Releases

Writing about a newsworthy event is covered in detail in the Public Relations Asset, but, instead of sending a press release that is basically an e-mail, there are Web sites that allow you to send releases which are embedded with links and upgraded with video capability. Such a service is provided by PRWeb, through their Web site: www.prWeb.com/sharenews. php. This is one of the best ways to gain one-way links and drive traffic to your site.

E-Newsletter Marketing

Many firms recognize the importance of staying in touch with their clients during and after their matter or case is complete. A great way to do this is to create a newsletter which can be e-mailed to clients – if you believe they would be receptive to receiving your news (clients of criminal attorneys or bankruptcy attorneys, to name just two, are sometimes sensitive about receiving e-mails that broadcast their association with certain law firms – especially if their only e-mail account is at their workplace).

The first page of the newsletter contains the first couple of paragraphs of several articles. If one of these articles attracts the reader and they want to read further, they can click on a link that says "Read more about this," or something to that effect. Once the reader clicks on the link, they are taken to the law firm's Web site where they can complete the article and have ample opportunity to explore the Web site further if they wish.

Some online newsletter systems provide templates for use in designing these kinds of e-mails. One that provides a great deal of tracking information is called "Constant Contact." It has been used widely by our clients and, indeed, many in the corporate world, preferred because it will track how many people received the newsletter, how many deliveries failed, how many people clicked on the newsletter for further information and how many people who clicked on the link then browsed through the Web site – all good information when you are trying to conduct an Internet marketing campaign. You can't manage what you don't measure.

Name-Squeeze Pages

This is a strategy that can be used with just a single page or as a page on your Web site. The sole purpose of the page is to get the name and e-mail address of the visitor. Sometimes the name-squeeze page is used as an entry into a Web site; unless you enter your name and e-mail, you aren't allowed in. This strategy is typically used with very content rich sites, meaning that the Web site is authentically used as a resource because it contains a great deal of information. Name-squeeze pages get double-digit conversion rates of visitors, while regular pages get about 1 or 2%. A well done name-squeeze page, geared to the right targets and combined with the right offer, can get more than a 50% response – making them very effective.

Social Networking Sites

This option involves a considerable amount of time, so it is not one to take on lightly. It is a bit like joining a service club. Only join if you intend to participate and have a passion for the vision of the community. You will need to spend regular time working the network on the site. Also,

it depends on your practice area as to what site might be good for you. These sites usually have systems for chat, voice chat, messaging, e-mail, posting, blogging, video, discussion groups, etc., to communicate with other members. For business-to-business practice areas, visit:

- *www.Linkedin.com (biggest by far)*

- *www.networkingforprofessionals.com*

- *www.moli.com*

- *www.perfectbusiness.com*

For law firms who seek younger clients who are more likely to use social networking sites, look here:

- *www.Facebook.com*

- *www.MySpace.com*

- *www.Twitter.com*

Facebook is currently the #1 most used social networking site among worldwide active users, according to a February 2009 study by Compete.com. The site allows users to join networks defined by city, workplace, school, and region, to connect and interact with other people. Facebook enables you to create an individual profile, which allows people to get a glimpse of who you are. To maximize the potential of Facebook, attorneys should create a profile that is both accessible and professional. The profile should include photos of themselves, a brief summary, and a link back to their firm's Web site.

Next to Facebook, Twitter is one of the fastest-growing social networking sites on the Internet. Twitter is a free site that allows its users to post messages of up to 140 characters known as "tweets."

Tweets can range in both length and content, and can include such topics as:

1 Publicizing an upcoming speaking event
Example: "Looking forward to speaking at the AR Bar Assoc Conference on 10/13."

2 Linking back to a blog post
Example: "Check out today's commentary on recent Supreme Court decisions. http://url.com/myblogpost"

3 Responding to (known as "@ replying") a follower's query
Example: "@lawstudent2011 for more information, look at the animal legal defense fund"

4 Recommending a book or recently read article
Example: "Great article in Houston Chronicle today! Check it out at http://url.com"

Twitter allows you to build a network of dedicated information providers who can offer immediate feedback to questions. By following the leaders in their fields, an attorney can track new trends in the law and participate in shaping those trends.

Twitter functions as a research tool which gives attorneys distinctive access to individuals she or he might never meet in person.

Sites such as Tweetlaw and Legalbirds make this access even easier by functioning as databases for legal professionals. These sites aggregate the most recent tweets posted by those in the legal field, and enable you to sort through these posts by category (i.e., environmental law, cyber law, small law firm). They are great resources for legal professionals who are interested in becoming more active in social networking and want to be part of discussions relevant to their interests or specific practice.

LISTSERV Or Discussion Groups

These are functions on various Web sites that allow you to join and participate in a discussion group on topics related to your practice area. Groups like these allow you to accelerate your learning process because you are able to tap the combined wisdom of your peers by simply posting a question for the group to answer. Include a robust signature line on each of your posts that includes your Web site link. For more information visit:

• *http://groups.yahoo.com/*

The Power Of Blogging

The ABA reports there are 70,000 new blogs posted online each day and approximately 6% of lawyers have a blog. Blogs are relatively easy and inexpensive to build and few technical skills are needed by those doing the writing.

For those of you not familiar with the term, a "blogger" has a special site on the Internet – most professionals make them a part of their Web site – where they post comments, opinions and ideas.

Some of this commentary is lengthy, formally organized and written much like articles in a newspaper or magazine – in fact, often journalists who work for large publications maintain blogs so their readers can read more in-depth commentary when they expand on a topic.

Much of the writing at this level complies with the normal rules of grammar and punctuation. Others write commentary that is looser and more like a personal e-mail, producing text that reads like a quick recording of their thoughts, ideas or opinions. Others approach their blogs as they would a diary, chronicling their daily experiences.

Despite its informal approach and relatively new form of public media, many bloggers boast huge followings, and their ability to influence public opinion should not be underestimated. The audiences of some bloggers eclipse those of traditional media, and easily outstrip the readership of many newspapers.

How can a law firm use a blog to their advantage? According to Nora Bergman, Atticus coach and former director of the St. Petersburg Bar Association, by using it as a tool to advocate for their clients, attorneys can demonstrate their expertise and encour-

age dialogue. "It's not appropriate for all firms to use blogging as a strategy to attract clients, but for some it is another means of adding to their Internet marketing plan," says Bergman. As a Public Relations tool, "It must be appropriate for the type of clients the law firm wants to attract. Those who practice in the areas of intellectual property, patents, trademark and entertainment law, to name just a few, have early-adopting, technically sophisticated clients who are more likely to use the Internet to search for legal services."

Attorneys who seek a forum for expressing their opinions and expertise can also use blogs to cultivate other attorneys; again, this is practice-area dependent.

TIP

Build a solid foundation by developing a basic Web site that serves both your needs and the needs of your clients. Then you can focus on driving your traffic and increasing your rankings.

There are some blogging programs that are set up to allow the reader to post feedback on an article, opinion or views posted. If you are considering starting a blog, it's important to think carefully about allowing this function. If a blog's intended use is to cultivate an exchange of views and the feedback is monitored and responded to frequently, then it's a good idea to employ the feedback function. If feedback isn't welcome or won't be monitored enough, don't allow readers to post comments. Negative, insulting or misleading comments may sometimes be written and should not be left there, unmonitored, for any visitor to read.

One advantage of blogging is that the

fresh content posted on a blog that is part of a law firm Web site will often boost the Web site's ranking. While Search Engine Optimization has many components, one thing that's easy to understand about them is this: search engines scan for new material, and any Web site that has recently been updated with new content is automatically ranked higher than those that haven't. This means when a potential client searches for a practice like yours, your Web site shows up closer to the top of the search results page.

Blogging also incorporates the use of "tags." In blogging, a tag is a keyword or term assigned to an entry that helps categorize it and allows it to be found again by browsing or searching. A blog may have a sidebar listing all the tags in use on that blog, with each tag leading to an index page. By looking through the index of tags, the average user can instantly find what she or he is looking for in an entry, rather than searching through the user's history to find what it is that s/he wants.

Another advantage of blogging is synchronicity. One example of this is linking to your Twitter account. By linking to Twitter, you are able to amplify your blog's presence on the Web. Visitors to your blog will be able to connect, or "follow" you on Twitter, thereby driving up your blog traffic and page views.

Many blogging sites are easy to use. They allow the user to customize and personalize a certain design, moder-

ate comments, and upload and store multimedia.

The following sites offer such services, and are completely free, mainstream and popular:

• *WordPress (www.wordpress.org)*

• *BlogSpot (www.blogspot.com)*

All together, having a well-designed Web site, whether or not it includes a blog, is how you acquire this Asset. It must broadcast your firm's brand and educate potential clients about who you are, who you serve, and the problems you solve. It should attract clients and inform Referral Sources. For many of you it is a very important marketing tool and should be considered by every firm, no matter how small.

In the next section, we address the many ways you can use Public Relations to help you attract clients, polish your firm's reputation, and raise your profile in the community.

ASSET #7

PUBLIC RELATIONS CAMPAIGN

*The only thing worse than being talked about
is not being talked about. ~ Oscar Wilde*

Generating A Positive Public Image

Oone day, many years ago, we received a call from an attorney we'd been working with for only a short time. "Have you been watching the news?" he asked with great urgency. "Yes, why?" we responded. "Have you been following the school shooting story?" We had – the whole nation was watching because at the time it was still a rare occurrence. The panic in the voice of this small town attorney started to rise, "I've represented the mother of one of the alleged shooters in the past and she's just asked me for help. Somehow the press got a hold of this and right now there are trucks from CNN and all the network news stations outside my office. I'm trapped.

***Should I go out and talk to them? Should I avoid them?
What should I do?"***

We worked to ease his fears and crafted a few statements he could use to satisfy the press while protecting his client. But this was just the beginning for him. For months his life was turned upside down and we received more secretive calls for advice as he sidestepped throngs of reporters in the courthouse and was imprisoned in his office by reporters clamoring for comments. He had hired us to help him with practice management issues and we became media consultants instead as this case overtook his life. He was hounded by countless phone calls from reporters and tracked everywhere he went by media people desperate for news.

Quite by accident, this normally very quiet and unassuming man was thrust into the national spotlight and gained a great deal of publicity that was unplanned, chaotic and quite invasive. But very effective.

How is this relevant to you and your practice? Because his experience (though most PR is not based on such high profile cases) illustrates a simple fact in a very condensed way: every single day hundreds of news correspondents, television journalists, reporters and writers across the nation search for new subject matter, interesting things and people to write about. They descend on the stories of the day because the media machine they serve is voracious: thousands of publications, news programs and talk shows need fresh material on an hourly, daily, weekly, or monthly basis.

When well planned and executed, Public Relations can greatly enhance your client development efforts. Being featured, quoted or profiled by various publications, appearing on radio talk shows, or being interviewed on television can be an enormous boost to your credibility. And the publicity you receive can serve as a significant means of attracting new clients to your door. You may never have the press show up at your door in the remarkable and unexpected way our client did, but there are ways to cultivate buzz and enhance your reputation in a more methodical way using various media.

Before we go any further with this discussion, however, it's important to understand that Public Relations, or "PR," as it is often referred to, is distinct from marketing and advertising. The purpose of Public Relations, whether used by corporations, business entities or law firms, is this: to

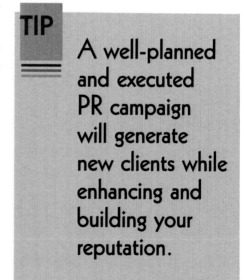

TIP

A well-planned and executed PR campaign will generate new clients while enhancing and building your reputation.

TIP

Becoming an active member of your community and volunteering for causes and fundraising efforts can help to build a well-rounded Public Relations effort.

generate and uphold a positive public image.

This effort serves to popularize any law firm successes, downplay any negative situations that may occur, announce important alliances, broadcast changes in leadership and promote firm-related activities. For smaller firms, most of this will occur in print media such as newspapers and magazines.

The *non-press* related activities in PR include becoming an active member of the community, being a sponsor of art events or volunteering for a grass-roots community cause. They also can include fundraising efforts for charity (separate from hosting a Signature Event) or being a school board member – activities and associations that present a picture of the lawyer as a supporter of the community vs. activities that are only practice-related. A well-rounded Public Relations effort would cover all aspects.

Marketing – as a client development activity – is based on creating a positive reputation through word of mouth and building referral relationships with those who can send business to you. It is generally carried out one-on-one or happens with small groups of people in various social and business settings. With the exception of larger events such as seminars or speaking engagements or Signature Events, marketing to develop new clients happens on a small scale within the confines of your social and professional circle and requires a highly personal approach.

Also distinct from Public Relations, using **advertising** as a way to develop new clients involves formulating a message about the services you provide and delivering it on a large, impersonal scale, via print advertising, radio promotions or television commercials. On the positive side, when you advertise, your message is conveyed to a significantly larger audience than simple marketing efforts can impact. On the negative side, though, advertising is generally very expensive, attracts a wide range of clients, both qualified and those who are price shopping, and is viewed with some suspicion by its intended audience.

While lawyers who advertise must

always fight the negative perceptions associated with it, appearing on television, radio or in various print media because you are being interviewed, quoted or profiled as an expert, has the opposite effect. It tends to build trustworthiness and adds, rather than subtracts, from an attorney's reputation.

When an attorney has paid for his or her appearance in the press, the public is suspicious. When an attorney is appearing at the behest of the station or is sought out by a journalist to discuss a case or provide commentary on a subject, he or she is viewed as an expert with valuable input.

Though advertising has its place, as does marketing, Public Relations provides one of the most inexpensive (it

generally only costs the attorney and team members the time it takes to write a story or be interviewed) and highly successful forms of creating Top Of Mind Awareness available. And it can do so on a large scale. The reach of publicity can equal that of advertising, though it will usually occur for a shorter duration.

TIP

Being quoted or interviewed as an authority on a particular topic, or as a reference source on radio, TV or in the print media, can help to build your credibility with current and potential clients.

Your Target Audience

Because it can be so effective when done correctly, thought must precede action when you want to generate a Public Relations Campaign. Before you begin promoting yourself through different media, you must first identify your target market or intended audience.

Each practice area will have its own set of ideal clients. In Asset #4 we discussed the elements that go into a successful Laser Talk: Who you serve, how you solve their problems and what makes you uniquely qualified to do so. We mentioned that it's important to have a separate talk for each area of practice – due to the fact you serve a different clientele with different problems to solve in each one. Likewise, for Public Relations efforts to be successful, it's important to analyze each media outlet to see what type of reader, listener or viewer it attracts. Then craft your message accordingly.

Newspapers

General print publications such as your local newspaper, for example, will be read by a wide variety of people whose demographics might be a good fit for potential clients and possible Referral Sources. In your local newspaper there are most likely opportunities for you to be quoted in front page news stories or features in the business, financial, real estate or lifestyle sections. Also, a smaller, local newspaper will be easier to contact and build a relationship with than obtaining space in a larger newspaper. A real estate attorney might contribute

> **TIP**
>
> Have your Marketing Assistant post your articles on the firm's Web site to increase its content.

to or write an article for the real estate section on how to avoid predatory lending practices. An elder law attorney might be quoted in a story on the "sandwich generation": middle-age parents who are trying to raise their children and care for their elderly parents at the same time. This would be a great story for the lifestyle section. A criminal defense attorney might comment on the link between illiteracy and criminal tendencies among young offenders. This could be placed in an article about a spike in crime rates. A firm we have worked with regularly places articles that educate the public about the inner-workings of the court system; placement coincides with Law Day every year.

Trade Publications

If, however, you are an estate planning attorney and wish to cultivate more CPAs, you might have more success if you target their local trade publications. It doesn't hurt to be featured in a publication for general consumption like the local paper, but being referenced by Referral Source-specific publications adds that much more credibility.

The question to ask yourself when contemplating your local newspaper's effectiveness as a Public Relations vehicle is whether or not your potential clients and Referral Sources will find you there. It's up to you – or your Marketing Assistant if you have one – to know where you should be featured to provide the greatest impact. Often, the publications most sought or trusted by your Referral Sources have the greatest impact.

Article Vs. Press Release

There is a difference between a press release and an article. A feature article is often what you'd submit to a trade journal. It is not usually as time-sensitive as a press release and covers an issue in greater depth.

Press releases are most often submitted to the local newspaper and cover the Five Ws: the Who, What, When, Where and Why that constitute news. Ideas worthy of a release: a new partner joins the firm who brings special expertise; a Signature Event with an interesting theme or charity tie-in; accolades or awards which are received.

Don't make your press release strictly self-promotional or it won't be published. Reporters and editors look for news that is of interest to a broad segment of the population and not obviously self-promotional. Don't expect to have a release published every week or every time it's submitted, and don't get too discouraged if it isn't picked up.

According to Nancy Butler-Ross, former columnist for *The Miami Herald,* you should "Cultivate a relationship with the <u>appropriate</u> editor and submit a release of similar length to those that usually run in the paper. Make the editor's job easy – don't make them read 1,000 words to find your pertinent 'news' – they'll pick and feature someone else's release, or won't want to open yours in the future." She goes on to say, "If your release is about an event you're hosting, make sure to extend an invitation to the editor – they may assign a reporter to cover the story." Her final words of advice: "Don't trust Spell Czech!"

Read through the form at the back of the Asset for an exact description of what to put where when constructing a press release. Once done, it can be used to distribute news to newspapers, magazines, and other printed publications, and television and radio contacts when appropriate. Compile a group of contacts to whom you can e-mail your releases with the push of a button. Keep in mind that 'Blind' e-mails (where the list of all recipients is hidden) are appreciated

TIP For added exposure, use your Marketing Assistant to send copies of articles you've written out to your Top Twenty and Farm Team members. Include a note saying: "I thought you'd be interested in this article...".

when sending mass mailings. Keep your list current, as editors and staff writers change; you want your releases to reach the proper person.

Where Should You Submit the Press Release?

If your news release is not hard news and doesn't contain "breaking" news, submit it as a feature dis-

tribution. Feature releases are often placed in the living or lifestyle section of the local newspaper and will be reproduced verbatim. If your news is business-related, submit it to the business section. If it's event-related, submit it to the calendar section, as well as to the appropriate editor.

An Alternative Method

If you have noticed your competitors are getting coverage which seems out of reach for you – whether they regularly appear in the local newspaper, on television or in business magazines – they may be using a different approach. While some might hire Public Relations firms, others develop their own expertise in-house.

There are two different approaches to media placement. One is press release driven. The other is to convince reporters and journalists that individuals within your organization are worth interviewing. This approach is "pitch" driven. Being considered an expert whom reporters call and rely on for analysis and insight demands that you look at the world through the reporter's eyes and figure out what interests their readers. Once you have performed that analysis, look at which individuals within your organization can satisfy these reporter needs, and what topics and presentations will be the best fit.

When you compose a press release, you're packaging your news for reporters en masse, but when you write a pitch, you're customizing your idea to fit an individual reporter, and selling yourself as the right person to interview.

This will only work if you've done your homework. You've read their articles, you've researched their work or you've watched their show many times, and you know what their preferences are. It is important to take a long-term perspective here and design your pitch in such a way that the recipient will respond to a future submission even if this one doesn't work for them.

TIP

Small and mid-sized firms can maximize their public relations efforts by hiring a publicist to focus on media placements and high-profile community activities.

You'll be considered a reliable source if you or others in your firm (i.e., your partners, if you have them), can consistently pitch good ideas.

If you want to be serious about this idea, perform an *Expert Audit* on yourself and other prospective experts in your firm. Meet with your colleagues to identify who can talk about which issues. Then profile your spokesperson(s) on your Web site, listing their credentials and where they have been quoted by the press in the past.

When a 'hot topic' hits the news, consider sending out a *Media Advisory* alerting reporters and journalists that your spokesperson is available to give his or her position on the subject.

Let's talk for a moment about what a Media Advisory does (see the Media Advisory Form at the back of this chapter): start out with a prominent headline announcing the topic and let the reporter know what the expert has to offer. Open with a short paragraph, then outline your premise below, using bullet points and sharp, to-the-point short sentences. Know that the reporters and journalists who receive these Media Advisories are going to scan them quickly, looking for the most important information and an angle they think their audience might find interesting. Make it easy for them to connect with you.

Make sure the information they need, including contact information, is available at a glance in an easily accessible format. If your Advisory is successful, you may get a phone call from the editor or producer, if you've sent your alerts to a television program. Be enthusiastic and engaging on the phone as this call may actually be a "pre-interview" in which your viability as a guest speaker or interview subject is being tested. Keep in mind you may eventually be interviewed via phone for radio shows.

If you don't receive a response from your Media Advisory, call and follow up on whether or not the information was received. Sometimes opportunities will arise in these conversations which are difficult to predict, and you should stay alert for them. In any case, your ability to sell yourself plays an important role here.

We've had matrimonial attorneys appear on CNN to comment on celebrity break-ups, and we've had criminal defense attorneys appear on local network news programs, giving their opinions on crimes that make national headlines. An attorney who was an advocate for the homeless made several appearances in the local press commenting on various homeless issues. There is a wide range of possibilities for this sort of expert appearance, but these kinds of efforts will be much more likely to happen if you are employing a Marketing Assistant to aid you in writing these Advisories.

To excel at this approach, you or your Marketing Assistant must cultivate relationships in advance with those reporters and journalists to whom you

can send a Media Advisory. In some instances, you'll be sending advisories to media people you don't know – national media outlets, for example – but if you are working more on a local level with your local television networks or local newspapers, you'll probably know the people you are targeting. This is where many of the same marketing skills you rely upon to build relationships with Referral Sources can help you – as long as you stay within the more restricted parameters of the reporter's world.

TIP

Before pitching a story to the media, do your homework and familiarize yourself with the reporter's work, the radio commentator's show or the TV personality's program. This will help you prepare your approach when making the initial contact.

TIP

Find out which way is best to communicate with your media contacts. Do they prefer being contacted by e-mail, phone, or face-to-face

- Be helpful and available to them on short notice.

- Be aware of their audience; formulate your message or comments so they are relevant.

- If asked to comment on a particular subject that is out of your element, refer them to someone else. This can be a great marketing device. If you recommend another professional to be interviewed, they are much more likely to remember you when they have a client to refer.

- When being interviewed, be yourself, and try to speak in short, quotable sound bites and resist the urge to give long, rambling answers to questions. Remember: your interviewer will be trying to take notes.

- Speak briefly and leave time for follow-up questions.

DOs And DON'Ts

Where you might thank a Referral Source for a client referral with a personal gift, you would send a reporter who mentioned you in a story a simple thank you note. Make it an acknowledgment of how well the reporter wrote the article or conducted the interview, as opposed to blatantly thanking them for featuring *you* in the story. While being as friendly and accommodating as possible, it is important to avoid the appearance that you are in any way trying to buy or win the affections of the press. To avoid alienating members of the press while trying to cultivate them, here are a few ways to maximize your chances of being on their call list:

Building Relationships

Communicating with your media contacts in the way they prefer is essential: while most rely heavily on e-mail, others may prefer the telephone. For court reporters, a face-to-face conversation with litigators at the courthouse would be logistically beneficial, but litigators must examine the ethical issues involved in speaking to courthouse reporters and only do so when it's advantageous to their clients. Remembering details about the reporters or journalists you work with – the stories they've written, what they typically report on – can provide fodder to help develop your relationship. Add these details to your Contact Management Software for future relationship development.

When attempting to build these relationships, you might – as you would when trying to cultivate a Referral Source – ask them to lunch. Some in the media are open to this level of contact, and some are not. Proceed slowly and look for signs that might indicate whether or not your contacts embrace having a more personal relationship with you. Several of our clients invite the reporters they know to firm-related social events and introduce them to other people in the community that they might view as valuable resources in the future. Others jealously guard their relationships with the media and are very careful not to introduce them to others. All in all, we believe reporters look more favorably on those who share, but can understand the protective instincts of those who don't.

Damage Control

There have been several incidents in which our clients received harshly negative press on issues they didn't cause and had no control over

as they unfolded: criminal clients who committed suicide and firm employees who got themselves in trouble with the law. Typically, after taking any damage control options that can be taken, they hunker down and hope the passage of time will blunt the impact of the incident. By all accounts, these attorneys report that even negative news raises their profile, creates buzz about their firm and brings in more business.

The first thing you should try to do if you know there will be negative press is to get in front of it. If a negative article is about to be published and you know about it ahead of time, ask to speak to the reporter so your side is heard. If an article comes out that is negative and you had no advance warning, talk to the reporter and offer your side of the story. It is important to counter the bad news and set the story straight. If you do get your side of the story published, and you want to broadcast your version of the story, e-mail the article to appropriate clients and influencers with a cover letter.

Writing a letter to the editor can also be helpful if you can't get the reporter to respond. Again, this is something you can e-mail or send to appropriate people. A lively debate in the press on some matter will normally help a firm's Top Of Mind Awareness and add to their image.

If someone in your firm has done something wrong the firm should publicize corrective actions, such as letting the involved parties go or sending staff members for training. Obviously, each situation has to be weighed individually and considered in light of the firm's liability. Actions that suggest the firm is guilty have to be weighed carefully – especially if a suit is possible. Talking with advisors is recommended if the situation becomes complicated.

When situations like this occur, it really pays to have cultivated a relationship with the press in the first place – your chances of having your side of the story told are much greater if you have existing relationships with the reporters and journalists on the receiving end of your calls.

We don't at all suggest you create negative press, but it reinforces the old adage, "I don't care what you say about me – just spell my name right," meaning that almost any publicity is good publicity. We prefer you use Public Relations to build the reputation of your firm in a positive way, to enhance your reputation as an expert and show your work as a force for good in the community.

To claim this Asset, you must set and achieve goals that are specific and measurable in the area of Public Relations that relate to and support your marketing plan. We'd like you to achieve a total of six media placements over the course of a year. In order to accomplish this, your goals might look something like this:

• In order to increase our credibility with Referral Sources, we will have one article placed in Referral Source trade journals once a quarter.

• In order to increase our exposure to other attorneys and increase our referrals, we will write a monthly column for our local Bar journal.

• In order to raise our profile in the community, our partners will each sit on the board of a community or charity organization.

• In order to enhance our reputation, we will cultivate our relationship with our local paper and submit one press release per month.

If you follow the tips in this chapter and seek publicity by forming a good working relationship with the press, you may be pleasantly surprised at where it will lead.

In the meantime, the next chapter on the interview process will teach you another one of the most important conversational strategies. Not a strategy for asking questions of a job applicant, as you might think; this particular conversation has the ability to deepen rapport with Referral Sources well beyond business as usual. Read on to discover the power of asking the right questions at the right time.

PRESS RELEASE
ATTICUS RAINMAKERS - SAMPLE FORMAT

FOR IMMEDIATE RELEASE
Capitalize all letters in this headline and place this title in the upper left-hand margin. Include the date of submission here. Try to keep the entire release to one page in length.

The Headline
A single sentence that summarizes the essence of your text. Put any articles, prepositions or conjunctions of three letter words or less in lowercase type.

The Dateline
List the date of your press release and the city it is issued from.

Lead Paragraph
Write a strong introductory paragraph to grab the reader's attention. Use the journalistic device of formatting your message to follow the Five Ws: who, what, when, where and why. While this paragraph should be a summary of what's to come in the rest of the text, if effectively written it hooks your reader and encourages them to read on. Keep your word count between 50 and 75 words.

Body
The main text of your press release is where you expand upon your news. Many journalists use the inverted pyramid technique in which the most critical information and any pertinent quotes are placed at the beginning. This will be the largest and most informative section.

Firm Information
End your press release with a brief paragraph that describes your firm and its practice areas. Include a short history of the firm.

Contact Information
List the name, e-mail address and phone number of the person who wrote the press release and their qualification to discuss the subject matter (i.e., Esq., Admin. Asst., etc.), as the newspaper's fact checkers will call to verify the info in the release before printing.

MEDIA ADVISORY
RAINMAKERS SAMPLE FORMAT

Directions: Following the format suggested below, compose your own brief Media Advisory to submit to reporters and journalists who **routinely** (this is important) write or report on the subject you'd like to comment on. Follow your submission with a phone call if you don't get a timely response. Be prepared to extemporaneously discuss the topic if you receive a follow-up phone call from a reporter. The same applies if a radio or television producer calls you to follow up — the phone call may actually be a "pre-interview" to test how you come across.

PROMINENT HEADLINE: Explain the topic and what the expert has to offer.

Example: CITY MOVES to BAN HOMELESS DOWNTOWN:
LOCAL ATTORNEY QUESTIONS the LEGALITY of THIS BAN

Attorney Bob Smith is available to address the controversy over the homeless which is currently occurring in the downtown area, and can shed new light on the legal perspective.

SHORT, EXPLANATORY PARAGRAPH: Briefly explain the view of the attorney.

Example: Bob Smith, local attorney and long-time advocate for the homeless, speaks out against the St. Louis police department for their treatment of the homeless population. Protected under present panhandling laws, Smith claims the homeless are not violating local laws:

- *The police department routinely arrests homeless men and women without cause*

- *Most homeless spend the night in shelters and are not loitering*

- *Only a small percentage of homeless panhandle, etc. ...*

CREDENTIALS: State the credentials and contact information for the expert speaker and supply pertinent facts about their background.

Example: Bob Smith practices criminal defense and is a founding partner in the firm of Smith, Butler and Ross, PA. At 51, Smith is a resident of St. Louis, Missouri and a frequent advocate for the rights of the homeless. Frequently quoted in The St. Louis Sun, The Missouri Resister and the Hometown Paper, Smith has represented...

Office Phone Number:
Cell Phone Number:
E-mail Address:

ASSET #8

THE INTERVIEW

You can make more friends in two months by becoming interested in other people than you can in two years by trying to get other people interested in you. ~ *Dale Carnegie*

Building Rapport With Referral Sources

H*ave you ever had a Referral Source just drop off the radar screen? Someone who used to send a lot of business, then stopped for some unknown reason? They haven't moved, died or changed how they do business, but the referrals just stopped coming? You must find out what happened. And next time, don't wait until something goes wrong. If you fail to notice when your Referral Sources are dissatisfied, they may send their clients elsewhere. As we've said before, with 42,000 new attorneys graduating every year, competition for referrals is on the rise.*

If you haven't thought about your Referral Sources as the valuable assets they are – take a moment to calculate their worth. Not just over the course of a year, but over the lifetime of your practice. Thousands of dollars of business every year, and hundreds of thousands over the life of your practice, can often be attributed to just one good Referral Source. They are much too valuable to ignore.

The Eighty-Twenty Rule

This is important stuff. As we have said before, 80% of your referrals probably come from fewer than 20% of your Referral Sources. It's likely your firm owes its existence to a handful of people who know you, like you and have faithfully sent you clients over the years. Unless you depend entirely on advertising, the very survival of your firm is tied to the continuing good will of these people.

Unfortunately, they're under no obligation to continue sending you business and can stop at any time. For any reason. No 30-day notice required. Given the delicate nature of this unspoken contract, wouldn't it be wise to treat them well? And to find out what they're thinking once in awhile?

Yes on both counts. We spend a great deal of time in marketing seminars and workshops trying to make attorneys understand the importance of their Referral Sources. Sitting down with Referral Sources to see how well you serve their clients is a direct method of obtaining honest feedback.

We routinely ask Atticus attorneys to interview 10 people who've referred business to them in the past. If you haven't been proactive in cultivating your referral relationships, we recommend you do two things:

• *First*, schedule lunch with your Referral Sources to let them know how much you appreciate their ongoing support. (You almost can't express your appreciation enough and starting off with a compliment is a nice way to lead into the conversation.)

• *Second,* ask their opinions on your practice and how it serves the people they send.

How To Start:

Appreciation

We recommend you start with referrers you feel comfortable with and use the first part of the conversation to reconnect and catch up. Then, to smooth the way for the next part of the conversation and bring the conversation back to business, acknowledge them for the business they've sent in the past. You can use your own words, or use ours. There are endless variations of acknowledgments, some of which we cover in other sections of this book. Just remember: it's best to keep it simple and sincere:

> •**We really enjoy working with your clients — thank you for all your referrals.**
> **Or**
> •**Thank you for sending us your business — we really appreciate your faith and confidence in us.**
> **Or**
> •**We appreciate your business and thank you for trusting us to work with your (clients, friends, family, etc.).**

Evaluation

Next, launch into the interview. Begin with one of the following statements:

> •**I'm always trying to improve the level of service we deliver to clients and I'd like to ask your opinion: Is there anything I can do to improve how I handle the clients you send?**
> **Or**
> •**I really appreciate the fact that you send such great clients. Is there anything I can do to serve their needs better?**
> **Or**
> •**I make a special effort to take care of the clients you send. Is there anything else I could do to take care of them better?**

Keep in mind you don't have to use these exact words. Just get your point across in a way that's comfortable for you. Though this may seem like a difficult conversation, our attorney clients are generally surprised at how well it goes. Making more follow-up calls is a suggestion they commonly receive, installing a handicap parking space or

> **TIP**
> Take good care of your Referral Sources. One Referral Source may send thousands of dollars worth of business every year — multiply that by the 30 to 50 years you'll be practicing law — it adds up quickly.

bathroom has been suggested for clients that are elderly, and making sure the receptionist remembers names of clients when they call is also a regularly reported suggestion.

Rarely can you go wrong thanking someone, then asking his or her opinion. The opinion-gathering part of the conversation proves useful for more than just gathering information. This exchange nurtures your relationship with your Referral Source. Believe it or not, better rapport and a new sense of familiarity are created from conversations like these. Your Referral Sources will come away complimented that you asked their opinion. From their perspective, it means you care about them, and value what they think. It indicates you're paying attention to their needs, and, most importantly, those

of their clients. Clearly, you aren't taking their referrals for granted, but recognize their importance to your success. Attorneys should always ask their Referral Source if they can refer back to them, if they are not doing so at the time. Reciprocity is important whenever it is possible.

Press Them Further

When you begin asking questions, your Referral Source may initially refuse to say anything specific, instead offering generalities such as "You do a great job," or "What you do now is just fine." Press them slightly by first asking more positive, open-ended questions, then move to more pointed ones:

> • In your opinion, what creates a positive experience for your clients?
>
> • What do you think we do well?
>
> • Could we improve on or add to any of those aspects of the client experience?

If that doesn't work, or you prefer another approach, say, "Is there anything you suggest I do more of, or change altogether, when dealing with your clients?" Alternately, you could say something more specific:

• **Were your clients comfortable in our office?**

• **Were your clients comfortable with our staff?**

• **Did your clients feel taken care of by our team?**

• **Were your clients seen in a timely manner?**

• **Did your clients feel they had our full attention?**

• **Did we answer your client's questions to their satisfaction?**

• **Would your clients be likely to recommend our services to their friends?**

These kinds of open-ended questions will usually produce more of a response. Nine times out of ten the Referral Source won't have anything substantially negative to say, but will be complimented that you asked their opinion.

It is of paramount importance, however, to refrain from a defensive posture if any negative comments are made. This will shut down the flow of information and indicate you weren't seriously interested in constructive suggestions. View any nuggets of information gleaned from the conversation, whether positive or negative, as very valuable, and thank the per-

TIP

Sit down with your Referral Sources and ask how well you are serving the needs of their clients. They'll appreciate that you care enough to ask their opinion and their clients will ultimately receive better care.

Your competitors will focus on delivering a high-level of *technically correct* service to clients of Referral Sources you might have in common. Edge out the competition by delivering the kind of service that also recognizes the human being behind the problem.

you demonstrate you care about their clients and are sincerely interested in delivering a high level of service to them. It's generally a safe bet most of the other attorneys they send work to won't go to the same lengths to be sure their clients are being treated well. This conversation gives you an edge over your competition who may focus on being technically correct and forget the human side of the equation.

This strategic conversation increases the likelihood that when that Referral Source has a client to send, they'll think of you first. You've heard us refer to it as Top Of Mind Awareness and you won't get many referrals without it.

son for their opinions. If, by chance, a negative comment is made that you think is unreasonable, don't fall into the trap of accusing a Referral Source of having impossibly high standards. They are entitled to have standards. Resist the urge to defend yourself or your team and instead say you'll use their comments to enhance the level of service you provide to their clients. This part of the conversation must be managed well or you could alienate the Referral Source who is only offering you the feedback you specifically requested from them.

In addition to the normally very useful feedback you get, this conversation opens the door to more referrals from those Referral Sources who spread their work around to several other attorneys in addition to you. Why? Because, in having this conversation,

To claim this Asset, schedule 10 interviews in the next month to deepen your referral relationships and gather important feedback to enhance the service you deliver. For motivation, remember that if you don't take good care of your Referral Sources, and their clients – someone else will.

In Asset #9, *An Accountability Partner,* we discuss the power of teaming up with another professional for the dual purposes of sending each other business and spurring each other on to more and better client development efforts. The power of having another person hold you accountable is an untapped source of additional motivation for most attorneys. Read on to discover how you can tap into this motivation for yourself.

ASSET #9

AN ACCOUNTABILITY PARTNER

There is no more sure tie between friends than when they are united in their objects and wishes. ~ Marcus Tullius

Teaming Up For Success

It's hard to make anyone do anything they don't want to do. Like many things in life, developing new business is easier if you don't do it all by yourself. Teaming up with even one other person can make all the difference. There is safety – and success – in numbers. Marketing is something some people absolutely do not want to do. Experience has shown us that for some attorneys, the idea of marketing – which requires taking initiative in the social arena and risking rejection on some level – inspires a great deal of anxiety. Unnecessary anxiety, and anxiety that's surmountable with practice, but an uncomfortable feeling, just the same.

Having an Accountability Partner, another attorney either inside or outside your firm, a practice advisor or another trusted professional, can support your efforts and help you overcome your feelings of discomfort. And, if you team up with the right person, they can hold you accountable for the marketing actions you agree to take.

Set Up A Structure Of Accountability

You are more likely to keep a promise you've made to another person than one you've made to yourself. When it comes to changing behaviors, or stepping outside of your comfort zone, having outside accountability is critical. Many attorneys team up with like-minded colleagues in their own firm. They use the relationship as a structure of accountability in that they will meet and discuss marketing ideas on a regular basis. Not only is this good for the brainstorming opportunities it creates, often the attorneys will make commitments to each other, such as, "I'm going to ask three potential Referral Sources out to lunch in the next two weeks," or "I'm going to the Bar luncheon on Friday and will try to meet two new people that I can network with."

These small, one-on-one partnerships can be very helpful to anyone strug-

gling to build a practice. But there are other forms of accountability which can be equally effective.

For two long-term partners and owners of a successful estate planning and elder law firm in Garden City, New York, attending their weekly networking meeting with other professionals and business people is a must. For these two attorneys, the meeting provides not only the opportunity to meet other business people in their area, it's one of the structures of accountability they've put in place to develop new business for their firm.

At the breakfast meeting, they hear from new members who talk about the services they provide to the group's collection of CPAs, a financial planner, people who own their own businesses and other types of professionals. the two partners also have an opportunity to talk about the types of clients they serve. This meeting exposes them to a cross section of business people in the area that they, unlike many of their colleagues, regard as an important group to know. They look for the opportunity to send other members business and hope they'll reciprocate. Over the years, this strategy has paid off. They've received numerous referrals from the group and credit their participation in the group with a significant portion of their business.

While these attorneys belong to a very formal national networking organization, it's not accessible in all regions. You can take a similar tack by forming your own group.

First, make sure your plans don't conflict with any local Bar regulations. Once you are clear on the rules, an easy approach to creating an alliance involves inviting one or two existing Referral Sources to lunch and discussing how you can help one another with referrals. A variation of this format is commonly seen within large firms where two partners, whose practice areas complement each other, such as estate planning and elder law, form an alliance and refer clients to one another. These relationships can easily serve as structures of accountability for their members as it's easy enough to make commitments to marketing steps you'll take between meetings. Making these com-

mitments public and voicing them in front of your marketing partners turns a marketing partnership into an Accountability Partner.

To avoid conflicting with Bar regulations, most small groups are organized on an informal basis and give multiple referrals. Since referral relationships thrive on trust – trust that all of you will take good care of each other's clients – it is smart to proceed with caution and know the other person's commitment to client service in order to avoid a negligent referral situation.

In 2001, a respected family law attorney in Dallas assembled a group of interested attorneys to discuss practice management issues. The plan was to meet once a month in a member's office and either discuss a business book or listen to a guest

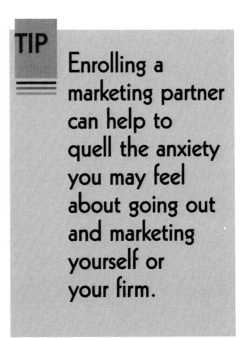

TIP

Enrolling a marketing partner can help to quell the anxiety you may feel about going out and marketing yourself or your firm.

> **TIP**
>
> Having someone hold you accountable works for one reason: you are more likely to keep a commitment you make to another person. Privately trying to change your own behavior and overcome your fears is much less successful.

speaker. What he didn't anticipate is that the group would develop into an informal referral network. As the group got to know each other, they became invested in one another's success, and referrals were the result. Without realizing it, our friend from the Lone Star state started his own marketing alliance.

Around the same time, a business and patent attorney in Jacksonville, Florida, actually set out to start a networking group. Comprised of solo and small firm attorneys, the once small group has grown over the years, both in size and in their ability to refer clients to one another. Crediting nearly a third of his business to members of this group, this attorney considers their referrals a tremendous boon to his practice.

Aware that there could be problems with competition, he handpicked the original members so their practice areas wouldn't conflict with one another and create trouble within the ranks. Now, when a new member is proposed, a five-person membership council reviews the candidate. If the candidate is considered to have high service standards and a good reputation, the council then invites them to attend a meeting. From there, the entire group votes on allowing the candidate to join. A unanimous vote is required for membership. This group, like the others mentioned, strives to pre-empt any negligent referral issues by maintaining high standards of service and competency. Though this is purposely an informal organization, the members want to protect what has become a source of camaraderie and good business for all of them.

In an alternate approach, an existing network of professionals, colleagues and business contacts who already send work to each other is brought together by someone in the group who recognizes the opportunity and takes the initiative to form a group. They institutionalize their collective relationship by meeting on a regular basis and making a point to look for referral opportunities for each other. Generally, alliances, both large and small, benefit from having a central theme or target market. A group focused on small businesses, for example, might include litigators who work with small business owners plus accountants, bankers and others who serve the small business community. Another target market might be financial services which would include estate planning attorneys, insurance brokers, CPAs, etc.

There Are Six Key Ingredients To Maintaining A Successful Marketing Alliance:

1 Each member should regularly attend all meetings, lunches or breakfasts that are scheduled. It should be an easy commitment to make for all parties. Examples:

• Lunch once a month.

• Breakfast every Friday.

• A meeting and tour once a quarter in one member's office

2 Each member should be genuinely committed to helping the oth-

ers succeed – mutual benefit should be a guiding theme.

3 Each member should be committed to referring high quality business to one another. The client's best interests should outweigh the attorney's interests when a referral is considered.

4 Each member should be committed to treating referred clients with great care:

• Clients should be seen as quickly as possible by the referred attorney.

• The referring member may call ahead or bring the clients and introduce them in person, when appropriate.

• Each member who takes a referred client should never steal the referred client.

• The referrer should be endorsed strongly and respected as the principal relationship.

• The referrer should be kept informed, when ethically appropriate, of progress, new developments or changes as they occur with the referred client.

5 Each member should be committed to giving honest feedback about the standard of care provided by each person, and receiving feed-

back about their own.

6 Each member should use the opportunity to make their marketing commitments public so that their marketing partners can hold them accountable to whatever client development steps they need to take.

Strategies For Marketing Alliance Partners

The most obvious and directly beneficial means of supporting other members is to provide them with client referrals. But that's not all you can do. Resourceful members can help their marketing partners in several innovative ways:

1 Alliance members can set up a lunch and introduce others to their law firm or professional partners.

2 Members can introduce others to their friends, family and community contacts, when and where appropriate.

3 If a member is part of a group, such as a Bar committee or a local Inns of Court, they may invite another member to be a guest speaker, allow them to make an announcement about an upcoming event, or invite them as a guest for a special meeting. By providing an additional platform, other members can help increase their colleague's visibility and credibility.

4 Those in the group can encourage their clients to use the services of others by handing out appropriate literature, be it a business card or brochure.

5 Members can co-lead or co-sponsor educational events such as seminars (the divorce attorney who joins with a family therapist to host a lecture on "Helping Children Survive Divorce," the banker who joins with the business lawyer to host a lecture for small business owners on "How to Avoid Costly Litigation," the Personal Injury attorney who joins with a bicycle shop to host "Safe Biking Day," and the elder law attorney who joins with a financial planner to host a "Don't Outlive Your Money" seminar).

6 *Large Signature Events* such as golf tournaments, an outdoor barbeque, a day at the races, a charity auction, etc., can be co-hosted by members.

In some cases you may be called upon to hold others accountable for their marketing actions and actually train them to become better Rainmakers.

Some firms will conduct a marketing discussion in their partner or practice group meetings to continually train their attorneys on client development habits and skills.

TIP

Referral relationships depend on a mutual desire to take good care of each other's clients. When beginning a new relationship, start slowly by sending a client over to test the waters and listen for any positive or negative reactions as to how they were treated.

lack the desire to market themselves or the firm. Their desire to learn is important to this process, so test their resolve before investing a great deal of time, money and effort on their training. If they have the desire, they'll challenge themselves to be a little uncomfortable, try behaviors that are outside the norm for them – and with your guidance, discover their own client development style. It is a worthy use of your time to help them with this effort and a necessary investment in the future of your firm. It is a rare firm that doesn't need to develop new clients to survive.

If you find yourself in the position to mentor other attorneys in your firm, you will run into roadblocks along the way. The following is a variety of problems and effective methods/solutions you might encounter in developing a team of Rainmakers.

Host a Marketing Retreat.

Sole practitioners can meet with their associates on a weekly or monthly basis to discuss marketing issues and opportunities. The formula for success goes something like this:

The more important the goal, the more frequent the meetings. And the more public a goal is made, the more likely it will be achieved.

No marketing methods will work if your partner or associates completely

As a forum to discuss firm goals and marketing plans, a firm retreat is an opportunity to spend focused time on learning how and why the firm must develop new clients. Firm-wide ambitions are rarely achieved without some type of marketing plan. A retreat is also ideal if you have more than a few reluctant marketers on board. Bringing in a client development specialist to lead part of the retreat may be more cost effective than sending everyone to a seminar.

TIP

If you create a referral alliance made up of different professionals, it's important you all focus on one type of client — such as small business owners. Your target markets must match in order for this approach to work.

Marketing Assistant is one solution if your would-be marketing partners or associates don't have the patience to make all the phone calls and plans that go into setting up lunches and other get-togethers. But they would show up and be quite charming if someone else took on the planning.

Do they feel socially uncomfortable?

Model marketing for them. Invite your associates or partners to accompany you and observe how you market yourself or your firm. Human beings learn new skills by watching and emulating others. Invite your partner or associate to lunch with you and an important client, or have them participate in a golf match with a Referral Source or two. Initially, they should be a friendly and active contributor to the conversation, but not take the lead in sensitive areas. As they watch you, and gain confidence, they should be better prepared to discuss firm services and the roles they play.

Do your associates perceive they lack time for marketing?

Usually, we say to block time — three substantial contacts per week — on the calendar every week, but they may need to ramp up to that level of frequency if they've done no marketing at all. One lunch a week might be an easier goal to achieve until they are ready and able to undertake three contacts. Start them at a level you think will work for them, then request more time as they progress. Hiring a

Plan to invite the partner or associate you are mentoring to quite a few events in order for them to get comfortable. The more shy they are, the more practice they'll need. If you really take this seriously and want to accelerate their learning curve, plan to strategize in advance and debrief them after each event to hear what they learned from the outing and to contribute your perspective on their performance. A lot of encouragement helps.

their rapport in small ways with every meeting.

Give out tickets.

Some marketing activities don't require the marketer to be present (for die-hard introverts). Giving important clients and Referral Sources tickets to sporting events, plays, openings, concerts, conferences and lectures can have a great impact on the recipient and require little effort on the part of the lawyer.

Focus on client service.

One of the more hidden aspects of client development happens when a client feels well taken care of by the firm with whom they're working. You understand that if they leave happy, they'll be much more motivated to use the firm in the future and recommend their services to others. This is especially helpful with a client who has the potential for a great deal of future work. Be sure your associates attend to clients by returning phone calls promptly, proactively communicating with them instead of waiting until the client makes contact, and being empathetic about the emotional stress the client may be feeling for the duration of their matter. They should learn to connect with clients on a personal but professional basis initially, taking the time to deepen

Initiate reverse seminars.

These are events in which important clients or Referral Sources are invited to be the guest of honor at lunch in the firm's conference room. Lunch is usually catered, but the meeting can be done in a formal or casual fashion – depending on the level of

TIP

Before teaching associates to market themselves, observe their willingness to step outside their comfort zone. Natural extroverts will often do well in unfamiliar social situations, but even the more shy ones can find techniques that work for them.

TIP

Giving tickets to Referral Sources and valued clients is one way for an attorney to score marketing points without actually being present at the event.

Plan a large, firm-wide event such as a Client Appreciation party, or Holiday Open House (for any holiday: Halloween, April Fool's Day).

If your associates and partners want to have their Referral Sources attend the big event, they will be motivated to contact them and issue invitations. The list of invitees they come up with can serve as a great marketing tool for future marketing. If they keep it accessible for future use, they can use it as a hit list of people to cultivate further in the future. Some of our clients park it on the desktop page of their computer for fast access, or file the information in their cell phones. If you are trying to mentor a partner in the area of client development, invite contacts to the event that may provide additional work in their practice area and make it a point to introduce them. A large event provides many opportunities for cross-selling and may be a great help to a partner who could use a kickstart.

formality in your firm. The purpose of the event is to get to know the client or Referral Source by having them be the center of attention, talk about themselves and answer questions – without feeling interrogated – in the genial atmosphere of your firm. This technique is most effective when hosting clients or Referral Sources that are business owners. Questions designed to get the guest of honor talking about themselves, such as, "Can you tell us why you started your business?," "What are your biggest challenges?" or "Why did you settle in this area?" are asked. In this situation, the whole firm does the marketing and the partner or associate who is learning to market themselves has a chance to participate as part of the group effort, removing much of the pressure. It's also another chance for them to observe how others handle this type of marketing.

For those who enjoy and thrive on networking and making contacts in social situations, something called a "marketing alliance" might be the perfect support mechanism. These are groups of two or more people who come together to provide marketing support and, best of all, referrals. As demonstrated by the examples just mentioned, there are several types of marketing alliances which range from large, very formal groups with structured agendas to casual get-togethers between colleagues. Regardless of the format, all of these groups provide that most important ingredient: accountability.

Business-savvy attorneys have depended on referral relationships for many years. Giving and receiving client referrals is a healthy business practice. An informal marketing alliance is created when attorneys and other professionals recognize that client development efforts are easier when they work together – and hold each other accountable to grow and step out of their comfort zone. Alliances are one of the most proactive forms of marketing, and one that requires trust in others to whom you are bound out of mutual benefit. Take a look around your universe. Are there individuals on your list of Referral Sources with whom you might form an informal alliance? It would benefit you to find out.

If, however, you are surrounded by associates or partners who don't or won't engage in client development activities, you must take action to support them. It is vital for the future of your firm to involve everyone in marketing and promoting firm services. Use the methods we've detailed to mentor your socially anxious associates and cultivate your reluctant partners. To make your efforts have more impact, don't fail to hold your colleagues to some form of accountability. By helping them grow in this area, you not only give them a gift that will serve them for all the years they practice, no matter where they go – you ensure the future of your own firm.

> **TIP**
>
> It only takes two people to form an alliance and provide support for one another in the area of marketing. Sometimes that support will take the form of giving advice; sometimes it will involve actual referrals.

A Practice Advisor As A Structure Of Support

A Practice Advisor is a coach that specializes in law firms. A good coach will guide you, direct you, and, when necessary, give you a polite kick in the pants to stay in action. There are a lot of different types of coaches in the marketplace; it is an exploding profession with little regulation or certification in the legal world. Most of today's coaches are "life" coaches and focus on balance in one's life. For accountability purposes, most types of coaches, as long as you have a good relationship and respect for them, will do fine. If you want marketing or practice management direction and guidance as well, look for a Practice Advisor who specializes in law firms and marketing. As an example, go to www.atticusonline.com and review the certifications and qualifications of the Atticus Practice Advisors. I know that is not very modest or humble, but we take great pride in our selection and certification of our law firm Practice Advisors. Also, look at the Atticus Rainmakers Programs, www.atticusrainmakers.com, as it includes a monthly Accountability Partner in the structure.

To acquire this Asset you must form some sort of partnership where you are held accountable for the goals you set in your marketing program. You can fulfill this by teaming up with another attorney, joining a networking group which has an element of structured accountability to it, or joining the Atticus Rainmakers program.

In the next section we'll discuss how you and your firm can stage a retreat to move forward. A yearly firm retreat is an important step for a firm to take when considering long-term client development goals. If your firm isn't taking advantage of stepping back to see the big picture at least once a year, it's missing a critical step.

ASSET #10

THE ANNUAL MARKETING RETREAT

In the business world, the rearview mirror is always clearer than the windshield. ~ Warren Buffett

The Importance Of The Marketing Retreat

Why take the time to have a Marketing Retreat? Aren't there more important things to do...like actually marketing? This is the sentiment expressed to us by partners who dislike setting aside a chunk of good, billable time to focus on discussing client development. Usually, their very enthusiastic partner has come to us with the idea of having a Marketing Retreat and they want us to help convince the reluctant one it's a good idea. Sometimes we're successful in this effort, and sometimes we're not, and the resistant ones show up – usually late, usually rolling their eyes, clutching files in one hand and their cell phone in the other, ready to dash out the door at the first remotely legitimate interruption.

But at least they show up. Because, for the most part, once they're exposed to new ideas for client development and able to hear how small shifts in their marketing strategies can make a huge difference – they're sold on the idea. By being forced to step off their treadmill for a few hours, they begin to understand that taking time to focus their efforts can lead to the kind of results they want for their firm. Granted, there are always a group of curmudgeons (young or old) who never see the value in planning and don't understand strategic marketing. But fortunately for them, others in their firm usually do and are willing to invest the time.

You may feel the same reluctance to set aside time, especially if you feel behind in everything else you have to do. No one can predict the future, right? So why spend valuable time talking about it? Is it reasonable to try to forecast trends and project results in an uncertain economy or periods of sporadic growth or change? We think it is. To paraphrase Winston Churchill, when all is said and done – even if you don't achieve all of your objectives – it's the mental exercise of planning that makes all the difference.

Many of the top-producing attorneys we work with meet regularly with their partners to check the relevancy of their goals, and inspire and challenge each other. A long-time Atticus client in the Chicago area who has the rare ability to lead his own firm's Marketing Retreat recently discussed the results of his retreat with us. This client, working with his wife and partner, heads up a rapidly growing tax assessment firm, and is an incredibly busy man involved in a great many pursuits beyond the law. In spite of a crushing schedule, he understands the power of stopping once a year, gathering up his team and talking about what worked and what didn't in the last year. It was particularly important this time around because last year his firm tried a couple new marketing strategies. For the first time ever, they hired a marketing person and charged her with not only re-energizing all of their marketing efforts, but cultivating new hotel and condominium business.

Determined to look back before he stepped forward, our client wanted to see if these approaches were working. His analysis showed – in no uncertain terms – that his investment in a marketing person and the focus on new business was indeed paying off. His business from hotels and condominiums showed record highs and he was able to attribute over $150,000 worth of new business to the efforts of the marketing person.

Beyond looking at these results, he decided to analyze all of the marketing efforts they made the year prior. He made a list of all their different client development activities and scored each category on 1) whether or not it deepened his relationships with his Referral Sources, and 2) whether or not it directly brought in new business. His categories included the following: what he calls 'lunches with lawyers' (he receives a great many referrals from his colleagues); small gifts given over the holidays; activities such as outings done with various property management companies; educational seminars directed at decision makers within targeted groups; staffing a trade show booth at an industry conference; and sending out his annual newsletter.

After scoring each of these efforts, he discovered most of the *face-to-face* activities garnered him the most direct business, with the exception of the trade show booth which produced no real results. The response to his newsletter, which he spends a great deal of time on, offered the biggest surprise as it stimulated substantial interest (he received over 100 calls responding to what he had written – an extraordinary result and not one easily duplicated by other law firms). Given this, in the coming year he will up the number of issues he produces in order to have one such piece in front of his Referral Sources per quarter.

After looking at everything on his activities list, he was able to make informed decisions on what strategies he'll carry forward and which ones are best left as interesting experiments. But the main point is this: he will move into the coming year armed

TIP

Planning for the future does not guarantee an outcome, but can get you much closer to your goals than if you allow your firm to drift along with no end in mind.

with accurate data. And the exercise he and the team go through in debating the right strategies helps to underscore the importance of client development and the need to take a strategic approach with marketing. His approach is the right mix of experimentation, coupled with a heavy dose of what has worked in the past.

Like this client, being willing to set specific and measurable marketing goals on a regular basis is one of the most important things you can do to ensure future success for your firm. Taking the opportunity to examine and retool your marketing efforts at least once a year will create a surprising effect on your results.

We ask you to take the time to hold a retreat because the legal landscape in which you live is not static. Referral Sources dry up, die or move away; you are joined by a new partner; legislation changes the services you provide; you take on a newsworthy case; or you decide to launch a new practice area. These are just a few of the many changes that can occur over the course of a year in your career.

Fortunately, changes like these are fodder for the creative marketer. Depending on what's happened in your year, you may need to adjust your marketing goals to compensate for a lack of referrals, to feature a change in the services you offer, or to publicize a new partner. Often what appears to be a stressful or dramatic change can be spun in a positive way.

In a large firm, a Marketing Retreat is an important time to coordinate responsibility for various clients, client types, or segments. If you are conducting seminars and workshops, or working strategically with another organization, it is a good time to establish dates for upcoming events such as co-sponsored seminars or Signature Events. It is also a chance to:

• Review last year's or year-to-date marketing results.

• Focus on marketing successes and acknowledge team members.

• Educate other partners or team members on marketing strategies.

• Establish next year's marketing targets: this is important for capacity planning and budgeting (it's hard to get where you are going if you don't know where you want to go).

• Make corrections from last year and establish accountability systems.

• Assess the effectiveness of using the Yellow Pages or other advertising vehicles.

• Assess your Rainmaker profile and see what assets or habits need to be developed or strengthened.

Who Should Attend?

Senior partners should be the first on the roster to attend any meetings about marketing. If there are associates who are being trained to market themselves, they should also attend. If the firm has a marketing director or assistant, they should not only attend, but also set up the meeting for the participants. A gathering like this is even useful for some staff members who are often in a position to cultivate much more business than they realize. Whatever group is selected to attend, the retreat facilitator as

TIP If you analyze the effectiveness of the relationship-building activities you engaged in during the past year, face-to-face activities will usually generate the best results.

well as firm management should place on the agenda exercises and discussions that allow the team to contribute their ideas on client development. Even if there is an already established direction which has been previously discussed by the partners prior to the retreat, the more the idea can seem to come from the team – the greater the buy-in and consensus.

Before The Retreat

Regardless of the size of your firm, an annual retreat in which marketing objectives are discussed and established helps keep the focus on the most important strategies for growing the firm. The Marketing Retreat is a time to assess your client mix, your firm's image, new opportunities for business, and determine who will carry out each of the responsibilities.

Making The Retreat Happen

The best way to make sure the retreat actually happens is to budget the time. Take time to look at potential date(s) for a Marketing Retreat, then commit to a date and hire a facilitator (it's hard to get a facilitator at the last minute). It is best to schedule next year's retreat the year prior, in September, October, or November,

TIP

Often the changes your firm undergoes during the year are fodder for your marketing plans: adding a new partner? Have a party to welcome her aboard.

you an authentic look at *your* strengths and weaknesses, or if you need some assistance in brainstorming and targeting, then it is a good idea to have an outside professional moderate your marketing meeting.

A professional facilitator – someone skilled in both leading group discussions and setting marketing strategies, who can be objective and keep things moving in a productive and constructive manner – is often a professor in a business school or a consultant to law firms. It is imperative that your facilitator be able to:

although holding a retreat in early January with new goals, optimism, and renewed enthusiasm is also fine. The marketing discussion may also be staged as part of a larger firm retreat, with a minimum of four hours dedicated to discussing the subject.

- Educate and bring context and credibility to the idea of marketing.

- Share ideas that other firms have undertaken so the firm is not re-inventing the wheel.

- Spark discussion on new ideas.

- Give realistic feedback on the frequency of marketing activities.

Retreat Facilitators

Most attorneys do not entirely understand what it takes to develop new clients. Even if there is a good Rainmaker in the firm who wants to lead the retreat, that attorney is often doing what they do unconsciously, and has a hard time breaking down the process and making it understandable, or in some cases, appealing, for other personalities. If you are personally reluctant to create the retreat, or you want someone to give

Prior To The Retreat

Assignments in advance of a retreat are an excellent way to motivate your group into action.

Creating a substantial assignment with an event-driven deadline – such as a retreat – helps to motivate and engage attorneys who may otherwise be distracted. Partners and associates are much more likely to participate in a pre-work assignment if they face the idea of having to admit to the rest of the group at the retreat that they failed to carry out their assignment.

The Top Twenty Exercise: Have the firm's bookkeeper print out a list of each of the firm's biggest clients, divided by attorney. Prior to the retreat, give each attorney an assignment to identify the influencer responsible for each big case and to create his or her Top Twenty list. (For more information on *The Top Twenty,* see Asset #1.)

The Laser Talk: Each attorney in the firm can be asked to prepare their own Laser Talk in advance. They should state what service they deliver, the benefits of that service to the client, how they deliver the service, and what makes them unique. Once a rough draft of this talk is constructed, it can be used as a marketing tool, but is also useful as a mini-marketing plan for the individual to refine at the retreat. (See Asset #4, *The Laser Talk.*)

Create a list of the most successful marketing activities from the prior year. What worked and what didn't?

Brainstorm a list of people or Referral Sources that each attorney wants to target. In addition, outline opportunities for cross selling between partners, where applicable.

Prepare a report on Web site or advertising successes, and work still needing to be done.

Compile a Client Service Innovation report in which any improvements to client care are listed, along with feedback from clients or team members about their effectiveness.

The measurements listed are some of the indicators you can use (see Asset #17, entitled *A Tracking System,* for a further discussion of key indicators to track) to monitor your progress:

• Track the number of inquiries generated by different sources, including print ads.

• Track the amount of clients that inquire based on your Web site.

• Track the percentage of phone inquiries that convert to in-office consultations.

• Track the percentage of consultations that convert to become clients.

At The Retreat

Demystifying Marketing. Of the many different disciplines required of an attorney, marketing can

be the most difficult to adopt. One helpful aspect of a retreat is the opportunity to educate the inexperienced – to bring the group together to perform exercises and hold brainstorming discussions that are not possible on an individual basis. Some topics to include:

• Discuss the principles of relationship-based marketing with an emphasis on how this type of marketing is the least complicated, the least expensive and the most ethical and effective way to conduct a marketing campaign. It should be made clear to those who are inexperienced that relationships form the basis for referrals.

• Refresh the team about client selection and A, B, C and D client distinctions, and how to design a marketing plan that targets the very best Referral

Sources that can deliver the A and B level client.

Setting Marketing Objectives & Goals

In addition to setting very specific marketing goals such as determining the number of new clients to be brought in during the coming year, and identifying the optimal number of referrals the firm will receive from past and present clients, the retreat is the time to establish the amount of marketing activities individuals will do on a daily, weekly, and monthly basis.

Listed below are activities that will support you in building rapport and relationships with your referral base. Your goal is to have each attorney commit to attend or initiate:

• One marketing-related conversation per day.

• No less than three contacts per week. (**Note:** three contacts a week will be between 100 and 150 marketing contacts a year; a significant jump-start to any practice.)

•One or two evening events per month such as charity dinners, theater events, wine tastings.

Cultivate Referrals

• *Spend more time with your Referral Sources to get to know them better.*
Sample Goal: Dedicate three lunches a week to cultivating Referral Sources.

• *Thank your sources for any referrals they send – whether or not the client engages you.*
Sample Goal: Put thank-you cards out on your desk to ensure you'll use them.

• *Invite your Referral Sources to events they'd enjoy, or give them tickets.*
Sample Goal: Purchase season tickets and give them to different Referral Sources.

• *Introduce your Referral Sources to people they can network with.*
Sample Goal: Use marketing lunches to introduce Referral Sources to one another. This is especially useful if

you don't have a lot of business you can send to them – and only applies when referrers are not competitors.

• *Refer business to your Referral Sources, whenever possible.*
Sample Goal: Reward Referral Sources with business, whenever possible.

• *Conduct satisfaction interviews to see how well your sources think you're taking care of their referrals.*
Sample Goal: Use your marketing lunches to check in with Referral Sources on their perception of your service.

Improve Client Service

To inspire more client referrals, you can discuss ways to focus on increasing your level of client service.

• *Make clients feel more welcome and taken care of during each visit to your office.*
Sample Goal: Offer clients a selection of beverages when they arrive.

• *Enhance your level of communication with clients.*
Sample Goal: Each client receives a check-in call on a regular (weekly, monthly) basis.

• *Build more rapport with key clients.*
Sample Goal: At the conclusion of each large case or matter, invite the client out to lunch to get to know them better and get feedback on your performance.

Build Your Reputation

Take a look at how you and your firm are perceived by the larger community. Have you done anything lately to build your reputation?

• *Increase your visibility by being quoted or mentioned in the papers your clients read.*
Sample Goal: Look at what you are doing that is noteworthy throughout the year and send press releases or write a column for a local newspaper or trade journal.

• *Increase your visibility on local or national television.*
Sample Goal: Cultivate television reporters and/or news anchors in your area so they turn to you for comments on local and national events.

Host Activities And Events

The events and activities you participate in often shape the perceptions of you and your firm. Commit to:

• *Hold a Signature Event every year.*
Sample Goal: Host a party to celebrate the firm's anniversary every year.

• *Begin a seminar or a series of speaking engagements.*
Sample Goal: Schedule one speaking

engagement a quarter.

Schedule Weekly Lunches

Set goals to use your lunch hour for marketing. You can:

• *Have lunch with people on your Top Twenty and Farm Team lists.*
Sample Goal: Meet influencers or potential Referral Sources for lunch two or three times per week.

Energize Your Bar Participation

If you, like most attorneys, get much of your business from other attorneys, Bar events are great places to:

• *Spend time with existing Referral Sources.*
Sample Goal: Use every event as a chance to invite another Bar member out to lunch in the following week.

• *Sit next to new people at Bar events to get to know them.*
Sample Goal: Meet one new person at every event who could be a potential Referral Source for you

• *Participate or lead a committee.*
Sample Goal: Join a committee and use it as an opportunity to meet and cultivate fellow members.

Join Your Client's Organizations

If you aren't a member of organizations other than the Bar, take a look at the kind of organizations that your clients join, both business and community related. Once you join, see if you can:

• *Become a high-profile presence in the group.*
Sample Goal: Arrange to speak to or teach the group on a regular basis.

• *Become recognized as an expert.*
Sample Goal: Write an article or column for their newsletter or trade journal.

• *Become a contributing member.*
Sample Goal: Sponsor hospitality suites, golf games or dinners in conjunction with special events.

Be A Sport

If you are a sports fan, **schedule a regular sports or hobby-related marketing event.** Calendar golf or tennis on Friday afternoons and invite different Referral Sources to participate.

Cross-Selling Opportunities

Partners may consider:

• VIP lunches and reverse seminars.

• A creation of a firm-wide Signature Event based on a holiday or some other theme.

Increasing Individual And Firm-wide Reputations

• Speaking engagements.

• Placement of a certain number of articles a year.

• Mentions in trade journals or Bar newsletters.

• Placement on business or non-profit boards.

• The achievement of titles, board certifications.

Marketing Assistant

If your schedule precludes it or you aren't good at initiating marketing activities and events, determine if it is prudent to recruit a paralegal or a secretary to act as your Marketing Assistant to:

• Schedule marketing lunches and speaking events.

• Coordinate your annual Signature Event.

• Manage or coordinate updates to your Web site.

• Write or coordinate others to write a firm newsletter.

• Capture new client data to gauge the effectiveness of your marketing efforts.

Create A Structure For Accountability

Though marketing is not complicated, it can be daunting for some personalities who aren't confident of their skills in this area. Many personalities are helped when an accountability structure is in place, and, when the personalities are involved in creating the structure, it is even more successful. If the firm has a Marketing Assistant, he or she should be a big part of this discussion and act as an on-the-ground support person for these efforts. Any accountability structure must have consequences for non-compliance, so a senior partner who is respected by the team must stay with the program to give it the appropriate weight.

The establishment of weekly or monthly accountability meetings can support those who are trying to adopt marketing habits. These meetings can then offer opportunities for further discussion and brainstorming about the firm's marketing activities. Further accountability might involve bonuses

that are based in part on client development goals. Partnership opportunities also often depend in part on the associate's ability to bring in new business.

Taking consistent action on the goals you've identified will dramatically alter your client development results. In order to claim this Asset, you must have an annual retreat and regularly review your goals to remember to act on them. The more accessible they are, the better – especially if the perfectionist in you resists making commitments for fear they aren't achievable.

Set yourself up for success by keeping these goals with your weekly planning materials so that you view them often. To help, read through the next chapter, Asset #11, *A Monthly Marketing Plan.* By creating a Monthly Marketing Plan which is based on your annual goals, you help to insure your long-term success and avoid getting bogged down in interesting tangents.

Keep in mind: even if you don't meet those commitments perfectly, in trying to achieve them you'll do much more than you would have otherwise. Set your goals high, because in the words of Ralph Marston, "Your goals minus your doubts equal your reality."

ASSET #11

A MONTHLY MARKETING PLAN

It is better to take many small steps in the right direction than to make a great leap forward only to stumble backward. ~ Chinese Proverb

The Mini-Marketing Plan

In Asset #10 we encouraged you to set annual client development goals, and in this Asset we also encourage you to set short, intermediate goals with their attendant deadlines subordinate to the annual goal. The additional urgency created by the more frequent short-term deadlines will keep you on track and enhance your chances of making your long-term goals. They also give you the opportunity to make many small course corrections along the way, should you go off course during the process.

At the end of this chapter you'll find the Mini-Marketing form (use it as a master and make 12 copies). It is the only form associated with this section and is one of the most important in this book. It is specifically designed to support you in your daily pursuit of new Rainmaking Assets and Habits. You can use the form in several different ways: to plan your marketing activities for the month, or, if you have an associate whom you are mentoring, they can fill one out and use it as a planning and reporting tool. If you are part of a partnership that conducts monthly marketing meetings, this form can also be used by each partner to report on their client development activities for the month.

es the chances you'll remember your goal. If you remember something, you are much more likely to do it. You can help this along by keeping the plan in a plainly visible spot and not allowing it to be lost in the piles of files on your desk.

Use The Form
On A Monthly Basis

Because the form requires each person (the attorney and/or the Marketing Assistant) to write down their intended actions for the month, it becomes an accountability tool. In our experience, plans committed to paper are much more likely to be acted upon than those that are not. The extra mental energy it takes, and the visualizing required to remember or look up names and then list them along with the intended outcomes, helps to solidify the idea, and increas-

Intended to be used on a monthly basis, you'll find that the Mini-Marketing form is very simple to use and helps you to produce impressive results. Numerous clients have reported back to us that they fill out this form religiously, and keep it out on their desk to remind them of their marketing goals. The Mini-Marketing form is where the rubber hits the road in your client development program. Filling it out forces you to assemble lists of your Referral Sources, study those lists to figure out who you want to invest time in, then actually take those people out to lunch or to some other event. Thinking about who sends you business, worrying about who sends you business, talking about who sends you business – these are all good things.

But nothing gets you the business like actually going out and spending time with existing and potential Referral Sources.

TIP

There is no substitute for action when you want to develop new Referral Sources. Thinking about it, worrying about it and writing down names only takes you so far. You have to get out on the playing field to score.

Being 'In Action' Matters More Than Anything

While strategic thinking must precede action, it will be the real-world actions you take that land you more business. If you ever catch yourself thinking about marketing but not actually doing any marketing, it doesn't count. It's important that your monthly Mini-Marketing form contains some activities that you find engaging, interesting or fun.

How To Use The Form:

At the top of the form there is a place to fill in the *Assets* and *Habits* you'll focus on for the month. If you have any doubts about which Asset to choose, they are listed in order of priority. Acquiring Asset #1, *The Top Twenty* should be your first order of business – in fact, filling out the Mini-Marketing form is impossible if you don't have a list of Referral Sources that you can refer to and assess.

Below the top box on the form is a larger section that allows you to fill in the names of the people you'll be meeting with during the month. It is set up with 12 horizontal blanks divided into three columns. Each of the

12 blanks in the first column, *Referral Contact,* provides the space for you to write the name of the person you'll be meeting. To complete this section you'll need your list of Referral Sources on hand – both your Top Twenty (Asset #1) and any other list of Referral Sources you may have, such as your Farm Team List (Asset #14). You'll use these lists to figure out who you want to get together with in the coming month. Ideally, you'll have your present Referral Sources on your Top Twenty list, and the Referral Sources with potential on your Farm Team List. You will want to allocate your client development time on a rotating basis between old, proven Referral Sources and new and potential Referral Sources.

TIP

When planning who you'll spend time cultivating, rotate between potential Referral Sources and those with whom you already have a relationship.

Next to each name, you can insert your intended outcome for each meeting in the next column entitled *Objective.* List your intended outcomes by using short phrases such as "develop more rapport," or "ask for referrals," or "conduct interview." Since you will have a different level of relationship with each individual, your intended outcomes will differ widely, but will generally be aimed at increasing the depth of your relationship.

One of Atticus' laws of client development is that the better your relationship with your Referral Source, the more likely they are to send you business. When you are merely an acquaintance of the person you will be meeting, your goal may be to get to know the person better. When you've known the person for quite awhile, but the person still hasn't sent you any business, your intention might be to develop more trust and ask subtlety for referrals. Perhaps you can say something like: "I would enjoy working with your clients if they ever need my services…" or "Let's talk about how we can develop a business relationship with one another. I believe I can send some clients to you and I'd gladly help anyone you send me…"

In the next column, *Action*, there is space to list the intended marketing action. For example, you may plan to take the Referral Source to lunch, have a phone conversation, invite them golfing or to dinner at your home. The idea here is to become proactive with your marketing activities each month.

In doing all of this, you must make sure the actions you take to connect with your contacts fit your hobbies, passions or interests. You want to anticipate the meetings on your list with pleasure. To do this they should have something to do with what you are interested in; otherwise, your monthly plan will become something you dread implementing. Lunches are the most popular marketing activity among our clients, but that doesn't have to be the sole activity you rely upon for meeting with your contacts. Your marketing plan can include much of your social life in the community.

The whole idea of finding *your* way to successful monthly marketing is simple: don't make service club meetings your marketing focus if you aren't genuinely thrilled with their agendas.

You may be wondering if the most successful Rainmakers are effective only because they have the *right* personality. You may have in mind Rainmakers you've seen at some point in your career: those men and women who navigate every social situation with ease and radiate such self-assurance that new clients are continually drawn to them.

You, on the other hand, might be someone who is decidedly not at your best in unfamiliar social territory. You might experience apprehension when asked to market yourself because you don't believe you're a natural at marketing. One attorney voiced it perfectly: "For me, marketing means I have to 'fake it,' and few things are more exhausting than having to fake my way through a marketing event that holds no interest for me. After a few events like that, I decided I didn't really have the personality to be a marketer."

If you don't have what it takes, however, are you doomed to always work for those who can make it rain? Or to join the ranks of sole proprietors whose firms limp along and never fully realize their potential? These questions are of critical importance: your ability to develop clients shapes your destiny in almost every practice setting. Instead of deciding you don't have

TIP

Invest time in your referral relationships: we believe that the more your Referral Sources like you, the more likely they are to send business.

> **TIP**
>
> Even introverted personalities can become successful marketers — they may favor small gatherings or one-on-one lunches instead of large social events. Find the approach that works best for your personality.

the right personality to market yourself, create a focus for your marketing that inspires you and fits your personality.

Sample Objectives

- Practice Laser Talk

- Thank the source

- Explain what you do in depth

- Request new business and/or contacts

- Build more rapport

- Define any issues

- Discuss how to work together more

- Catch up

- Determine how to work more effectively together

Sample Actions

- Coffee/breakfast

- Lunch

- Dinner

- Phone call

- Cocktail

- Golf

- Other sporting activity

- Cultural event

- Community function

- Religious function

- Charity event

Never forget that the ability to market yourself gives you power. With power, you can direct your career the way you want to. Options that aren't available to grinders exist for finders. To market yourself with authenticity, do what you enjoy, share it with other people, and the business will follow. Be sure to use your Monthly Mini-Marketing form to support you, your partners or your associates in these efforts.

To claim this Asset, you must use this form on a monthly basis to capture your marketing goals for the month. To borrow a phrase from Nike: Just Do It. Many small steps add up to a big result.

In the discussion of Asset #12, *Creating A Signature Marketing Event,* we'll outline ways in which to customize your approach to marketing even further by staging an event that is a distinct reflection of you and your firm.

Mini-Marketing Plan

Month: _____   Name: _____

**Current
Rainmaker Score:** _____   **Current
Rainmaker Profile** _____

Marketing Asset to focus on this month: _____

Marketing Habit to focus on this month: _____

Referral Sources to Cultivate:

REFERRAL CONTACT	OBJECTIVE	ACTION
1.		
2.		
3.		
4.		
5.		
6.		
7.		
8.		
9.		
10.		
11.		
12.		

Fax to: _____

ASSET #12

CREATING A SIGNATURE EVENT

Excess on occasion is exhilarating. It prevents moderation from acquiring the deadening effect of a habit. ~ W. Somerset Maugham

A Good Reason To Celebrate

S*everal years ago, Atticus clients Steve Eichenblatt and Gregg Page, personal injury attorneys in Orlando, Florida, decided to parlay their love of golf into an annual tournament. They teamed up with the "Make a Wish" Foundation, one of the charities they are most passionate about, and sought out a course interesting enough to lure their Referral Sources, mostly doctors and other attorneys, away from their busy practices.*

The inaugural event attracted 80 players, raised money for their charity, and was a huge marketing success. Says Steve, "We had no idea this thing would take off like it did. Our attendance was great and continues to build every year." These two tapped into a classic win-win marketing scenario because their passion for golf and their interest in helping out the community coincided with that of their Referral Sources. As a result, attendance was high, a good time was had by all, and the firm's profile got a significant boost.

TIP Your Signature Event must have a distinguishing theme or type of food or entertainment that sets it apart from the run-of-the-mill open house.

Energize Your Marketing

In coaching solo and small firm attorneys on marketing, we usually look for ideas that will energize their rainmaking efforts, help them develop new Referral Sources, and raise their profile in the community. Asset #12, the Signature Event, does all of this, and more. To qualify as a Signature Event, a gathering must be distinctive in some way – either because of the theme, the entertainment, or the food. In addition, a Signature Event should showcase you and your staff and take place on an annual basis. The idea is to create a gathering that people look forward to – you'll know you've succeeded when your event becomes a sought after invitation and you see an uptick in post-event referrals.

There is a broad range of possible themes for Signature Marketing Events: everything from casual client appreciation events, to elegant affairs promoting a charitable cause, to unusual holiday celebrations. The best themes spring out of the passions, interests and hobbies of the host. What is the best theme for your firm's event? Atticus graduates from across the nation have been doing various events. Use their ideas to inspire you to plan your own Signature Event.

Happy Halloween

Diane Holmes, a family law attorney also in central Florida, wanted to host a holiday open house, but feared her gathering would be lost in the end-of-the-year frenzy of parties. To stand out from the competition, she took a chance on a holiday that's been a favorite of hers since childhood: Halloween. "It might seem like an unusual choice for a law firm party, but everyone loved it. We sent out invitations in tubes that made a ghostly sound when opened. We held the party at noon and invited all of our Referral Sources, along with some clients. A surprising number of them showed up. It was a hit and now we do it every year."

Mardi Gras, Thanksgiving And April Fool's Day?

In a similar vein, a law firm in Nashville chose a Mardi Gras theme for their Signature Event and personally delivered tasty "king cakes," a traditional Mardi Gras pastry, with each of their invitations. Farther south, in north Florida, the owner of a small firm invited a group of Referral Sources that he's known for many years to an "After Thanksgiving Party." Everyone was invited to bring his or her leftover turkey, cranberry sauce and pumpkin pie along. April Fool's Day was the theme chosen by another Atticus client who wanted to do something fun and unusual. At this party, a costumed jester circulated through the crowd and a prize was

given for the best lawyer joke. A week or two after the party, the jokes were e-mailed to all of the invitees whether they attended the party or not.

Sumo Wrestling Party

Former Atticus clients, a multi-partner business law firm decided to throw a party in their parking lot under a large tent. The food was catered by a local vendor, and enter-

TIP

Choose a holiday outside the norm to celebrate. Your party will get lost in the crowd if you hold it between December 1st and January 2nd.

tainment was provided by the firm's normally staid attorneys who donned giant, padded sumo wrestling costumes and battled one another in a roped off area – to the delight of everyone watching. This was one of the most unusual approaches we've seen to a Signature Event, but, according to the reports, the party was a big hit.

Charitable Events

Another way to host a Signature Event is this: invite Referral Sources and others in the community who would be interested in learning about a cause you are championing and stage a promotional event. The event might involve a guest speaker, a panel of speakers, or a performance of some kind. It might be a dinner, a cocktail party or a brunch. Take time at the event to inform those in attendance about your cause and why it's important to you. There might be a suggested donation, a ticket for admission, or it might be free. You get to design something that works for you and the cause you are promoting.

Lawyers For Literacy Launch Party

Lucas Fleming, a leading criminal defense attorney in St. Peters-

burg, Florida, believes that the opportunity to promote his firm and a cause he believes in is worth all the extra effort he invests. "It takes time to plan, but once we settle on a theme, I delegate the majority of the party planning to my Marketing Assistant. We meet regularly to discuss the catering arrangements, the tent we'll erect in our parking lot, and who we'll invite." Three weeks before the event, his Marketing Assistant will mail the invitations, which will then be followed up by personal phone calls. This year, they'll invite over 200 local attorneys. For Lucas, this party is about more

TIP
Choose a charitable cause that your entire firm can authentically embrace. Ask your team members for suggestions if you lack ideas. Also notice the charities with which your Referral Sources are involved. Find something that moves you.

than just socializing. "We've created a program for attorneys to mentor at-risk kids with poor reading skills. Over the years, I've seen the connection between illiteracy and crime and wanted to do something about it. *Lawyers for Literacy* was the result. Every year we try to enroll more attorneys, and this fall we'll host our largest launch party yet." The benefits of hosting your Signature Event are sometimes instantly visible, but will usually unfold in the weeks and months to come. Keep an eye on who refers business in the months following your event.

TIP

The benefits of hosting your Signature Event are sometimes instantly visible, but will usually unfold in the weeks and months to come. Keep an eye on who refers business in the months following your event.

Bike Safety Day

A plaintiff's practice in New York State took a similar approach. They focus their marketing approach primarily on community service. In the spring, they sponsor a "Bike Safety Day" to promote safe cycling and the importance of wearing a helmet. Having seen the damage that can happen to children in simple bicycle accidents, it was their goal to pre-empt as many future accidents as they could by raising awareness among children and their parents. Though it's difficult to track the direct benefits of an educational event like this in terms of accidents prevented, the good will generated by the firm is invaluable.

Client Appreciation Events

A number of Atticus graduates hold annual client appreciation parties because the majority of their business comes from past and present clients. If your goal is to build rapport with and thank people who send business to you, you'd naturally invite your top Referral Sources, and encourage your partner or partners (if you have them) to do the same.

The guests for your Signature Event will differ according to your marketing goals and your theme. The idea is

TIP

Handing out small gifts as tokens of your event adds to the overall impression made by you and your team. The gifts don't need to be elaborate to be effective.

to thank clients who have been faithful Referral Sources over the years. These affairs may be held in a park, a hotel ballroom, or your own office. They don't have to be lavish affairs, but make sure enough effort has gone into the planning, decorating and entertainment so clients feel genuinely appreciated.

A Celebration Of Diversity

One firm decided to host a "Celebration of Diversity" party that featured food from many different ethnic backgrounds. Since their clients come from many different cultures, it was quite well received. The gathering was serenaded by a couple of the firm's clients who happened to be working musicians. This party was also held in a large tent in the firm's parking lot.

Circus Party

Another firm will be using a tent of a different kind for their event. A "Circus in the Big Top Tent" is the theme for their family–oriented client appreciation party, which will feature circus foods, face painting, and games for kids. A dunking booth for the attorneys is planned and no doubt will be the highlight of the event.

The Champagne Campaign

A family law attorney in Calgary, Canada wanted to thank his Referral Sources with an open house. To encourage circulation throughout his townhouse-style office, he placed food stations in offices both upstairs and down. As a special touch, a member of his staff handed out small bottles of champagne, tagged with the law firm's name, to departing guests.

According to Balbi, the parting gift made a big impression and garnered the most compliments in the post-party buzz.

engraved with the firm name, to take home.

Wine, Wine, Wine

A firm in upstate New York is fortunate enough to have a partner who is a wine enthusiast. They capitalize on this knowledge and his connections by holding a wine tasting event in their lobby on a regular basis. Several local wineries participate and each guest receives a wineglass,

Other Reasons To Have A Party

If you've just hired a new associate, or brought in a new partner, use this occasion as a reason to throw a party. Invite a mix of Referral Sources and have your new associate or partner also invite people that he or she knows in the community.

TIP

Having your Signature Event serve as a celebration of something that you are passionate about — such as food or wine — guarantees you'll be motivated to make it memorable.

Show Off A New Office

If you've just moved to a new space, show it off. A move like this offers a great opportunity to invite a mix of Referral Sources, special clients, friends and family to see your new office. Planning a party to show off a new office will also provide great motivation to get the place organized and appropriately decorated.

A Piggyback Party

If the idea of an event on such a grand scale is not for you, consider the local events that might occur in close proximity to your office. There may be an opportunity to "piggyback" a small gathering based on these annual local events. Attorneys with offices in prime viewing locations for parades, in walking distance of art festivals, and close to outdoor community concerts can invite a select group of Referral Sources to park at their office, attend the event and join them for refreshments before or after. The small investment in food and beverages is minor compared to the good will experienced by those who will gladly stop by for a drink and think you are generous to share your hospitality and parking.

The Hidden Benefits

If you are contemplating the idea of hosting your own Signature Event, it is helpful to know there are a couple of unexpected benefits that occur prior to the actual event. The first benefit occurs when you establish the guest list. To create it you'll have to think about and list out or notate (or record or catalog) your best Referral Sources. This provides you much helpful data for future marketing purposes.

The second benefit is more surprising: your practice will receive referrals even from people who don't attend your event. Why? It seems that just receiving an invitation is enough to increase Top Of Mind Awareness in the minds of your influencers, and often leads to referrals.

When you combine both the unexpected benefits of this event with the real opportunity it provides to spend time with clients and Referral Sources in a convivial atmosphere, the Signature Event can deliver sure-fire results in "branding" your firm and encouraging future referrals.

Conclusion:

To acquire Asset #12, Creating A Signature Event, you must plan and host an event with an interesting theme which helps you promote your firm and raise its profile in the community.

The affair must be something that can be repeated on a yearly basis and so becomes your Signature Event. Creating a Signature Event can do a great deal of good in the community, provide an opportunity to interact with many Referral Sources, and help create some "buzz" about your firm. Whether you base the theme on your hobbies, passions and interests, or a local community event, you will ensure that your firm is noticed, and you will have created a gathering people will remember and look forward to, year after year. Party On!

General Event Planning Sheet

WHAT YOU NEED TO BUY OR RENT:

- Invitations
- Scented Candles
- Tables/Chairs
- Space (Home, Office, Hotel)
- Name Tags/Table
- Tents
- Entertainment

FOOD
Consider:
- Glazed ham
- Fresh smoked turkey
- Sides of salmon

DRINKS
- (Full serve or self-serve bar)
- Wine
- Cocktails
- Specialty coffee/teas
- Egg Nog
- Soft drinks
- Spring/Tonic water, Club soda

WHAT TO DO BEFORE THE PARTY:

2 weeks in advance:

- Wrap gifts
- Schedule a massage for the day
- of your party
- Schedule appt. with hair stylist
- Purchase/rent party attire
- Order flowers

5 days out:

- Courtesy call to those who haven't RSVPed

1-2 days out:

- Set up room
- Pick up/receive centerpieces
- Cut checks for help
- Get cash for tips

Golf Tournament

WHAT/WHY
<ul><li>A high profile event that is good for positioning the law firm positively in the community and enhancing their image. May be held in support of a charity. Could be combined with a silent auction.</li><li>To build know/like/trust and rapport with your influencers.</li><li>An opportunity to meet new influencers as you will invite your players to bring their friends.</li></ul>

WHO	
Guest List Options • Your Top 20 List • Other attorneys • Judges • Sports celebrities • Bar officials • Physicians • CPA's	Invite those people with whom you would like to build rapport. As the tournament host, plan on NOT playing in the tournament. This will allow you to visit all the golfers during the event. Enclose a registration form with your written invitation. An open invitation, accompanied by a registration form, can be published in your bar news.

WHERE
A highly desirable local golf course that guests would be excited about playing.

WHEN
Once a year. Plan for a time of year when the weather will accommodate.

AWARDS
<ul><li>Create a trophy or an award plaque inscribed with the tournament name.</li><li>Imprint giveaways with your firm name – golf tees, hats, shirts, umbrellas, etc.</li><li>If it's a morning tournament, present awards during a luncheon ceremony.</li><li>If it's an afternoon tournament, present awards during the cocktail hour.</li><li>Invite the president of your local bar, or a judge, to present the trophy/award.</li></ul>

The Reverse Seminar
or "VIP" Lunch

WHAT/WHY
A lunch-time event that gives the guest(s) of honor a chance to be "center stage" and talk about themselves and their business. This can be an informal event with "brown bag" lunches, or a more formal, catered affair. ➤ A chance to build know/like/trust and rapport. ➤ A creative way to discover how to help the person in the future. ➤ An opportunity for cross-selling other firm services to the client

WHO
A new or existing client who is capable of sending recurring business; or an influencer who is capable of influencing others to use your services. Be sure to invite any firm partners that might have an interest in getting to know the guest of honor. Examples: A small business owner who recently hired the firm for a project or a CPA who brings along a partner from his firm.

WHERE
➤ At your law firm in the conference room -- if you have sufficient space to hold the guests as well as your firm members. ➤ A quiet corner/private area of a nice local restaurant, if you don't have space at the firm.

WHEN
12 PM – 2 PM is typical, though an after-hours event can work as well.

IMPORTANT!
Be sure to provide a good showing of firm members or the event will be a disappointment to the guest of honor. Invite the appropriate members of your law firm. If your firm is small, include your Designated Hitter/Paralegal and other staff members to increase attendance.

Firm Open House

WHAT/WHY

> Show off remodeled or new office space
> Showcase new technology
> Introduce a recently hired new attorney
> Introduce a new partner
> Chance for your partner's Top 20 to meet your Top 20 & cross sell
> Celebrate an award, honor or special recognition given to the firm
> To build know/like/trust and rapport with your influencers

WHO

Guest List Options

> Your Top 20 List
> Other attorneys
> Your Farm Team List
> Judges
> Bar officials
> Selected clients

Note:
Your invitations can be written or verbal, made at least two weeks prior to the event.

Ask invitees to RSVP at least 5 days prior to the event so food orders can be adjusted.

WHERE

As this is an "open house," your firm is the only option for a location. Use your entry, waiting room or conference rooms to set-up drinks and finger foods to encourage circulation throughout the entire facility (close off unsightly areas). Your food and beverages can be catered to lessen the work done by the staff, or made by the attorneys and staff if they have the requisite time and talent.

WHEN

These events are typically held during the workweek between the hours of 4:00 and 6:00. Invite people to stop by after work. Plan to wrap up the event by 8:00 or 9:00 in the evening.

Holiday Event

WHAT/WHY

> ➤ A festive event to celebrate the holidays with referral sources, friends of the firm, past and present clients.
>
> ➤ To build rapport with your influencers, reconnect with referral sources and further your relationship with clients.

WHO

Guest List Options

➤ Your Top 20 List
➤ Other attorneys
➤ Judges
➤ Past and present clients
➤ Staff
➤ Family members

Note:
Inviting spouses is optional due to the nature of the event. Some firms use this opportunity to introduce spouses to their referral sources and clients.

WHERE

Choose a location that is roomy enough to accommodate the size crowd you intend to invite. Your firm may fit the bill and this could be an opportunity to showcase a new or redecorated office. If your office doesn't fit the bill, your home might if it is spacious enough and has adequate parking. If you belong to a club, you might be able to hold the party at their facility. Generally, the more formal the facility, the more costly it will be. Consider the pros and cons of each location before deciding.

WHEN

Once a year during the holiday of your choice. Consider other occasions beside the busy end-of-year holidays. The competition for party-goers is most intense then and your party will not stand out as much as you would like. For maximum attendance choose another time of the year.

HOLIDAY FOOD IDEAS

Wine and Cheese Theme
Holiday Homemade Theme
Local Artisianal Food Showcase

Seafood Buffet
Rustic Italian
Chef attended food stations w/ display cooking

Marketing Event Guest List

Guest Name	RSVP	Guest Name	RSVP
1		26	
2		27	
3		28	
4		29	
5		30	
6		31	
7		32	
8		33	
9		34	
10		35	
11		36	
12		37	
13		38	
14		39	
15		40	
16		41	
17		42	
18		43	
19		44	
20		45	
21		46	
22		47	
23		48	
24		49	
25		50	

Marketing Events Budget Form

Instructions: Meet with staff 45 to 60 days prior to discuss details and create a budget. Record the maximum amount you are willing to spend on each category listed below. Empower staff to work within the confines of the budget to accomplish the desired outcome.

Category	$ Budget	$ Spent
Room/Space		
Tables/Chairs		
Rentals		
Entertainment		
Food		
Drinks		
Hired Help (Tips Included):		
Caterer		
Bartender		
Clean-up		
Photographer		
Decorations		
Eating/Drinking Utensils		
Parking Valet		
Invitations		
Name Tags		
Table Tents		
Flowers/Centerpieces		
Gifts		
Other:		
GRAND TOTAL		

Marketing Event Resources

Use the following resources to order awards, trophies, gifts, logo merchandise and cards of all kinds.

Successories

www.successories.com

800-932-9673

HRdirect

800-346-1231

www.hrdirect.com

(awards, cards)

Best Impressions
Promotional Products

800-635-2378

www.bestimpressions.com

(imprinted golf balls)

Lands End
Corporate Sales

www.landsend.com

(The art of imprinted business casual)

Awards

www.awards.com

800-5AWARDS

Baudville

www.baudville.com

800-728-0888

Recognition/Team Building/Special Events

Invitation Tips

BASIC INFORMATION TO INCLUDE:

☐ Host's name(s)

☐ Type of event

☐ Date

☐ Time

☐ Location

☐ Reply telephone number

Note: If there are special guests whom you want to attend your event, call and extend a verbal invitation. Send the written invitation as well to provide all the pertinent details.

OPTIONAL:

☐ Rain date

☐ Special parking arrangements

☐ Map to your office

☐ Tell something extra, like what to wear

WHEN TO MAIL THE INVITATION:

Formal dinner..............................	4 weeks ahead
Informal dinner...........................	2-3 weeks ahead
Luncheon or tea	2-3 weeks ahead
Cocktail party	3 weeks ahead
Big bash	4 weeks ahead

APPROPRIATE TYPES OF INVITATIONS:

Specially printed	Any type of party, semi-formal to casual
Handwritten on blank cards..........	Small personal parties, formal or informal
Email	Casual get-togethers/informal events

Reference: Entertaining for Dummies

ASSET #13

CLIENT INTAKE MATRIX

*Watch the little things; a small leak
will sink a great ship. ~ Benjamin Franklin*

Building The Client Base YOU Want

*"You know, I had a bad feeling about that client. He questioned my fees
right from the start and asked if I would reduce my retainer at our first
meeting. Foolishly, I let him pay half, then bent over backward to help him
resolve his problem. He never paid me another dime."*

Does this situation sound familiar? A client comes
in with a story about how they've been wronged
in some way and, despite the fact they cannot pay what
you ask, you are persuaded to take their case. Perhaps
because you know you have what it takes to resolve the
situation, or perhaps you are emotionally drawn into
the situation, or perhaps your bank account is low that
day. Ultimately, when the errant client doesn't fulfill his
part of the bargain, you end up writing off the fees and
becoming just a bit more jaded about the human race.

The client selection task that faces attorneys is more difficult than that of many professionals. People who initially present themselves as nice, well-grounded and cooperative individuals will engage in uncharacteristically extreme behavior during the course of a trial or in a battle waged over a contract. It can be very difficult to tell the good clients from the bad when they are on an emotional roller coaster.

If you think you are alone in your inability to sort the good clients from the bad, don't worry. Variations of this scenario happen with alarming regularity in firms across the country, to attorneys in all practice areas. Client selection is one of the most important non-substantive skills every attorney should master. Carefully selecting the clients you work with not only helps to protect you against malpractice problems, it has the added benefit of improving office morale, minimizing collection problems, and restoring peace in an otherwise crisis-driven practice. Proper selection of clients has widespread consequences as it impacts not only your team, your profitability and income, but also your ability to manage your time and well-being.

Your Ideal Clients

As important as knowing what clients you *don't* want, is knowing what clients you *do* want to attract. Answering the following questions will give you a demographic profile of our ideal A and B clients.

Age Range: What is the age range of your ideal client?

Income Range: What is the income range of your ideal client?

Value of Home: Where does your target/ideal client live?

What Counties: What counties do your ideal clients live in?

Asset Values: What assets do your ideal clients typically have?

Family Size: Are your ideal clients married; do they have children, etc.?

Education: What level of education have your ideal clients achieved?

Title at Work: What positions do your ideal clients hold in the workplace?

Associations: To what associations do your ideal clients belong?

Remember, there may be no distinctions between your ideal and worst clients in any of these demographic attributes if your worst clients have personality-based problems, or if the kind of work they bring you is out of your area of practice. We will give you a tool to help you distinguish those problems. The idea behind understanding their demographic profile is to sharpen your ability to identify them through their background and personal details quickly, and to distinguish them from potential C and D level clients.

Pareto's Principle

In Asset #1, *The Top Twenty*, we spoke of Vilfredo Pareto and the 80/20 Rule as it applies to your Referral Sources. You saw that 80% of your business probably comes from 20% of your Referral Sources. Not surprisingly, this rule also applies to your client base, in that 80% of your income usually comes from 20% of your clients. Hidden among the clients that you serve, this 20% is a small, quiet, but vitally important group. How important are they? Typically, they will generate a hefty 60% to 80% of your revenues and only take up 20% to 40% of your time.

Fortunately, for those of you who have a hard time telling the good clients from the bad ones up front, your Top Twenty group exhibits certain characteristics. It is our belief that when you learn to identify those characteristics, you can target them as future clients and increase the number of more profitable clients in your practice. We have a scorecard, called the Client Intake Matrix, designed to help you rank your clients so you work with only the best.

The Four Client Types

To keep this process simple, we classify clients into four categories: A, B, C and D clients. Each level is judged on pre-determined criteria:

payment habits; loyalty; having needs that fit the attorney's expertise; the ability to cooperate and trust the attorney; their opinion of attorneys in general; whether they are high or low maintenance; their ability to be satisfied with services rendered; and the likelihood of their sending more work or quality referrals. We also ask you to carefully consider the Referral Source who sent them - and on occasion the opposing counsel, if their identity is known at the time of intake.

In this framework, which you can customize to your particular practice areas, A and B clients are the good, C clients are the bad, and D clients are downright ugly. In short, the A and B clients are those you actually enjoy working with! They are the low maintenance clients that bring you the kinds of matters that fit your expertise. They don't hassle your staff, are not crisis-driven, and they trust your opinion. Unfortunately, these are also the clients that tend to get lost in the shuffle as you scramble to handle the constant demands of your C and D clients.

TIP

If you don't believe in the validity of the 80/20 Rule, take a look at your closet. You probably wear 20% of your clothes 80% of the time. Think how much room there'd be if you didn't keep all of those extra clothes. It's the same with your practice.

Red Flags

Your C and D clients don't sneak into your practice unannounced. They usually arrive at your door waving several red flags. They often:

• are excessively needy and talk about their situation endlessly to attorneys and/or staff members;

• refuse to take responsibility for their actions and any contribution they may have made to the current breakdown, problem or dispute;

• can and will be deceptive in an attempt to protect themselves and their interests;

• will withhold information or stall in complying with your requests due to mistrust;

• `may be so focused on their dilemma that they cannot focus on or follow through with your instructions.

Often, because you need the money, you welcome "C" and "D" level clients into your practice and close your eyes to the red flags. But remember: for every negative characteristic you can attach to a client, you will spend more time with that client - persuading them to trust you, calming them down, or trying to get paid.

TIP

One of the most difficult scenarios you may face is the decision to take a C level client from an A level Referral Source. If the client has a need outside your area of expertise, however, you should not take them on.

How To Tell The "Good" Clients From The "Bad"

The client scorecard enables you to rank clients as to their standing in certain critical categories. By making it more scientific, you may be able to save time by having associates or members of your staff pre-interview prospective clients on the telephone (this only applies when you have highly experienced team members whom you trust to handle this task). Especially if your initial consultations are free, this will eliminate your spending many unproductive hours interviewing what may turn out to be a C or D level client.

Adopting The Client Scorecard Method Of Selection

We encourage you to modify the client scorecard to suit your own needs, while still acting as a filter for C and D clients. Some attorneys may assign a different weight to each category. Many attorneys weight the ability to pay pretty heavily, as well they should. A client who scores as an A in every category, but who cannot pay for your services, is immediately downgraded to a D level. For

> **TIP**
>
> Using the client scorecard can dramatically shortcut the training of a new intake person because it offers tangible guidelines to use during the intake process.

some attorneys, the opposing counsel can be a deal-killer. Their experiences with some opposing counsel have been so negative, that even if a client is a high-scorer in every category but this one, they refuse to take the case. Alternatively, some attorneys simply raise the cost to the client based on what they fondly call the "jerk premium." They know that the extra work generated by the opposing attorney's tactics warrants the higher fee and openly discuss this with the potential client.

On the opposite end of things, many attorneys will opt to take in a C or D level client because of the Referral

Source that sent them. In this case, because the Referral Source is so valuable, they will suffer with a less than wonderful client because the inconvenience is worth the continued referrals. We encourage this type of decision only under the following circumstances: (1) the C or D level referral is a rare occurrence, and (2) the Referral Source would not be amenable to sending the client to another attorney. In many cases the fear is that the Referral Source will stop sending clients if you do not take the good with the bad.

This is understandable to a point, but when the C or D level client is so ranked because they either have no money or they need help in an area outside your typical practice, you should carefully weigh your options. If the fees attributable to a certain source are so significant that their discontinuation would be disastrous, the obvious choice is to work with the referred client. Many older and more established attorneys give these clients to younger associates, but, for maximum leverage, associates shouldn't be used this way too much.

A generic version of a client selection scorecard, otherwise known as our Client Intake Matrix, follows. Use it as is, or modify it to suit your particular practice. To help you in this process, think about the clients you consider to be A level, and those who have been D level clients – then variations in-between. Add your own criteria to the scorecard to ensure that it reflects

A, B, C & D Client Selection Scorecard

Rank	Client Personality	Type of Work	Case Value	Ability to Pay	Referral Source
A	Cooperative	Most Preferred Work	High Fees	No Problem	Very Good Source
B	Cooperative	Semi-Preferred Work	Medium Fees	Slight Problem	Medium Level Source
C	High Maintenance, Not Cooperative	Not Preferred Work	Low Fees	Low or Slow to Pay	Yellow Pages or Referred by C Level Source
D	High Maintenance, Very Difficult	Work Outside Your Expertise	Low or No Fees	Very Low or No Ability to Pay	Yellow Pages or Referred by D Level Source

the issues you must consider before working with a client.

Putting The Client Scorecard Into Practice

With the client scorecard, you can now score incoming clients and make a logical decision whether or not to take them on. You can do this during or right after your first client interview, but you risk wasting time. There is an even better way, if you create a system based on this form that allows you to score the clients on the phone prior to their first visit; then, if they appear to be qualified, continue the scoring process when they come in.

As you begin to formalize your system, keep in mind that it is not usually the best use of attorney time to screen potential clients on the phone. That is best left to staff trained in how to use the client scorecard. The best situation is to have a designated intake person. The receptionist always transfers the call to this person, who is practiced in client intake and on the alert for desirable levels of clients, and who possesses a keen discernment for financial and personality-based red flags.

The following sections are excerpted from our book, *Time Management: A Lawyer's Guide To Eliminating Interruptions, Decreasing Stress And Getting Home On Time,* (Mark Powers and Shawn McNalis, 2008) in which we discuss the financial and personality-based warning signs displayed by not-so-desirable clients. Also, we give you sample scripts to guide the intake conversation, and sample declination letters to use with those you may choose to turn away. We have consistently found that clients who have been pre-screened have a much higher conversion rate than the non-screened clients.

Financial Warning Signs

What makes many clients the wrong kind of client is their habit of not paying for services rendered. Your accounts receivable report might indicate that you have not been the best at judging a client's ability to pay. The questions that follow in "Financial Warning Signs" are very important. The answers to these questions are either going to point you in the direction of the client's financial stability or instability. Any that indicate instability should be seen as red flags.

It is possible to have a plan to filter out prospective non-paying clients, clients

Financial Warning Signs

• Did the client find you in the phone book?

• Was the client referred by a local Bar referral service?

• Was the client referred by other C and D clients?

• Is the client's first question "How much is this going to cost me?"

• Does the client mention that he/she knows another lawyer who is cheaper?

• Does the client resist paying a consultation fee or a retainer, or only pay half?

• Does the client hold out the promise of other work in order to get a fee discount?

• Does the client mention that he/she is switching attorneys or has switched attorneys midstream?

• Is the client a distant family member with a large matter?

who have no access to assets. If any of your clients exhibit these warning signs while on the phone or in your office, think twice about working with them. Note: for very large matters, many law offices will conduct a credit check before they take on a new client. Some even take credit cards, which automatically removes the collection burden from the law office, in case of non-payment. Sometimes one red flag is reason enough to reject a client, but usually each one should be considered in light of other criteria.

Look For Personality-Based Warning Signs

Whether or not a financial risk is spotted, there might be personality-based warning signs that indicate future cooperation problems. Pay attention to these signs before you admit these troublesome clients into your practice.

Given the emotional state of many clients, you must be particularly selective, since extreme behavior can manifest itself in many ways that negatively impact you and your staff. Many of these behaviors translate into large amounts of time lost and scheduled time being displaced.

Clients with these signs will likely be excessively demanding, time consuming and, in spite of your best efforts, unable to be pleased. These kinds of

Personality-based Warning Signs

• Did the new client show up with a full-blown crisis and demand your full and immediate attention right from the start?

• Did the client display a level of anger totally out of proportion to the matter?

• Is the client seeking revenge or does he/she have some other hidden agenda?

• Does the client want you to guarantee a particular outcome?

• Can the litigation client hear an objective, realistic appraisal of his/her case?

• Does the client have a bad attitude toward lawyers?

• Does the client act displeased no matter how well you take care of them?

• Does the client refuse to take responsibility for his/her own actions?

• Did the client arrive late to the first meeting and neglect to bring documents that you requested?

high maintenance, crisis-producing clients are considered to be "time-bandits" because they take up a disproportionate amount of time and energy. And when they don't pay you, they become a significant drain on both your time and your cash flow. Even if they do pay you, it may not compensate for the drama they have inflicted. To top it all off, these clients are the quickest to file a Bar complaint or bring a suit against you. When you encounter any of the red flags listed in the Personality-based Warning Signs, run the other way!

Suggested Scripts For Client Intake

When your designated intake person is conducting a client intake interview, he or she should ask questions whose answers point to problem areas. It is suggested that the attorney and an experienced team member develop a script to follow. The script provides consistency, thoroughness, and can serve as a training aid. A sample script, with potential red flag and preferred answers, follows:

New Client Intake Initial Script

Caller: "I'd like to talk to an attorney."

Receptionist: "I am going to put you through to _____. She can help you set up an appointment and also answer any questions you might have."

Intake person gives the first test: (The intake person should have the **New Client Scorecard** in hand to evaluate the caller for this exchange.)

Intake person: "Hello, this is _____, and I can help you set up an appointment. But first, whom may we thank for sending you to our office?"

Caller: (Potential Red Flag Answers)
- "I found you in the phone book."
- "The referral service at the Bar sent me."
- "My friend, (names a C or D client), sent me."

(Preferred Answers)
- "You were highly recommended by (names a good Referral Source)."
- "My friend, (names an A or B client)."

The red flag answers tell your intake person to proceed with caution, and move gracefully into mentioning the consultation fee. Often, the clients who come from the red flag sources will most likely be very price-sensitive, with the rare exception of the caller referred by your past C or D clients. When they hear the fee for the initial consultation, they may realize they've called the wrong law office. Your staff may then want to give them the names of some other attorneys they can call who don't charge for their initial consultations. The tone of the conversation should always be friendly, helpful, and not condescending when turning away a client.

The preferred answers are the first indication that this may be a very good client and your intake person should proceed with the conversation. Some offices prefer to mention the consultation fee here, just to save time in case the client still is not a good candidate. Alternatively, some mention fees after they go through a subsequent fact-finding conversation (below).

The next part of the screening intake script requires a helpful, gently inquiring tone and shouldn't be rushed, as the intake person is inquiring about very personal issues. Not all attorneys are comfortable having their staff take it to the next level of questioning. This must be undertaken by someone with experience in dealing with clients, who is sensitive to their situation, yet knows how to gracefully ask for just enough information

TIP One of our clients, determined to rid his office of "D" level clients, brought all of his files into his conference room and physically divided them into piles labeled A, B, C and D. The As and Bs went back into the files. The Cs and Ds were quickly completed or terminated.

to qualify them. A long-time paralegal, or an associate who has experience with clients and who is trained to shoulder much of the lower level communication tasks for the attorney, qualifies.

The initial intake and the appointment pre-qualification are the first level of ranking using the scorecard. All of the information gathered by the intake person is preliminary. However, it should be adequate to determine that an appointment with the attorney is either warranted because the client scored highly enough that they look like an A or B client, or that referring them to another attorney is more appropriate.

The attorney will gather much more detail about the case value and type of work in the actual initial consultation with the client. It is helpful for the attorney to go into the consultation prepared for the client, armed with the facts, advance information in hand, and ready to make a good impression.

You don't have to stay up all night to do your housecleaning, but it may keep you up at night until you do. To conduct the housecleaning, you can choose a time after-hours when you are alone in the office, or you can make it a group effort and go through the client list with the staff. The staff, by the way, will usually have an unerring sense of who the A and B level clients are. They take the abuse that sometimes comes from C and D clients and know exactly whom the more vocal or demanding ones are.

Transitioning To A Practice With Only Good Clients

Once you have initiated an intake screening process that will help you move from selecting problematic clients to desirable clients, you may be thinking about cleaning up your present caseload. One attorney we counseled became so obsessed with the idea of finding out how many problematic clients he had that he went to the office that evening and spent most of the night ranking his clients. As he suspected, the reason he was becoming so disillusioned with his practice was due to the fact that 80% of his caseload was made up of C and D level clients.

Take A Quick Look At Your Caseload

Before you go through each file looking for C and D clients, you can take a look at the following quick checklist of symptoms signaling an overload of this type of client:

Symptoms of a Practice with Many C and D Level Clients

Instructions: Read through the following checklist. Place a check beside the situations that occur in your practice.

☐ High outstanding receivables — doing quite a bit of work that you or your team will not be paid for.

☐ Clients leave prematurely or often threaten to seek the services of another attorney.

☐ Clients fail to show for scheduled appointments.

☐ Clients fail to bring requested documents or follow direction.

☐ Staff feels abused by clients who misdirect their anger and scream at them or act unreasonably.

☐ There is a constant sense of crisis and tension that is attributable to specific clients and/or specific opposing counsel.

☐ Staff and attorneys dread going to work and dealing with certain clients.

☐ Staff and attorneys are conscious of not meeting the high expectations of some clients.

☐ Staff and attorneys never hear "thank you" or any acknowledgement for their efforts — even when major victories occur.

If you do see a need to initiate a housecleaning, the following steps will assist you, and you'll be surprised at how energizing it is to take control of your practice in this way:

Step One: Using the client scorecard, go through your case list and rank your current clients as A, B, C or D, Note the A and B clients which you'll keep, and identify the C and D clients.

Step Two: If you think any of your borderline C clients can be "rehabilitated" and upgraded to a B level, sit down and have a straight conversation with them about what they are doing that is a problem (i.e., they need to make payments, produce necessary documentation, stop canceling meetings, etc.). Some will respond positively to this approach; some will not. Take the rest of your C clients and refer them to another attorney if their issues are personality-based, not payment-based. Avoid sending clients who won't pay to another attorney.

Step Three: Take your D clients and let them go. You can write them a letter; you can let them know in person; or you can phone them. Check your local Bar rules to be sure you follow the proper protocol. If you decide to write a letter, your Bar association has sample disengagement letters you can use. (Sample letters are included in this chapter for your reference.) If you decide to decline representation after research or investigation, you

TIP

Continually refine your client intake abilities — deciding which clients you'll work with is one of the most important business decisions you'll make and can mean the difference between a profitable year and a disastrous one.

should protect yourself and your client by (1) promptly advising the client in writing of your decision not to take the case or matter; (2) be certain to inform the client of his or her right to contact another lawyer for a second opinion; and (3) inform the client that his or her prompt attention is required. Disengagement and non-engagement letters are especially critical when a lawyer decides not to continue past a specific stage in the case.

If you decide to let the client go in a face-to-face exchange, you need to have a plan. To help you prepare, refer to the guidelines in the following section: "How to Fire Clients Face-to-Face.

How To Fire Clients Face-To-Face

Protect yourself up front: follow your local rules regarding releasing a client, especially if you are currently in litigation. (Your local rules supersede any advice given here.) Consider having a paralegal or legal assistant present in the meeting if you feel the client may react irrationally and later accuse you of misconduct. Under normal circumstances you won't have to take this extra precaution, but don't fail to document this meeting by summarizing the discussion in a letter and sending a copy to the client. Put a copy in your own file to protect yourself in case of a complaint. Follow these steps:

1 Gently set the client up for the firing conversation and limit their reaction by saying, "You may not like what I am going to tell you, but…"

2 Give the client the context for your decision so they will not think it is completely arbitrary. Link your decision to their attitudes and/or behaviors. Give specific examples of where the communication failed, where they were uncooperative, where they were rude or abusive to you or your staff, or where they failed to pay.

3 Explain why the behaviors and/or attitudes expressed by the client make it uncomfortable, unethical or inappropriate for you to continue representing them. Be factual and objective.

4 Give them an opportunity to respond, ask questions or express their anger. Resist being pulled into a discussion that escalates into a fight. If they become defensive it will intensify their emotions. Stay in control of the conversation by managing your own emotions.

5 If appropriate, act as a helpful resource for the client and make recommendations as to how they should proceed. You may recommend counseling, a legal service agency, or offer the names of other attorneys who may help them. (Remember to be very careful when referring unstable personalities and non-paying clients to your colleagues.) Call and discuss the situation beforehand to be certain the attorney wants to take them on.

Use the following Declination Letters with every client with whom you meet but decline to represent. Required in many states, the use of letters of this type will protect you from clients who claim they acted on advice you gave them. We also include a sample letter that terminates a client due to unpaid fees. To be certain that these letters arrive at their destination, they can be sent via certified mail, with a return receipt. We recommend that you take every precaution available to protect yourself when dealing with difficult clients, so keep copies of everything.

SAMPLE NON-ENGAGEMENT LETTER

Dear _____ :

You have contacted this firm and requested that I evaluate whether the firm will represent you in the above referenced matter. I met with you on ____, 200__ and have also reviewed the various copies of documents you left with me. I herewith return those documents for your use.

I appreciate the confidence you have expressed in our firm, but, for various reasons, the firm has decided not to represent you in this matter. However, if you have a need in the future for legal assistance, I hope you will again consider our firm.

You should be aware that the passage of time might bar you from pursuing whatever, if any, claim you have in this matter. Accordingly, because time is always important, and could be critically short in your case, I recommend you immediately contact another firm for assistance.

In declining to undertake this matter, the firm is not expressing an opinion on whether you might prevail if the action is pursued. You should not refrain from seeking legal assistance from another firm because of any interpretation you may place on this firm's decision not to go forward with this matter.

In accordance with our standard policy, we are not charging you for any legal fees or expenses. While we do charge for evaluating cases, that is only when we express an opinion on the merits of the matter to the client. Since we are not expressing an opinion in this instance, no charge is being made.

Although I believe this letter fully covers all pertinent matters, please call me if you have any questions.

Sincerely,

Reference: Law Office Management Section, The Florida Bar

DECLINATION AFTER REVIEW

Dear _____:

You have contacted this firm and requested that I evaluate whether the firm will represent you in a claim you believe should be filed against [insert appropriate name(s)]. I met with you yesterday and have reviewed various documents you left with me. I enclose those documents for your file.

I appreciate the confidence you have expressed in our firm, but, for various reasons, the firm has decided not to represent you in this matter. However, if you have a need in the future for legal assistance, I hope you will again consider our firm.

You should be aware that the passage of time may bar you from pursuing whatever, if any, claim you may have against [insert appropriate name(s)]. Because time is always important, and could be critically short in your case, I recommend you immediately contact another firm for assistance.

In declining to undertake this matter, the firm is not expressing an opinion on whether you will prevail if a complaint is filed. You should not refrain from seeking legal assistance from another firm because of any interpretation you may place on this firm's decision not to go forward with this matter.

In accordance with our standard policy, we are not charging you for any legal fees or expenses. While we do charge for evaluating cases, that is only when we express an opinion on the merits of the case to the client. Since we are not expressing an opinion in this instance, no charge is being made.

Although I believe this letter fully covers all pertinent matters, please call me if you have any questions.

Very truly yours,

Reference: Law Office Management Section, The Florida Bar

SAMPLE DISENGAGEMENT LETTER
UNPAID FEES

Dear_____:

When I undertook to represent you concerning [describe nature of representation, including case number, if any], you signed a Fee Agreement, agreeing to pay for the legal services provided to you and the costs and disbursements made on your behalf. At the present time, our records reflect that you have not paid our invoices in a timely manner, as you agreed you would.

Our records reflect that you have paid [report amount], leaving a balance of [report amount], which is now due and owing. Due to the apparent breakdown in our professional relationship, enclosed please find a Motion to Withdraw as Counsel, which I intend to file. I will be happy to continue to represent you if we can make acceptable financial arrangements in the very near future. Otherwise, my further representation of you has terminated.

If you wish to be represented in this matter, you should contact another attorney immediately. Keep in mind that, if your case is not filed in a timely manner, you may be barred forever from pursuing your claim. [Include specific time limit, if known]. You may wish to call the Lawyer Referral Service at [provide number].

Please contact our office to make arrangements for the return of your file. I will be happy to give it directly to you or to forward it to your new attorney, if you wish. It is our policy to maintain a file such as yours for [insert number] years, after which time it will be destroyed. I look forward to hearing form you soon regarding these arrangements.

Very truly yours,

Reference: Law Office Management Section, The Florida Bar

The Quality Of Your Practice = The Quality Of Your Clients

We believe the quality of your practice is determined largely by the quality of your clients. Imagine how different your practice would be if you worked with nothing but A and B level clients.

The scorecard, or Client Intake Matrix, becomes a great tool and asset when you take what you learn as you create your scorecard, and use the information to educate yourself and your team on what components determine an A & B client. It also helps you focus on your ideal clients.

Carefully selecting the clients you work with not only helps to protect you against malpractice problems, it has the added benefit of saving a lot of time, improving office morale, minimizing collections problems and restoring peace in an otherwise crisis-driven practice.

To claim this Asset, manage yourself, your time and your practice better, develop your client selection skills by using the Client Intake Matrix with each new client. The impact will be significant.

In the next section, Asset #14, we discuss *The Referral Map* and explore innovative ways to look at the community of professionals and network of local businesses where your present and future Referral Sources are found. This method of looking at your potential marketing contacts will be, for many of you, a novel but enlightening approach.

ASSET #14

THE REFERRAL MAP

You must give some time to your fellow men. Even if it's a little thing, do something for others — something for which you get no pay but the privilege of doing it.
~ Albert Schweitzer

Cultivating The Farm Team

The Referral Map is a tool to help identify and grow your referral network. Dan Sullivan, of The Strategic Coach, coined a term, Farm Team, in referring the referral network. It's a great term. The Farm Team is the group of people in the tier just below your Top Twenty List Referral Sources; basically, this is everyone else in your referral network. Just like your Top Twenty, not all of these Referral Sources are equally productive. Some may have great potential, some may not, but as the Farm Team metaphor implies, they are waiting to be developed. That this group sends fewer referrals than your Top Twenty Referral Sources could be the result of one of the following reasons: they may have recently met you and are testing your services.

Keep in mind that **Referral Sources who appear to be minor players may well be able to send you a higher volume of business in the future. But because they don't know you well, they'll start slowly and use a low risk strategy to determine the level of care and service you provide. Since these people feel a professional responsibility to their clients, they will want to assess how well you handle small referrals before sending substantial business.**

If you think you're being tested by someone on your Farm Team, treat their clients well, keep them informed of progress when ethically appropriate, and thank the Referral Source for their trust in you — in other words, treat their clients the way you should always treat referred clients, but make an extra special effort to reconnect with the referrer after the case is finished. Ask them out to lunch, if possible, and then look for opportunities to further the relationship.

One of our attorney clients, we'll call him Steve, loves to give Referral Sources books. A highly literate man, it's his way of connecting with people. As someone who is a voracious reader, he loves to discuss books — especially business books that he's found helpful in building his practice. If he thinks his Referral Sources will benefit from certain books, he'll buy a fresh copy, sign the inside with an appropriate message such as, "I hope this book is as insightful for you as it

was for me..." and send it off. Usually, the Referral Source will call to express his or her thanks and the attorney will suggest they get together and discuss the book when they've completed it. For Steve, giving a small but useful gift is a great way to extend a new relationship.

Years ago, another one of our clients received a small piece of business from a potential Referral Source testing the waters. During a phone conversation with the source who happened to be a physician, our client, whom we'll call Susan, listened carefully for insight into what his interests were. The doctor mentioned that his son loved basketball. Our client happened to jointly own season tickets for the local basketball team. Before the next game, she sent the physician an envelope containing the tickets accompanied by a note indicating that the tickets were for the doctor and his son. This is another great strategy that anyone can adopt as a means of getting to know someone better. Physicians are especially difficult to cultivate, but Susan's thoughtful gesture won her a great deal of good will with this particular one.

They may have recently moved to the area and haven't built their client base yet, which limits the number of people they can send.

If you think a potential Referral Source would be a good person to cultivate, the best thing you can do when they are new to the area is to send business to them and introduce them to others in the community for networking purposes. They'll be grateful for your introductions and may return the favor in the future.

They may have longstanding reciprocating relationships with your competition.

Don't feel you are wasting time getting to know people who have long-standing relationships with other attorneys, because the attorneys they like today may let them down in the future. We aren't suggesting you steal these referral relationships, but it doesn't hurt to develop a personal relationship with these Referral Sources in case something goes awry in the future. Your competitors will have problems from time to time that interfere with their ability to serve their clients. One of the most common problems is that they will overestimate their own capacity and will fail to keep their promises. Many of our attorney clients sit on community or

TIP

Be vigilant in your efforts to spot potential clients you can recommend to new Referral Sources — there is no better way to get their attention and inspire their sense of reciprocity.

charity boards and frequently have the opportunity to meet and work alongside potential Referral Sources who have long-standing relationships. There's no harm in developing personal relationships with their fellow board members in situations like this. Sometimes they'll turn into business relationships, sometimes they won't, but there is nothing wrong with demonstrating your expertise, reliability and friendliness in the meantime.

The business they send is all they are capable of sending.

Sometimes, all they send is all they can send. They may not be in a position to cross paths with the kinds of clients you want. However, if they like the way you've handled the few referrals they've sent, they may still be able to influence others professionals they know to send you business.

Keep an eye on the Farm Team.

Clearly, it's vital to cultivate the people on your Farm Team. From their ranks will come new additions to your Top Twenty list. It may take six months or ten years, depending on the circumstances, for a Farm Team member to become a more important Referral Source – but don't give up on them. You need the better ones to eventually fill in The Top Twenty list group, which will diminish through attrition over time. No matter what your practice areas are, you have probably received referrals

TIP To automate contact with some of your Referral Sources, you might include them in an e-mailed newsletter or send them articles of interest.

from the categories listed below. Scan the list to see the broad network of people who can act as a referral of sources and identify the categories of people who have sent you business.

Internal Networks

- Existing, satisfied clients
- Staff connections
- Adjacent office contacts

Informal Networks

- Family
- Friends
- Religious groups
- Local colleges and universities

The following list is an overview of the types of Referral Sources not usually thought of but useful to attorneys. Your particular mix of referrals will vary according to your practice areas. Look to see which categories of referrals are appropriate for your practice in each of your practice areas. Check off the ones that apply to you.

Referral Sources:

- ACLU
- Addiction counselors
- Adoption agencies
- Bankers
- Building associations
- Business brokers
- Claims adjuster
- Consumer groups
- Consumer protection agencies
- Corporate HRD departments
- Corporate meeting planners
- CPAs, accountants
- Detox units
- Embassies
- Entrepreneurs
- Ethnic churches
- Ethnic community leaders
- Financial planners
- Franchise owner/president
- Homeowners' associations
- Hospital administrators
- HRS department

TIP In most practice areas, your Referral Sources are more than willing to introduce you to people in their network. To make the introduction easy, you can arrange a lunch meeting and suggest they bring the person along.

- Immigration agencies
- In-house legal departments
- Insurance associations
- Insurance companies
- Juvenile agencies
- Large-size company owner/president
- Local event convention planners
- Local politicians
- Mental health counselors
- Mid-size company owner/president
- Minister, clergy

- Minority-owned businesses
- Mortgage brokers
- Newspaper reporters
- Nursing home administrators
- Physicians
- Real estate agents/brokers
- Real estate developers
- Senior citizen groups
- Shelters
- Small business networks
- Social service agencies
- Stockbrokers
- Television advertisements
- Therapists
- Title companies
- Venture capitalists
- Workers' Compensation departments

Professional Groups

- Local Bar: committees, speaker's bureau, referral service, attorneys
- Lead clubs
- Alumni clubs
- Service clubs
- Associations related to your practice areas
- Legal referral agencies
- Pre-paid legal groups

To cultivate more Farm Team members, look at those people who have been most successful in sending you business, then see if you can meet more people who do what they do. Target these groups and ask for introductions from those you know who may have relationships with your targeted group. Sometimes, if the Referral Sources are colleagues and not competitors, you can ask existing Referral Sources to introduce you to their network. You'll be surprised at how many are willing to do this for you. As we've said before, even though networking can be daunting for attorneys, most of the business world thrives on building and extending their networks.

To cultivate your existing Farm Team, keep them fully informed about their clients (in a way that is ethically appropriate), take them to lunch, consider giving something to them at holiday time, and put them on your newsletter list (if you send newsletters). Since they will value their relationship with you more highly if you can send referrals to them, keep your eyes open for appropriate clients to refer. There is almost no better strategy to develop the relationship and make them feel a little indebted to you. Also, spend time with them at your earliest opportunity in order to build and deepen the rapport you have with them.

To earn this Asset, you must identify the various categories of Referral Sources in your community that influence your ideal clients.

The traditional way many lawyers mar-

ket their services – through word-of-mouth referrals – is still the best way to gain new clients. Clients referred to your practice tend to be more loyal and less expensive than those who come from any other source. The people that make up your Top Twenty list deserve to be recognized as a big part of your marketing plan and treated as such. To be effective in your dealings with them, you must nurture the relationships and build on whatever level of trust and rapport exists between you. Use the Top Twenty exercise to plan your marketing activities, follow your plan faithfully, and you will see a surge of new referrals.

In the next section we'll talk about retaining clients who may have future business to send or who may be able to tell others about your services. Those attorneys who fail to cultivate an ongoing Top Of Mind Awareness program with past clients are wasting their marketing dollars. It's much less expensive to retain and stay in touch with clients for the long term, than to generate new ones. Read on to make the most of every marketing dollar you spend.

ASSET #15

A CLIENT AFTERCARE PROGRAM

*Unless you can find some sort of loyalty, you
cannot find unity and peace in your active living.*
~ Josiah Royce

Maintaining Your Client Base

As a marketing asset, the Client Aftercare Program is one of the most advanced and least understood. This Asset focuses on creating lifelong clients by providing value, whether paid or not, in the form of additional products and services. It is designed to have clients stay connected to you after their primary legal work is completed, to send referrals, purchase products, or use additional services.

A simple, non-law firm example is Atticus. After attorneys become clients with Atticus, they are automatically enrolled in our Graduate Network where we provide free monthly teleclasses. The teleclasses deliver high value, real world, practical advice on operating a successful, profitable law firm. Whether a past client attends the monthly teleconference or not, they get an e-mail flyer notifying them of the call and reminding them that they are important to Atticus and still part of our world. Now, let's look at law-related examples of law firms which take a similar approach.

One of our clients, an elder law and estate planning attorney, says, "I don't want clients to hire me to solve a one-time problem, I want them to hire me for life." He seeks to provide his clients with service and support for the long-haul – both while they are active clients and after their initial issues are resolved. Everything, from the name of his firm to the way he packages his services, is designed to elevate his services above that of lawyer-for-hire to that of long-term advisor. Because he is determined to deliver life-long service, you could say his Aftercare Program begins when the clients first come in the door.

He isn't concerned that surveys peg CPAs, not attorneys, as the most trusted advisors in the United States. He believes the approach he takes and the level of service he provides are comprehensive, and the trust his team engenders in return is well deserved. He's at the leading edge of a trend that has been growing among entrepreneurial attorneys who see the benefits of serving a broader spectrum of past clients' needs in-house, and who do it so well that clients regard them as their most trusted advisor. This approach avoids the limitations, not to mention the considerable time and expense, of constantly originating and working with new clients.

According to David Maister, Charles Green and Robert Galford, authors of *The Trusted Advisor* (Simon and Shuster, 2000), the evolution of the client-advisor relationship is a four-step journey that starts the day an attorney hangs out his or her shingle.

This concept is new to many attorneys who have performed with excellence within their chosen field, but have taken care to not step over the narrowly defined bounds of their practice area and have therefore limited the scope of what they can offer. In addition, they didn't try to stay in touch with their clients after their initial needs were met. Many traditionalists stay at this stage for their entire career.

Entrepreneurial attorneys, like the estate planner mentioned earlier, challenge themselves to broaden their services beyond the confines of their initial expertise and seek to care for their clients for the long run. Once they move to this level, which authors Maister, Green and Galford point to as the second step in the process, the attorney starts to offer advice in affiliated or complementary practice areas – all the while increasing intimacy in their client relationships. If they do this in such a way that they enhance their credibility, their clients begin to consult with them during the early, "defining stages" of their problems, a clear sign of increasing trust, instead of delaying their consultation until problems are fully formed.

According to our previously mentioned estate planning attorney, if you only deliver the service requested by a client, and offer nothing more, you've missed an opportunity. When he was just getting started, his practice did just that – though to him it was never a satisfying way to operate. A naturally inventive person, he began to study how other professional service firms inspired loyalty among their clients and were rewarded with repeat business.

He discovered that in order for clients to trust you, you've got to deliver *more* than what they request *and* you have to design your services to appeal directly to their needs. Having a significant emphasis on client care, from the initial consultation all the way through to the resolution of the client's case, sets the stage for clients to return. Consequently, Riley raised

TIP

It is much less expensive to cultivate new business from old clients. Once they've done business with you, the investment it took to land them as clients is typically covered. Any future business with them is thus more profitable.

the level of service he was delivering, expanded his offerings, and reengineered how he worked with clients.

Because of this change, clients now seek his advice proactively – well in advance of their actual needs. Typically, this signals that the attorney's advice is even more highly regarded, and he or she is now viewed as a valuable resource in the client's eyes. In this phase, the attorney is trusted to put issues into context, offer new perspectives, and interact with the client on a strategic level.

When the highest level of trust is present, what Maister, Green and Galford have labeled the *pinnacle relationship*, the depth of the relationship is matched only by the breadth of the issues the client is willing to discuss.

If you believe that offering broader services and deepening your relationship with clients is easiest in practice areas such as estate planning and elder law, you'd be right – but interesting variations are evident in other practice areas as well.

Take the forward-thinking criminal defense firm that has developed an expertise in addiction treatment centers. Painfully aware of the role addiction plays in the life of their clients, they study which treatment centers will best serve the needs of their clients. They then make recommendations to the family (there is an additional fee for this) to help them sort through the alarming array of avail-

able options.

What drove this firm to innovate this approach to client care? Three things: the clear-cut connection between criminal activity and addiction to drugs or alcohol, the confusing number of treatment centers that offer various types of services and differing lengths of stay, and, most importantly, the desire to do more than just handle the client's immediate legal issues. The firm's clients perceive them as not just attorneys, but as advisors who offer life-altering advice.

TIP

You'll know that clients have begun to trust you and value your input when they consult with you in the early stages of a problem instead of waiting until a full-blown crisis has occurred.

How do your clients view you? In order to analyze how you and your firm are viewed, and what image you present, ask yourself the following questions related to the issue of "branding" yourself:

What do you think your "brand" or image is now?

Do your clients see you as:

• A professional with a narrowly defined expertise?

• Someone who offers a wide range of services?

• A confidant, friend and/or long-term advisor?

Personalized exit surveys can be useful for learning what your clients think (see the exit survey in Asset #18). You can also ask your staff members to report back to you any comments they've heard about you and the level of service your firm provides. Be sure to capture both good and bad comments, as all remarks are instructive.

TIP

What complaints do you commonly hear from your clients? Listen carefully. Among these complaints lie clues to additional services they may need.

How is your firm perceived by the local community of professionals who send you business? In other words, what is your firm's reputation?

Are you considered to be a firm that:

• Can achieve results that other firms cannot?

• Cares about and works closely with its clients, serving them on many levels?

• Bounce this question off of a few of your close colleagues or Referral Sources to benefit from their outside perspective.

What image do you want people to think of when they hear your name?

Do you want clients to view you as:

• Someone they confer with on a broad range of issues, or as someone to hire on an as-needed basis?

• The wise, gray-haired senior partner who has long-standing relationships?

• An enthusiastic attorney who presents cutting-edge solutions?

• ... or something in between?

Ask yourself how you'd cultivate your image if there were no barriers to re-inventing your professional brand.

Consider ways to build on your present image to bring it closer to your ideal:

•Add to your knowledge base by attending workshops and seminars so you can expand what you offer your clients.

• Devote a portion of your client meetings to building rapport (instead of focusing only on business).

• Dress differently or work in a better office.

No doubt, there are some aspects of your personality and the way you present yourself that already fit the image you are trying to convey. What else could you add that would further round out your image?

Emulate someone who presently embodies the image you'd like to convey:

Think of one or two people who could serve as role models for you. The human brain is wired to learn by imitation. Just observing how colleagues or partners relate to

TIP

Here's how to decide whether or not gearing up to provide an ancillary service is wise: calculate the potential cases on a yearly basis then subtract what it would cost to train yourself. If by the second year you will be profitable, go for it.

their clients and gain their trust can be very instructive. Interviewing (see Asset #8) those you admire is even more effective, if and when it is appropriate for you to do so. As an added advantage, asking these questions of Referral Sources you admire will also increase the depth and strength of your relationships.

Here's how to look for areas in which to supply or expand your 'aftercare' services:

Be aware of additional frustrations your clients may mention when you are dealing with their legal issues:

Client complaints, comments and off-hand remarks can hold great promise if viewed as clues to client frustrations and unserved needs. Out of frustrations and needs can come ideas for your expanded services. Offering help with these unmet needs may not only exceed your clients' expectations, but can create an additional stream of income.

One attorney we know noticed how all of his clients call up to ask "one quick question." To him, this indicated a desire on the part of the client to check in with him – but not be charged. However, he also noticed many of the questions led to new projects. When he later created a bundled package of services for clients who pay him a monthly retainer, he

> **TIP**
>
> If you form a Client Advisory Team, take them to lunch once a quarter and gather their feedback on what you are doing now and what you plan for the future.

added an option he calls "One Quick Question." With this option, the client's monthly retainer covers them if they want to call and talk about issues with him. This is a good example of how to take a client frustration and use it to inspire a new service.

Expand your present offerings to provide ethical, ancillary services:

For some attorneys, offering more means you must acquire additional training or hire additional expertise for a more well-rounded firm. If you are presently in the habit of advising clients on issues ancillary to your typical services, could any of this additional value be offered as an additional fee-for-service offering? Analyze your present services and see how you can repackage, bundle or "productize" them.

Cultivating Clients For A Lifetime:

Your job is not only to use your skills to help your clients through a legal situation, but to ease their minds and build their trust. Begin this trust-building process right away by asking clients what outcomes they seek, so you know their expectations up-front. While they're still in your office, explain each stage of your work together. After the consultation, send an engagement letter to educate them as to your full range of services, and reinforce your desire to build a long and productive working relationship.

As time goes on, don't forget to pay close attention to select past clients (those who may be in your Top Twenty list or Farm Team) with regular check-in calls and notes. Obviously, if you haven't taken the time to get to know your clients, these efforts will seem insincere. You've got to authentically engage in building relationships with them or this won't work. Develop a file on each client which includes not only information on their current matter and the legal services they de-

sire, but also contains names of family members, marital status, colleges, hobbies, etc. Make sure this information is easily accessible each time you talk to your clients. (See Asset #2, *Contact Management Software.*)

While gathering this information, search for areas of common interest that can serve as the foundation for building your relationship. To further the bonds between you, try inviting clients with whom you have a great relationship to join you in non-work-related activities. Sports are obviously great opportunities to build these bonds: golf, tennis and fishing are excellent activities for building rapport because they aren't so intense that there is little chance to interact. Similarly, taking special clients to watch football, baseball, basketball, hockey, soccer or any number of other games is a wonderful rapport-building opportunity.

Client Advisory Teams:

Some particularly progressive law firms go well beyond the norm in cultivating their clients and making them feel a part of the firm. Several we know have Client Advisory Teams made up of past clients. Not all firms have a culture that would allow them to be this transparent and let clients in on their inner-workings. But for those firms who are committed to a level of client aftercare that is extraordinary, the advice they get is invaluable, and for the clients concerned, to be invited to be on one of these teams is flattering. They give the attorney and staff feedback on what they are doing right, and what's not working. These teams are given periodic updates on any new directions or services your firm is interested in incorporating. No remuneration is given to the clients for their time and input, so it's important to treat them well and not waste their time.

maintains close communication with them and they develop a great deal of trust in her. In addition to family law, this attorney also happens to do estate planning. At the end of each case, she presents a gift certificate to the client for a free estate planning consultation. If for some reason the clients didn't receive theirs in person, they are sent one as part of the package each client receives at the end of their case. The package contains copies of their documents and a cover letter. Some divorce firms include copies of past editions of their newsletters and even booklets giving advice on how to handle the aftermath of divorce.

Cross-Selling Your Client Base:

Once you've started seeing clients in terms of a lifetime relationship and not just as clients for one matter, your next step is to rate your existing client base and learn strategies for upgrading or cross-selling to them. You'll soon realize there is a great deal of hidden revenue to uncover in this process. Ask yourself which clients are candidates for further services. Most of the firms we work with have complementary practice areas; it's likely yours does as well.

For example, a family law attorney we've worked with closely for a number of years does a great job of serving her mostly divorcing clients. She

Many real estate attorneys we work with also practice estate planning because the two practice areas are complementary. We've coached many to

TIP The ability to search your database of existing and past clients for those who could be cross-selling candidates is another good reason to use Contact Management Software.

include a thank you letter at the conclusion of each case that reads something like this:

> **C**ongratulations on the purchase of your new home. We enjoyed working with you and hope you are settling into your new neighborhood. Keep in mind that acquiring new property may change your estate plan and insurance requirements. In addition to real estate, we practice estate planning and would welcome the opportunity to help you with any needs in this area...

Once you establish criteria for the services or products you wish to promote to past clients, develop a list of attributes that are reliable predictors of these client needs. If your client information is in a database that allows you to sort by given parameters or fields, it will be easy to generate reports or lists of those clients who meet your chosen criteria. The criteria for higher-end estate planning services, for example, could be: income above $3,000,000, ages above 50 and those who have family-owned businesses.

If your information is not computerized, delegate a staff member to hand-sort your files using your list of criteria.

Once you have a list of candidates for selected additional services, strategize on your own, or with other attorneys in your firm, about cross-selling or upgrading these groups. To do this, create an offer that will interest them. For example:

• Call clients and schedule a brief, complimentary appointment to update their files or discuss a particular legal concern.

• Invite a small group (either by letter or phone call) to attend a complimentary informational session at your office on a specific legal issue. Open with a question-and-answer period after the initial presentation. Let clients know you will meet with them individually after the session.

• Host a VIP lunch in your conference room or at a restaurant. Select a very important client to be the guest of honor and to meet the other attorneys in your firm. Invite higher profile clients who have worked successfully with one member of your firm and who you think may benefit from other firm services.

• Create a questionnaire or needs analysis that you can mail or give to your clients in person. Design this questionnaire as a legal evaluation checklist that allows clients to discover where they currently stand on select legal issues. Offer them a complimentary session with you to discuss the results.

• Send a cross-selling letter to clients informing them of further services provided by the firm. For example, tell them that in addition to employment law, your firm has expertise in a wide variety of legal matters including estate planning and family law. Offer your clients complimentary consultations in any of these areas.

As you implement these techniques with existing clients, pay close attention to how they respond, as you may need to change your approach if the results are not what you expected. If you aren't getting a strong, positive response to a mailed letter – better than a 5% response rate (most direct mail pieces receive less than a 5% response rate) – you may need to alter the way it's written.

However you decide to nurture your clients, know that it is an effort worth investing in. In our work as practice advisors, we are constantly exposed to innovative attorneys who aren't satisfied with the status quo and have developed programs that exceed the average client's expectations. These

are proactive personalities who identify and serve their client's larger needs instead of only reacting to their most immediate issues. By using the techniques described, you will be able to join their ranks.

To acquire this Asset you must have a Client Aftercare Program in place which generates new business from old clients. Aim for a 10% – 20% increase over the previous year.

You've heard us use the term Top Of Mind Awareness, or TOMA, but do you really know what it means? If your clients and Referral Sources don't have it, they won't think of you first when they have a referral to send. In the next Asset, we discuss what it is and how to use it to your advantage.

ASSET #16

TOMA: TOP OF MIND AWARENESS

Without promotion something terrible happens...
Nothing! ~ P. T. Barnum

Staying Front And Center

Having Top Of Mind Awareness, or TOMA, means that a potential Referral Source remembers you when it comes time to make a referral. Being in contact with past clients and existing Referral Sources at least once a quarter, through written correspondence of some kind, is the goal in our formula for TOMA success. If a client or Referral Source has a potential referral, they will often send it to the attorney or firm they most remember, or the one who is freshest in their mind. Assets #7 and #12 discuss ways to maintain a high profile in your community. This chapter offers more direct methods of utilizing newsletters and other forms of communication to expand contact between you and your Referral Sources and ensure that they think of you FIRST.

Client Newsletters

Though some firms try to send newsletters more frequently than once a quarter, they can become intrusive, given the information overload most people are dealing with these days. Also, it takes time to write a newsletter that is worth reading, and to produce one more often than quarterly can be difficult.

For your newsletter to be most effective, it should address the questions, concerns and hot-button issues of most interest to your readers. In other words, it should be relevant in addition to being well written and succinct. Some attorneys feature clients' stories (written with permission) in their newsletter, and others

will choose a Referral Source to interview, which allows for an interesting bit of cross-selling. You can also insert any pertinent additions to your firm, awards, or accolades received by members. What you write about will be dependent on several things:

• Your clients' interests.

• Your ability to think of interesting angles and ways to present your topics so your audience will actually be inspired to read them.

• Your ability to capture and translate changes in the law for your audience – this is always a popular topic for a firm newsletter.

• How much your clients' stories will be of interest to others (published with their permission), and whether or not you feel comfortable writing about them.

Some firms have been successful at sending out simple newsletters that take up no more than the front and back of one page; others go with the standard four-page (two pages, front and back) format. Whatever the length, the page layout should contain a good ratio of white space to written text, and feature prominent, interesting headlines in order to capture your readers' attention.

It's important to have someone who understands newsletter templates work with you on the construction of your newsletter – it must look profes-

> **TIP**
>
> **Creating your own newsletter is a valuable exercise, but can be very time consuming to do on a monthly or quarterly basis. For ready-made, client-focused newsletters tailored to specific practice areas, check out www. lawyersweekly. com/newsletters/.**

sional and continue the look of any graphic images you already have on your letterhead and/or Web site.

Newsletter Formats

If the demographics of your clientele include those who use and like e-mail, then consider producing an e-mail electronic newsletter. If you haven't already acquired the e-mail addresses of your clients, include a space on your intake sheet that requests this information so you can start adding this to your database. If you want to drive people to your Web site, you might send a teaser e-mail in the e-newsletter that includes the first couple of paragraphs of your key articles, then asks clients to click on a link that will take them to your Web site where they can finish reading the information. You may link to a blog format as well (we explain blogging in more detail in Asset #6, *A Professional Web Site*).

Many attorneys have used "Constant Contact," an on-line service that provides ready-made and customizable templates for e-mail newsletters, with great success. Not only is there a great variety of templates to choose from, you are also able to track important statistics on your mailing, such as: what percentage of recipients clicked on the link to read further and what percentage of e-mails were rejected due to undeliverable addresses. These functions give you the ability to see what your clients are most interested in – which is valuable when contemplating new topics – and to continually refine the addresses in your database. Without this kind of feedback, your e-newsletters will be less effective as TOMA tools.

Whether you produce a newsletter printed on paper, or publish it electronically, be sure to involve someone who is knowledgeable about graphic design to establish your masthead and layout. If you have certain colors, fonts, letterhead designs or a logo associated with your firm, the newsletter's design must match these ele-

TIP

Use a service such as Digg.com or Google Alerts to notify you when topics you are interested in pop up in the news. This will help you generate fresh content to write about in your newsletter or blog.

ments for the sake of continuity and branding.

Newsletter Language

Be sure to match the language used in the newsletter to your intended audience. If the articles are for clients, omit the legalese. If you are sending your newsletter to a group of industry-specific Referral Sources, use the terminology they typically use. Some firms create separate newsletters for separate audiences in order to address the issues most relevant for each group. Clients of elder law practices may be interested in learning about Medicaid issues; clients of

firms that specialize in business litigation might appreciate hints on how to manage employees in full compliance with the latest laws. Study the demographics of your clients and Referral Sources. Listen to their concerns and questions – they will indicate where their interests lie.

Piggybacking

If the thought of producing, writing and editing a quarterly newsletter makes you anxious, consider utilizing an existing newsletter to keep your name in the public eye. Can you contribute a short article to your church newsletter; write a helpful "How To" piece for inclusion in your civic organization's membership news? Many 501(c)(3) organizations welcome small advertisements in their publications. Think about your current memberships – film society, arts councils, historical and charitable organizations – and explore ways to connect your name to their newsletters.

E-mails

You can utilize both personal and group e-mails to connect with clients/Referral Sources (Asset #6) for a more detailed discussion on this topic.

TIP

Electronic newsletters generated using Constant Contact are easy for your Marketing Assistant to produce. Their templates are flexible to customize and they provide easy-to-use tracking reports.

Expanding Professional Publications

To maintain a high profile, you can send articles you have already published to colleagues who are on your Top Twenty list. This is an easy way to remind Referral Sources that you are an expert in your field and – best of all – it can be delegated to your Marketing Assistant. Any time you have an article published in a journal, a newspaper or an on-line publication, you can ask your assistant to acquire copies. Often the publications will e-mail you a PDF which you can then forward to the group of Refer-

ral Sources and/or clients. If you prefer, you can produce hard copies of the article and mail it. Either way, the article should be preceded by a cover-er letter from you with the receiver's (your Referral Source or client) name merged in the salutation line. This helps to personalize the letter. While some of our clients are appalled at the suggestion that they 'toot their own horns' by sending out articles they've written, we believe that the cover letter should emphasize the usefulness of the article to the Referral Source by saying something like:

"Dear Tom,
I recently wrote an article for the *Chicago Sun-Times* on the new zoning laws that I thought you might be interested in. I've attached it to this e-mail and hope it proves educational – the new laws can be difficult to understand..."

TIP As of the date of this publication, Twitter, Facebook, MySpace and LinkedIn might be the ultimate tools to maintain TOMA with large networks. Since social media networking is just catching on with attorneys. These sites can help you connect with clients, potential Referral Sources and the leaders in your practice area.

comes institutionalized in your marketing system, and automate the process. We know, as do you, that if a referrer or past client can't remember your name, they will send their business elsewhere. Don't let this happen to you!

You officially acquire Asset #16 when you have a newsletter or similar form of correspondence that promotes Top Of Mind Awareness and is sent to clients and Referral Sources, at least, on a quarterly basis.

In the next section, we'll discuss how you can measure progress in your marketing efforts. There are all sorts of small, marketing-related measurements that, if read properly, can tell you what's working and what's not. Read on to decipher what your marketing statistics say about you.

Remember: the whole point of maintaining TOMA with your past clients and Referral Sources is so the next time they have legal business or a client to send, they think of you before any of your competitors. Be sure your name is placed in front of your Referral Sources' and past clients' eyes at least once a quarter. Maintaining TOMA is an ongoing process. Systemize it by creating a well-crafted piece of correspondence which be-

ASSET #17

A TRACKING SYSTEM

However beautiful the strategy, you should occasionally look at the results. ~ Winston Churchill

Keeping The Numbers Straight

Here's a question we hear quite often from frustrated attorneys who are new to the client development process: *"Just how many times do I have to go to lunch with someone before they'll send me business?"* It's a great question. And one that's especially difficult to answer. Sometimes the results of your marketing efforts show up swiftly, such as when you take a Referral Source out to lunch and he sends a client the very next day. Boom. The ratio is one lunch to one client and the payoff is clear. When business shows up this quickly, and sometimes it does, it's a gratifying experience.

Then there are the times you connect with a **Referral Source four or five times and they send you nothing. Ever. Your repeated attempts to cultivate a relationship fail miserably. You believe you have good rapport because they appear to like you - but no new business has resulted. In stark contrast to your earlier success, the ratio here is five lunches to zero clients.**

Making Marketing More Predictable

There are many variables that come into play: the level of relationship you have with the Referral Source, their access to good, referable clients, whether or not they feel you can reciprocate, their standing relationships with other attorneys, their desire to see you succeed, etc. The interplay of all these variables leads to wide-ranging results, making it difficult to answer the "How many lunches does it take?" question. But let's take it one step further: how can you tell if your marketing efforts ever pay off?

It's helpful to think of marketing as a game in which the scores accumulate over time. How you judge whether or not you are winning is by keeping score.

To win the marketing game you've got to focus on two areas of play: getting clients to call your office, then converting the clients from "potential" to "paying" clients. If you're following our advice on engaging in three substantial marketing contacts a week, you'll have over 100 targeted contacts over the course of a year. This level of activity with the right kind of Referral Sources will get potential clients to call.

Once they've called, the game changes and your job is to lead them through the chain of events involved in signing them up. Measuring how you perform each of these steps is critical to improving your effectiveness. All of these statistics can be tracked on a simple monthly chart, The Client Development Tracking Form, at the end of this chapter. The statistics can then be compiled weekly, monthly, or quarterly and analyzed at the end of each year to evaluate whether or not progress was made.

You Can't Manage What You Don't Measure

By keeping track of certain key measurements, you will be able to tell what's working and what's not when it comes to your client development efforts. You may have a general feeling about whether or not a new tactic is successful, but you won't be able to fine-tune your marketing efforts without taking measurements.

Keeping track of your numbers and reviewing them regularly will allow you to make intelligent marketing decisions – quickly. When a negative trend begins and you see, for example, client referrals falling off, or your total number of client inquiries declining, you should be poised to take remedial action. Keeping track of your numbers will show these trends early. It will also, after you've kept track for a year, give you last year's numbers as a comparison. This is invaluable in mapping out your business cycles. Keeping your eye on these numbers will help you maximize your marketing and grow your firm intelligently.

To start, you must gather the data for eight key indicators. The Client Development Tracking Form, at the end of this chapter, is typically handled by a receptionist who is charged with capturing much of the initial data from calls and appointments made by po-

tential clients. If your office employs a Marketing Assistant, it may be a part of his or her job description to gather this kind of marketing data, working with the front desk person. This is easily accomplished in one of several ways: you can use a copy of our Tracking Form placed on a clipboard, an Excel spreadsheet placed next to the telephone, or a report generated by your Contact Management Software (if it has this function). A basic spreadsheet format, in whatever level of technology works for your office, is fine for this task.

The sample Client Development Tracking Form is set up to capture a month's worth of information and contains areas at the top for totals, as in "Total # of Inquiry Calls," "Total # of New Clients" and "Total # of Marketing Activities." Reading across the sample chart from left to right, there are spaces to capture the date, the po-

TIP

Never under-estimate the power of three substantial marketing contacts a week – it is considered one of the most powerful rain-making habits because it delivers results.

tential client's name, where the client originated (YP stands for *Yellow Pages*, AD stands for advertising, RS stands for Referral Source, CL for client and WS for Web site). You, your marketing intake person, or your receptionist must always ask, "Whom may we thank for sending you to our office?" or "May I ask how you heard about us?"; then indicate the source on the spreadsheet. If a Referral Source sent the client, their name can be written here as well.

In the next column – "Qualified Client?" – list whether or not the client is qualified. This is something the receptionist won't always know; an attorney will have to help make this determination, unless it's clear the

caller is price-shopping. Next, in the column entitled "Consultation Meeting Set?," you can record whether or not the caller signed up for a consultation, followed by a column entitled "Convert To Client?" in which you can capture whether or not the potential client became a paying client. Our model spreadsheet is truncated due to space limitations – make yours long enough to handle all your monthly inquiries.

Now that you understand the mechanism for gathering the data, the following section describes how to utilize it to your benefit:

1 The total number of marketing activities occurring on a monthly basis: The equation is very simple: typically, the more marketing events of a high-quality nature you and the members of your firm attend or initiate, the more referrals you'll get. When the total number of marketing activities goes up, expect to see an increase in the number of new clients in the coming months (there is usually a lag time between the marketing event and the referrals that will come from it). Unfortunately, the reverse is true when you slow down your marketing efforts. If the firm is large enough to have several attorneys, each attorney may have their own sheet. If it is small, the form can be a combined record of the firm's marketing activities.

2 What percentage of your clients are referrals? Out of everyone who dials your office to inquire about

your services, how many referrals come from a live person – another attorney, client, business network, family member or friend – as opposed to an advertisement of some kind? It is generally accepted that clients who are referred by people who know you and heartily recommend your services are easier to work with, more loyal and less price-sensitive. If you were retained by 100 clients last year and 25 came from client referrals, 25% of your clients come from Referral Sources. Typically, the higher this number, the less stressed and more profitable you are. As mentioned before, referred clients are generally more desirable. If this number is low for you, ramp up your marketing efforts and focus on face time with Referral Sources.

> **TIP**
>
> **Make it easy for your receptionist or Marketing Assistant to gather data on incoming calls by using the New Client Tracking Sheet Form at the end of this Asset.**

3 What percentage of your new clients is referred by past and present clients? Clients show their approval by telling others about you and your firm. This is a statistic that shows how closely related customer service is to marketing. In fact, we believe delivering a high level of customer service is marketing. If you want to know how your clients feel about the service they receive from your office, look at the spreadsheet to determine the number of referrals they send. To calculate your percentage, compare this number with the overall number of referrals sent.

An attorney in South Carolina that we know boasts a client satisfaction rate in the high 90s (they survey their clients religiously) and, not surprisingly, receives a huge number of client referrals. If you want to fine-tune your marketing without ever leaving the office, focusing on client service is a great place to start.

4 What percentage of your clients comes from the Yellow Pages? And how many are only price-shopping?

Probably your largest client development expense is your advertisement in the telephone book. Wouldn't it be nice to know if it was paying off?

Tracking the number of clients that call from the Yellow Pages is the only way. If the caller is overly intent on finding out the price of your firm's services before going any further, and appears uninterested in scheduling an appointment without hearing the fees, or passes upon hearing the fees, note that the caller is probably unqualified, or a price-shopper.

Phone book ads are notorious for bringing in a great many price-shoppers, but, once in awhile, they do deliver a substantial client. To figure out whether or not your phone book ad is worth what you spend, look at how much your phone book originated clients bring in compared to what you spend on the phone book ads. You will want to do this calculation once every six months, and then once a year, in order to have enough data to make an effective comparison. If you find the income from phone book clients is less than the cost of your ads, you are spending too much. Your fees should exceed your expenses by a 10% to 25% minimum in order for the ad to be considered profitable.

5 What percentage of the potential clients who call your office inquiring about your services are qualified or desirable clients? They are qualified if they appear to be able and willing to pay and meet all of the rest of your client selection criteria. (See Asset #13, *Client Intake Matrix*)

6 What percentage of the qualified clients who call actually make an appointment to talk to a lawyer? This tells you how successful the person who's conducting the intake calls is at bringing interested clients in the door. It may be you, it may be your associate, or an experienced staff person – whoever it is should aim to get 80% to 90% of qualified clients in for a consultation. Keep in mind the clients who are price shopping shouldn't be scheduled. In any given month, if eight out of the 10 qualified potential clients who call to inquire about setting an appointment don't end up booking one, something is wrong with your inquiry call script. Whether you are handling the conver-

TIP

Your receptionist or intake person will know when a client is "price-shopping" as their first question usually sounds something like, "How much is this going to cost?"

sation, or someone else in your firm is, you could be turning off potential clients by saying the wrong thing. Problems in this area happen more often than you'd imagine. If you are going to spend the time, money and effort to get clients to call in the first place, don't allow the system to break down at this point. Refine your intake scripts (Asset #13). There is a delicate art to converting an inquirer into a client and any breakdowns here are worth investigating.

If you don't have an official script, take the person in the office who ranks the highest in conversions (usually the person who has been doing it the longest), and create a script out of what they say. To do this you can have a paralegal or secretary sit in on several meetings and take notes on the questions they ask and the issues they explain. Other members of the intake team can sit in on consultations and observe the intake person in action in order to polish their own approach.

7 What percentage of those who schedule a consultation actually become paying clients? Next you want to track the number of consultations with potential clients who then become paying clients. This measures the effectiveness with which you are converting them. No one is successful 100% of the time, but attorneys who are the most successful typically convert 85% to 95%. If you or your intake person aren't converting at least 75% of the qualified clients who come in for an initial consulta-

tion, something is off. If you don't know what you are doing wrong, have a partner or a paralegal sit in on a consultation and evaluate your performance. Sometimes the problem lies with the way in which the attorney explains how they can help. Sometimes the attorney doesn't spend enough time listening to the client's story and the person feels unheard. Sometimes the attorney doesn't engage well or doesn't devote enough time to building a sense of rapport with the client. Many elements go into a successful

TIP

Pay attention to the types of callers who found you on the Internet. You want to determine how effective your Web site, or other on-line sites, are at delivering the kinds of clients you want.

consultation and any number of them could be off.

If someone like Tiger Woods, who at the top of his game broke down his swing and rebuilt it to be more effective, can do that, you can do the same thing with your consultation. It's well worth spending time to sharpen these skills. If your marketing efforts bring in 10 clients a month, but you only convert 50% of them, you've lost all the time, money and effort that went into getting half of them there. Life is easier on those who convert a greater percentage of potential clients. They don't have to market twice as hard to make up for their inability to close the client.

8 Your average fee per file: Most attorneys watch for an increase in the raw number of files they open, but we advise you to take it a step further. Why? Because opening 100 files at an average fee of $5000, for example, is not as good as opening 75 files with an average fee of $7000. The first scenario generates $500,000 in revenue – which is not bad, but the second gives you an additional $25,000, for a total of $525,000 – and you opened fewer files. Do the math using your own numbers. This approach typically translates to working fewer hours and generating more income.

There is no space to capture this statistic on our tracking form because the fees are not always known at intake. If your fees are clear from the beginning, feel free to pencil them in

TIP

To train a second intake person, the attorney should allow him or her to sit in on new client meetings. As the person learns more, the individual should be allowed to direct more of the interview until the attorney is satisfied with his or her abilities.

on the form next to the right-hand column, or modify the form by adding an extra column.

If you don't know your fees up front, you'll want to capture this information another way. To begin, establish what your average fee per file was last year by looking back at the cases you opened from January to December of that year. One way to do this is to have your bookkeeping software print out a list of cases, files or clients for last year and then add up all the fees and divide by the number of cases you opened. You can do the same for this year to see if your average fee per file is trending upward. This is a critical statistic to keep your eye on.

Practical Applications

With solid data in hand, you can see where you may want to set specific goals or make changes to your marketing game plan. Perhaps, like one of the attorneys we work with, you want to increase the number of referrals you get from a certain type of Referral Source. We met with this particular client at the beginning of the year and examined his list of Referral Sources. We saw that certain types of attorneys provided his best referrals. We asked him to further cultivate those he knew and to get to know more attorneys practicing in the same area. He became somewhat discouraged after a rough start in the first quarter, but he stuck with his plan and increased his efforts to build relationships with this group.

Toward the end of the second quarter, the referrals started to pick up. Not only did he prove to himself he could successfully market to a targeted group; he was inspired to set larger goals.

If your data shows that one CPA, psychotherapist or tax attorney sends you great work, clone them. Get to know more potential Referral Sources in the same field. The fact that you have one good Referral Source of this type means you can cultivate others. If your Referral Sources are not competitive with one another, ask the one you know well to introduce you to his or her colleagues. If it's not appropriate to ask for an introduction like this, get to know other professionals on your own. Targeting those who will not only send business, but will send very good business, is the essence of smart marketing.

Make sure your marketing efforts translate into dollars by doggedly capturing and reviewing your marketing statistics to understand and improve your conversion rates in the chain of events that lead a client from potential to paying, and target your Refer-

TIP Tracking your average fee per file – and seeing it increase year after year because you are providing added value – is the key to working smarter, not harder.

TIP

"Cloning" your best Referral Sources, by meeting others in the same profession or practice area, is an excellent strategy for increasing the number of high-value referrals.

To acquire this Asset you must have a tracking sheet in place and track the key indicators mentioned in this chapter. You should review your numbers once a month, then compile and review them on an annual basis so you have the data you need to tweak your marketing plan and spot client development trends.

In the next chapter, we zero-in on one of the elements of marketing we alluded to in this section – client care. It is our belief that increasing client care increases the number of referrals clients send. When they are genuinely pleased with how they were treated by your firm, they will tell their friends. When they aren't pleased, they will also tell them – often in greater numbers. To keep your clients singing your praises, read on.

ral Sources intelligently. Keep in mind that this spreadsheet must be reviewed on a regular basis. Either the Marketing Assistant and the attorney, or the attorney and his or her partners, or the attorney alone, should look at this form often during the month to track progress. Once data from a number of months has been captured, the firm will have an invaluable record of their key indicators and a tool to help them decide how to proceed with their marketing efforts. To win at the game of marketing, you've got to be good at every aspect of the game and learn to keep score. In the words of Yogi Berra, a man famous for playing games, "You can see a lot, just by watching."

New Client Tracking Sheet

Month: _____

Name/Date of Inquiry	Consultation Date Set	Scope or Fee Agreement Sent	Inquiry	Referral Source Name

ASSET #18

THE CLIENT-CENTERED OFFICE

*The way to gain a good reputation is to endeavor
to be what you desire to appear. ~ Socrates*

It's All About The Client

It is essential that your office environment portray you and your team as professionals focused on one thing: taking care of your clients. It is the stage which will shape your client's experience and further reinforce your brand. Consider the state of mind your clients are in when they come to your office. Rarely are clients in a law office because they want to be. Typically, they are dealing with a crisis of some kind, or attempting to forestall one in the future. How much better could you make the clients feel just by changing a few elements in your office? What kind of initial impression do you want your firm to make? Do you want to be seen as trustworthy, professional, dependable, stable, and reassuring? Ask yourself if the look and feel of your office sends that message.

When the airline industry was making money, they routinely re-invested in maintaining the look of their planes. The seats, carpet and wall covering in every plane were consistently replaced and kept looking good.

Why were they so particular about the look of their airplanes? It was good business.

Managing Client Perceptions Equals Good Client Care

When passengers see stained carpets or frayed fabric on the seat in front of them, they immediately begin to question how well the airline maintains the engine. The thought of a poorly maintained engine produces anxiety. A smooth, pleasant and safe experience is what the airlines are after for their passengers; the perception that the plane is in shoddy repair does not help.

That customers leap to such far-reaching conclusions is not limited to the airline industry. In the absence of any real information about a service or product, consumers will look to the quality of whatever surface features they see. We do this with politicians, too – the less we know about their abilities, the more we vote based on their physical appearance. A worthy candidate suffers if they don't look good.

What does all of this have to do with your firm?

Managing client perceptions about the care they will receive is as important for lawyers as it is for airlines or politicians. Many potential clients are nervous and feel at a distinct disadvantage when seeking legal services. They generally have a problem and want someone they trust to help them. As they sit in the reception area, their eyes wander as they unconsciously form that all-important first impression.

During their initial survey, if the reception area is full of mismatched furniture, and a disinterested receptionist sits behind the desk, what kind of an impression do they form about the attorney who works there? Is a worn décor or lack of hospitality a true indication of the firm's professionalism or concern for clients? No; but it might as well be.

Contrast that experience with one in which a potential client walks into an office, is impressed by the décor, and feels warmly welcomed by the staff. Their first impression is a positive one and confers all manner of wonderful attributes on the firm – whether they deserve them or not. Here the power of perception is made to work for you, not against you.

> **TIP**
>
> First impressions are key – in both life and in the workplace. Make your first impression a lasting one by ensuring that your office environment is a clean, bright and welcoming space for your client.

It is relatively easy to manage the perceptions of your clients. Keep foremost in your mind that they are drinking in the look, the feel, and the sound of your firm at all times. Your signage, how hard you are to find, what the parking is like, whether or not your Web site and letterhead match, the sound of the receptionist's voice when she answers the phone – all must be welcoming and consistently professional in the look and feel.

According to B. Joseph Pine and James Gilmore, authors of several best-selling business books, among them one named "The Experience Economy," consumers have an ever-growing awareness and high standards about how they should be treated.

Today's sophisticated consumers seek an elevated experience when they buy goods or services, and given the widening array of services they are able to choose from, they can get what they are willing to pay for, and many are willing to pay more. Starbucks, for example, can charge four bucks for their coffee because they deliver it in a more hip environment than the diner down the street.

Dentists, who face enormous challenges in offering their consumers a good experience as they poke them with needles, drill out cavities and install new pieces and parts, have learned to quell the anxiety of their patients by installing massage chairs, earphones and television monitors that run movies or cartoons to dis-

TIP

The "mystery shopper" technique is one effective way to determine your office's first impression. Ask a trustworthy, non-staff member to come and evaluate your office environment and report back to you at a later date.

tract patients from the anxiety they feel. Some dental offices even offer a choice of anesthesia – allowing the patient to choose their level of consciousness.

A theater near you no doubt features superior sound systems and seats that pulsate to the movie soundtrack. Design and technology are being employed at every turn to enhance the customer experience.

Many Atticus graduates have taken this idea to heart and have worked hard to create a better experience for their clients. One such firm that specializes

in divorce for high net worth clients is set in the South, where hospitality is sometimes elevated to an art form. Upon arrival, clients are surrounded by soothing sounds from music piped into the parking lot. Inside, the office is comfortably furnished with plush, upholstered chairs and harmonious colors.

This attorney knows his clients are in pain and surrounds them with a relaxing, calm environment. Once they've entered, clients are not only offered something to drink, they are provided with a menu of different beverages. Once their selection is made, the beverage of choice will be delivered on a small tray by a smiling assistant. This firm's commitment to service doesn't end here – they try to address the emotional needs of the client as well. To deal with the emotional trauma most of these clients feel, the firm employs individuals who are expert at handholding anxious clients. Think this is too much? This is one of the top divorce firms in the state. They must be doing something right.

A personal injury firm we know has taken a page from retailers and others who use scents for the psychological cues they invoke. Microwaved chocolate-chip cookies are made periodically through the day. The comforting, reminds-you-of-home smell of these cookies wafts through the firm and clients clamor to have them. As intended, the comforting scent takes the edge off whatever tragic circumstances the clients are there to discuss.

If you can't tell what kind of impression you make, use the "mystery shopper" technique: ask someone your staff doesn't know, but whom you trust, to call your office, make an appointment and come sit in the waiting room. When you bring them back to your office, they can tell you how they were greeted on the phone, whether or not they were put on hold, how easy it was to find the office, and what it's like to sit in your reception area. If asked, many of your spouses can tell you the same thing.

You can also take the Client-Centered Office test below to help you identify problem areas.

Client Reception

• All clients are greeted warmly and offered a beverage upon coming into your reception area.

• When meeting a client, the attorney or Designated Hitter comes to the reception area and escorts them to the conference room or office.

• The client is introduced to the Designated Hitter at the first meeting. (This is the paralegal or associate who works closely with the attorney and will bear much of the communication burden.)

• New clients are given a tour of the office and introduced to key people on their first visit.

• The clients are given some kind of token gift with the firm's name on it.

Facility Or Office

• The overall office decor sends the right message to the client in terms of credibility, permanence, and trustworthiness.

• The reception area chairs are in good condition and comfortable for sitting.

• There is adequate and easily accessed parking for clients.

• Any offices that the client sees are neat and orderly.

• The office decor is matched to the type of client that frequents the firm.

Materials And Signage

• New clients receive maps or written directions in advance of their first visit.

• Firm signage is clear and not difficult to follow.

• New clients are given a "Welcome" package of information to familiarize them with the firm.

• Firm letterhead or logo is well designed and consistent on all materials.

• The firm Web site has a look and feel similar to the rest of the firm materials, without being a duplication of the firm brochure.

Telephone System

• Clients are greeted warmly by a real human being when they call.

• The voice mail system is adequate to the clients' needs and always presents the option to speak to a real person.

• Attorneys never take a call when meeting with a client unless it is an emergency.

• Staff monitors their voice mail frequently.

• Telephone calls are returned the same day, or within several hours.

This test is taken from the point of view of the firm. The Client Satisfaction Survey, at the end of this section, is a form you can give to clients to get their point of view. This form can be mailed out with final copies of documents or given to the client in person at the last meeting you have with them. The most successful firms, however, ask the client these questions in person or over the telephone. Clients are much more responsive when they are your captive audience. Once the surveys are completed, the answers should be tabulated and discussed on a weekly or monthly basis to quickly catch and resolve any issues. Don't

make the mistake of gathering data from your clients but then failing to learn from it. Going through the motions won't work here.

The following section addresses the need for each member of your staff to excel at their telephone communication with clients. Since much of the firm's communication is handled over the phone, everyone should be sensitive to how they are being heard by clients. We've all dealt with staff who have poor communication skills and it leaves a lasting (and negative) impression. Follow our rules for telephone etiquette, and don't let this be the case in your office.

TIP

Give your clients the Client Satisfaction Survey directly: either over the phone or in person. Your client will respond more positively when you use this method.

Telephone Etiquette

1 Pick up the phone within the first three rings.

2 Add "How may I help you?" at the end of your normal greeting.

3 Techniques for putting a client on hold:

- Ask if you might put them on hold.

- Wait for their response.

- Tell the client why you need to put them on hold (I need a moment to get the file. This will just take a minute).

- Thank them for holding when you return.

4 Leaving a client on the telephone over three minutes seems like an eternity. If your task is going to be delayed, be sure to check back after three minutes to give them an update and the choice to hang up, speak to voice mail, or have you phone them back.

Control The Level Of Crisis In Your Office

U nfortunately, many offices are stacked with paper, piled with files, and riddled with evidence of one crisis too many. When clients see the mess, it doesn't inspire confidence, and degrades their level of trust in the quality of care they'll receive.

A number of different factors contribute to an office crisis – some of which you can control, and some you cannot. Clients, even A and B level clients, will have unexpected problems. And you can count on Referral Sources, partners or your opposing counsel to have issues that will demand your immediate attention. The control you have over crises instigated by external influences is limited by your ability to choose your clients, Referral Sources and partners wisely.

Whether or not you've mastered the talent for choosing whom you'll work with, you must do what you can to eliminate crises that arise internally. Issues such as poor office protocol, a lack of written office procedures, piles of files, all increase the chance of something falling through the cracks and creating a problem.

Why Systematize?

T aking a systematic approach ultimately enhances client care and the Client-Centered Office. In this section, the focus is on creating systems for three areas that commonly create problems. We'll provide direction to help you:

1 Establish a system of checklists that directs the sequence of activities in each type of file you commonly handle.

2 Establish model files for each type of case or matter that you typically handle.

3 Establish an efficient filing system on your desk to process paper.

Law offices tend to rely upon "customary" ways of doing things. This occurs most frequently in what we'll call the 'personality-driven' law office. In these situations, the attorneys rely upon long-standing employees who have supported them for years. Perhaps the attorney trained his or her staff to work through a file a certain way; perhaps the staff uses procedures observed at a former law firm. Many times the customary office procedure is something that is not necessarily trained, not something that attorneys or staff learned in school, but something they have observed and gotten into the habit of doing year after year. Unfortunately, the "customary" ways are not usually written down.

So what happens when new hires come in and try to work their way through a file? The training they receive is dependent on how those around them articulate the process. Training is especially difficult and somewhat unreliable when organized, written references don't exist. Since the rate of staff turnover is ever increasing (currently staff is only loyal for about three years in a typical law office), this is a critical issue not only for training, but also quality control.

How Does A Checklist System Work?

Checklists are written procedures that are created to demonstrate the best way to work through every type of file in your office.

The paperless office is not a reality quite yet and those "piles of files" on your credenza, floor, and desk are

TIP

Resolve internal office problems using a systematic approach. This approach will drastically improve the manner in which your client is treated in the client-centered office.

> **TIP**
>
> Start keeping a daily detailed checklist — it is easy to do, and will give every member of your staff the satisfaction of knowing no task has been overlooked.

not going to disappear on their own, making the checklist a critical element of the systematized office. For every major type of file that you work on, there should be a checklist. The checklist is a step-by-step list of each activity or task that occurs within that file in the appropriate sequence, with a place to denote the due date and a place for staff to initial when the task is complete.

The goal is for any person who picks up the file to be able to know exactly what has been done in that file. This is true because every task has been identified, put in sequence, checked off and initialed upon completion. Everyone, including the attorney who refers to the checklist or the paralegal

who works on the checklist, has the peace of mind that nothing has been missed.

Once the checklists have been thoroughly analyzed and found to be efficient, they should be termed master checklists. For ease of reference, for training new hires, or retraining, these "master checklists" should be stored in two places:

• On your computer in the appropriate directory.

• In a binder for each type of file (i.e., uncontested divorce, contested divorce, etc.).

Create Easy Access To Master Checklists

By putting the master checklist on the computer, you make it accessible to everyone. You can create a folder labeled "Checklists," with subfolders that are labeled with each type of file, i.e., contested divorce. Encode each individual type of checklist to reflect the latest versions. There are a couple of benefits to having them on the computer. One is that everyone can access them quickly. The other is that it serves as a backup for the forms in the binder. If you have invested in case management software for your practice, you may be able to incorporate your checklist into the software if it doesn't already provide this function.

TIP

Keep both digital and printed copies of all your important forms and checklists. You'll stay organized and prevent any potential crises that may arise in the future.

Printed forms in a binder can be used as a backup for the computer version. You can divide the sections with tabs to allow for ease of use. Here is a suggested tab system for your binder, listing the name of the tabs, their order and the purpose of each:

1 Master Checklist: behind the first tab, include a copy of the master checklist.

2 Procedural notes: behind the second tab, include procedural notes – anything that is too lengthy to explain in the checklist itself. This allows the reader to obtain a more lengthy explanation of certain steps in the checklist.

3 Samples: behind the third tab, include samples of the documents referred to in your checklist. These will be documents commonly used in this type of case, such as sample

pleadings, affidavits, orders, questionnaires, and letters.

The ability to train and retrain people in your particular procedures is critical to pre-empting crises. Having checklists like this serves as a reference tool for existing employees and as a training and ongoing reference tool for new employees.

Ways To Create A Master Checklist

There are three approaches to creating a master checklist for your files. When you, the attorney, analyze and list the tasks for specific cases or matter types and construct the checklist, it is referred to as the "Analyze and Create the Checklist" method. In the second method, you select another individual in the office to participate in a process called "I'm a File." The final method is called the "File in Action" approach in which the checklist is created by the entire team.

The "Analyze And Create The Checklist" Approach

If you, the attorney, decide to create the master list, follow these steps:

1 Select a common type of file or matter.

2 Write the protocol (non-substantive activity) for opening the file based on how that file is typically opened.

3 Write the protocol (non-substantive activity) on how that file is typically closed.

4 Look at the most commonly repeated activities within the file and determine the steps (substantive activities) that take place as the matter or file is worked (i.e., prepare documents, acquire records, schedule depositions).

5 List the steps in outline form.

6 Provide a place beside each step to mark the due date and a place for the person who is working with the file to initial when completed.

7 Where it is appropriate, list references to relevant documents by name or by their location in the computer.

The "I'm A File" Approach

You may decide to create the master checklist using an exercise called "I'm a File," where you, the attorney, would delegate the task of writing the actual checklist in order to save time.

To begin, assign one staff person the task of walking through the office, stopping at every location that a particular type of matter, case or file would travel as it is being worked. By interviewing each person that works on the file, the staff person can come up with the steps that are most commonly taken, and in what sequence, in each type of case. The interview may take place with two people or five people, depending on the size of your office and the breakdown of the workflow.

Once a rough draft of this file has been created, the staff person can submit it for review. This review can be by the entire staff at a staff meeting or by the attorney alone. The next step is to make the recommended changes based on the review.

The "File In Action" Approach

If you decide to create the steps of a master checklist by using the "File in Action" approach, you still write the protocol (non-substantive activity) for opening and closing the file based on how that file is typically opened and closed, and delegate the task of writing the protocol. Next, have all relevant team members keep a yellow pad on their desk and jot down notes as they work through the file. Instruct them to accumulate all the notes into a draft. Lastly, you and your staff review the draft and incorporate any changes to develop the master checklist.

No matter which approach is used, once the master checklist is approved, it should be put on the computer and into a binder with any other explanatory material. At that time, copies of the checklist should be attached to the inside flap of each file as it is opened. Some members of the staff clip it on; some staple it in. It is a permanent fixture in the file and everyone in the office uses it to direct the work done in the file. The checklist then becomes an up-to-date snapshot of all the work currently done on the case.

Adding Options Within The Checklist System

Once your master checklist is in use, a focus on client service can be built right into your system. Here are prompts for items you may want to include:

• Keeping clients updated on the status of their case through preemptive phone calls and/or update letters.

• Touring clients through the office and introducing them to the people they will be working with.

• Giving Referral Sources a thank you (by phone or in writing) and updates when appropriate.

When your systems are built not only around speed and efficiency, but specifically around serving your clients well, then everyone benefits. Often clients cannot judge the quality of your work product, but they can tell if you care about them by the way that you or your office keeps in touch.

Evaluating And Measuring The Success Of The System

A checklist should be considered an ever-changing document. There will always be improvements that you can make toward perfecting your checklist. When a new checklist has been put into use, it will contain some mistakes and some omissions. The job of the people who are using the checklist for the first several times is to catch those mistakes, fill in any information that has been omitted, and to generally upgrade the list. Of course, any new versions should be posted in the appropriate computer directory and an updated copy inserted in the binder. Versions can be created as they are updated so there is always the latest copy of the checklist available to be used without confusion.

A checklist is not working right if it complicates your process. Three criteria by which you can measure the success of your checklist system are if it:

• Streamlines the process and eliminates extra steps.

• Eliminates guesswork about what is to be done next.

• Creates peace of mind regarding details not being overlooked.

When you have a system in place, your speed is increased, your profits go up, and your clients and influencers are pleased with your turnaround time and the accuracy of your information.

Boost Your Checklist Time-Savings With A Model Folder

Together with the checklists, create a model file: an example showing the way you want your files to be organized. It is helpful to use pocket files or multi-partition files and to designate which areas of the files are to be used for certain types of documents. For example, the checklist would always be in the front of the file and the documentation would be placed in agreed-upon locations throughout.

When the attorneys and staff pick up a file, they can immediately refer to the checklist to see the status, or quickly find the backup documentation they need.

Establish An Action-Oriented Filing System On Your Desk

The second aspect of systematizing your office is to institute an action-oriented filing system for processing the paper that comes across your desk daily. With the introduction of the personal computer, it was predicted that we would all be operating in the paperless office well before the year 2000, yet researchers today say that we are dealing with 10 times more paper than when this prediction was made. The average American executive loses six weeks a year trying to retrieve information from paper-laden desks and misplaced files.

For most attorneys, the time loss is probably greater. It is not unusual for attorneys to have piles of files on their desks and their credenzas, with more boxes of files on their floors. A client once dropped by unexpectedly to see her attorney – one of these disorganized folks. She had never been to his office before as he always met with clients in the conference room. Stunned with the mess she walked into, she remarked that she didn't know he was getting ready to move. He was ashamed to admit that he wasn't, and soon after called for help in getting organized.

When faced with the tremendous influx of paper that comes to you in the mail, from the fax machine, the copier, and your computer's printer, it can be a daunting task to organize it all. The most important pieces of paper generally get attended to, but the rest get stacked, shoved aside, stored away or pushed out of sight.

Personality Pro-'files'

A unique approach to broadly categorizing individual filing system methods is personality-driven. One attorney referred to other attorneys who pile their desks with files as having an "Everything Out" personality. Lacking a filing system that they feel confident in, these attorneys store their files where they can see them. This gives them the false confidence that they will not forget anything. Piles of files are created and distributed according to their importance. Each individual attorney has his or her own formula, but usually the more important the file, the more prominently it is displayed. This means the urgent files sit on the desk and the less time-sensitive items are relegated to the

floor, gaining urgency with every hour that passes.

On the other hand, what would an "Everything Away" personality's desk look like?

For starters, these attorneys put things away because they have trust in their filing system. A clean desk usually indicates a well-organized filing system. All files that are not currently being used are stored away in either a holding file in their desk or credenza, or given to their staff to file in the outer office. These attorneys rely upon the calendar and to-do list to tell them what to work on. Because they follow their time template religiously, they have faith that they will touch on every important file in their case status review meetings and weekly planning sessions. Every night, before leaving the office, they take a few minutes to clear their desks. It takes discipline, staff support and a good system to operate in this way, but it is possible to see the top of your desk.

It's Time For A Paper "Triage"

From examining the phenomenon of the "Everything Out" attorneys, it was discovered that piles are a function of three things:

• *Lack of a destination*: Not having institutionalized stations for paper as it is being processed.

• *Indecision:* Not deciding on what to do with a piece of paper immediately.

• *Horizontal paperwork storage:* Storing paperwork horizontally, in piles, greatly restricts access to it.

One solution that can help with all three of these paperwork problems is to set up a standing file into which you and the staff triage incoming paperwork: determine the priority for treatment of each piece of paper. This is an "in-box on steroids" that can be used to process incoming mail, faxes, computer printouts, and any other papers that come across your desk. This solves the destination problem and the horizontal storage problem.

This standing in-box should be placed where the attorney can comfortably use it without getting up. The staff should also be able to access it easily. It should contain four files that open at the top, which are set in a file folder stand:

• Hot file

• Delegation file

• Holding file

• Reading file

The Hot file can be color-coded with red or orange and will contain the high-priority, truly urgent, deadline-driven paperwork that must be dealt with immediately by the attorney. When the staff needs to have paperwork of any kind addressed by the attorney, it goes into this file, appropriately flagged. When the attorney is opening mail, the items requiring immediate action go into this file. To insure that nothing is overlooked, the attorney should be in the habit of touching this file frequently throughout the day. This Hot file setup eliminates what would otherwise be lots of urgent paperwork sitting in random order, or worse yet, buried in a pile

TIP

Your master checklist is a vital part of your workplace. Always make sure your desktop and print versions are up-to-date. That way, your staff can effectively determine the work being done on the case.

TIP

Don't forget to take advantage of the often under used circular file/ wastebasket in your effort to organize your work space.

somewhere. With this method, all of the urgent items are centralized into one easy-to-access spot.

Into the *Delegation file* go the items that the attorney delegates to the staff. The attorney will need to set up a Delegation file for each staff member to whom they delegate. Upon receipt of paperwork that must be delegated, the attorney attaches a Post-It Note, or in some cases a delegation form, to direct the staff as to what action is to be taken: "call this person back," "pay this invoice," etc. The delegation form must include indication details regarding date due, priority level, and other helpful information. When the attorney holds a meeting with that person, the file folder is ready to go. Or, the attorney can keep the items in the delegation file until ready to delegate them individually. This is now a station for this category of pa-

perwork, and several more piles are eliminated.

If you are someone who relies upon the to-do list function in your case management software, and you have access to your staff to-do lists, you can easily post your delegated items electronically. It is recommended that most staff members need more information than is provided by the simple posting of a task. In this case, combine a meeting with the staff person to explain the tasks and answer any questions.

The *Holding file* contains all the items that are lower level priorities: important, but not time sensitive. Paperwork should not linger here too long. This file should be checked on a weekly basis to see that the items within have been dealt with. Routinely block time on your calendar to handle this weekly ritual.

The *Reading file* includes reading material, seminar notifications, Bar publications and the like. Scan publications and pull out the article(s) that interest you, instead of the entire publication, to be stored in this file. If that seems sacrilegious to you, a secondary method is to drop these publications into your briefcase for reading on the go. Another important file in this paperwork triaging process is the often underused circular file or wastebasket. Be ruthless here. Force yourself to toss out paperwork that is redundant or can be reproduced if you absolutely have to get another copy in the future. You do not have to save every issue of that trade journal; you can go online in many cases and download any article that you need - when you actually need it.

Using your new paperwork triage process, you should be able to work in a more organized fashion, especially when you pair this system with the discipline of cleaning your desk every evening. Even more effective is the idea of having a staff person "sweep" your desk once or twice a day when they meet with you. For some attorneys, opening the mail with their assistant keeps them from creating piles, and they can immediately hand off the items to be delegated to the assistant to distribute. Meeting religiously with your assistant once every morning to go through the piles on your desk is an effective way of keeping it clean.

When you are truly organized you'll be able to walk into your office each morning and sit at a clean desk. You will feel much more in control of your practice when you don't have to face piles of files everyday.

Merely having the systems in place does not insure that they will be used. Leadership on your part is the key to their effectiveness; stress the importance of completing checklists religiously and working with your desktop filing system.

There is no substitution for the feeling you get when you begin getting your office systematized. You will recognize it by having these three solutions (checklists, model folder, and paper triaging/standing inbox system) in place. Clearing the clutter will allow you to focus, be more efficient, and concentrate on client care. All of this leads to an office that is truly client-centered.

To master this Asset you must have an office space that conveys a sense of professionalism and competence, but remains friendly and welcoming in appearance. You've achieved this goal when you can successfully check off every item in the Client-Centered Office test given earlier in this chapter.

Once you've gotten your office whipped into shape, it will be time to take a long, hard look at your personal appearance. Your grooming, your wardrobe, and how you communicate with your clients and colleagues speaks volumes. Read on to learn how to put your best foot forward.

Client Satisfaction Survey

		Yes	No
1	Were the firm's staff members friendly and prompt in assisting you with your needs? Comments:		
2	Was your attorney attentive to your needs? Comments:		
3	Were phone calls to the attorney and staff returned promptly? Comments:		
4	Did the attorney and staff keep you informed on the progress of your case? Comments:		
5	Did the attorney and staff explain legal issues clearly so you could make informed decisions? Comments		
6	Did the service at our firm exceed your expectations? Comments:		
7	Would you recommend the firm's services to others? Comments:		

ASSET #19

A PROFESSIONAL IMAGE

Every person is the creation of himself, the image of his own thinking and believing. ~ Claude M. Bristol

All The World's A Stage

What can a mouse teach us about personal presentation? Perhaps quite a lot. Visit any Disney property throughout the world and you'll encounter cleanly-scrubbed, well-groomed employees who'll give you directions, sell you a balloon, or serve your meals. Every person you meet is costumed according to the role they play, and all conform to rigorous standards of appearance.

Supporting this effort are extensive backstage facilities dedicated to making, cleaning and distributing thousands of custom-made costumes each day. To complete their look, each employee is given written grooming guidelines to follow – and management doesn't tolerate deviations. Sporting facial hair is a firing offense.

Why does Disney spend millions of dollars and a great deal of effort maintaining the look of their employees?

The answer may surprise you. Prior to the opening of Disneyland in California, Walt is reputed to have had a recurring dream haunt his sleep: he dreamt of walking down his newly constructed Main Street and being accosted by surly, cigar-smoking carnival-types trying to entice guests into the shops. Carnival "barkers" were the antithesis of how he wanted his employees to dress and act. Though theme parks are a familiar concept today, he was breaking new ground in the mid-1950s, and feared his multi-million dollar entertainment complex would be mistaken for some sort of carnival-like operation. Carnivals, in his mind, sat on the bottom tier of the entertainment hierarchy, far below Hollywood and the theatrical traditions with which he wanted to be associated. Driven by his fears, he instituted grooming standards for all his employees to follow.

So what does this have to do with you and your law firm?

Managing Client Perceptions Equals Good Client Development

If the office is the stage, then you and your staff are the actors, and grooming counts. Every day you don a costume of some sort to play your role as an attorney. As we discussed in Asset #18, *The Client-Centered Office,* it is important to manage the perceptions of those who come to you for help. Not only does your office need

TIP

You don't need to work at the Magic Kingdom to learn the rules of good personal presentation, but the Disney model is a successful one. Take it from the Mouse: manage your personal appearance well and your clients will respond in a positive way.

to look good, so do you. Everyone you meet in a professional capacity will rely on their first impressions to set the tone for any ongoing relationship they may have with you. Their initial impression will be based on a number of factors, including your personal grooming, how you are dressed, the manner in which you speak, and how you interact with them.

Whether you stumble into the closet and emerge dressed in a new blue suit, a skirt and jacket or old khaki pants and a sport shirt, you pick out something, put it on and present yourself to the world. Your staff members do the same. You may make an effort to put together something nice; others

may not give it much thought. What you put on to fit your market may be different if you are an attorney in Key West, Florida or one in New York City.

Unfortunately, whether you think about it or not, your clothing and style of grooming make up your image and telegraph a message that clients, colleagues and others can clearly read. If you look clean, well-groomed and dressed to fit your law firm's culture, everyone will believe you to be intelligent and trustworthy. If you aren't appropriately put together, people will, rightly or wrongly, regard you as less capable and won't be as inclined to enlist your help with their problems.

When they sit before you, potential clients will silently decide whether or not to buy your services during your first meeting with them. It is critical that they form a positive first impression. Upon first meeting you, potential Referral Sources will also perform their own silent evaluation of your trustworthiness. It's essential to make a good first impression in both situations. Your opposing counsel and the jurors you may need to persuade will subject you to the same evaluation process – quietly and perhaps even more harshly.

Because the learning style of most human beings is visual, meaning their bias is to learn new information by processing images as opposed to those who are auditory and learn best through listening, or those who are kinesthetic and learn best by being hands-on, it's important to make sure your appearance sends a clear and appropriate message. The impression one quick image can make can be startling and long-lasting.

For example, have you ever made the mistake of peeking inside the kitchen after dining in a restaurant? Say you are on your way out and the kitchen door happens to swing open as you pass. One quick glance at the "back of the house" operation can either leave you feeling good, or slightly nauseated, wondering when the first signs of food poisoning will set in.

TIP

Most human beings learn new information visually — that is, they process images before everything else. Make sure your personal image sends a clear and professional message to your clients. It is essential that their first impression of you is a good one.

To take this one step further, the sight of the chef who presides over the kitchen should be clean and pristine. We've all seen a well-meaning but sloppy-looking chef who emerges from the kitchen every now and then to greet the patrons in his restaurant. Despite his welcoming, friendly manner, his unshaven face and dirty, disheveled appearance aren't reassuring to the diners. His appearance sends an incongruent message to his patrons: his friendly manner draws them in but his grubby appearance repels them.

At Atticus, we take a very broad view of marketing. We believe that everything about your personal presentation either adds to, or detracts from, your marketing efforts. Most of the good marketers we meet seem to also know this and are caught by surprise when their team doesn't display good judgment in this area. Baffled attorneys all over the country have turned to us to educate their staff and young associates on how to look, dress and act in a professional manner. In trying to help, we've dealt with fashion emergencies of every kind, including tattooed receptionists, associates who wore mismatched suits and bad shoes in court, and — to the horror of their firm's partners — young, male associates who stripped off their shirts at tailgate parties sponsored by the firm. Even with our broad view of marketing, that's showing a little too much enthusiasm.

The little things are important: telephone demeanor, general social graces

– saying please and thank you, calling clients Mr. & Ms. instead of using their first names – where it is appropriate, count for a lot. Good table manners are also important when dining out with clients or other attorneys – people notice if others treat the wait staff with respect. In fact, when advising our clients on hiring new team members and associates, we tell them to go out for lunch or dinner with the person. Character flaws will often reveal themselves in social settings more readily than in another office interview. General civility, especially in the courthouse, is critical – some attorneys have had to take instruction in anger management

because their in-court behaviors were so aggressive.

Just like Walt, you can't expect all your team members – especially the younger ones – to possess grooming, dress and professionalism standards suitable for a law office. Many don't yet realize how their personal appearance speaks volumes about who they are. Compounding their lack of awareness is their lack of funds. To remedy this situation, we frequently advise partners to pay bonuses to team members in the form of gift certificates to assist with the financial burden of upgrading their wardrobe. (This has the added benefit of avoiding any "fee-splitting" concerns for bonuses given to non-attorney staff.)

We also advise that team members meet with Personal Shoppers in department stores who can be very helpful in assembling a business wardrobe that is flexible, looks professional, but isn't overly expensive. By coordinating pants, jackets and tops that can be worn together or separately, they maximize the number of outfits they can put together.

Most people don't require a major makeover, but every now and then it's a good idea to check your look. For most, a good rule of thumb to follow is: dress slightly better than your clients.

If you are concerned that your staff won't react well to grooming guidelines if they are dictated by you, bring

TIP

Think of your personal appearance as an extension of your firm's marketing efforts. Remember: you are a reflection of your firm. Learn to "be your own brand" by maintaining a polished and Professional Image when you greet your clients.

them together for a discussion on the subject. To maximize the chance that they will buy into the concept, ask the question: what kind of grooming guidelines can we create so we look as professional as possible at all times? How should we dress if we want to dress a little bit better than our clients? As you gather their input, you may have to push for more conservative dress than they will suggest, but, if you don't see clients on Fridays, you can offer a dress-down day as a bargaining chip. When you've received the team's suggestions, you can craft some guidelines of your own.

Following are some guidelines you can use as is, or modify for you and your staff. These guidelines can be put in

TIP
If the state of your office's professional dress is in question, arrange a staff meeting to discuss appropriate grooming guidelines. Keep their thoughts and concerns in mind as you establish your own rules.

your policies and procedures manual, handed to new recruits as part of their orientation, or posted somewhere in a back office where staff can see it but clients can't.

Also included are rules for clients who must appear in court – where their personal appearance can make a huge difference in how credible they look and how well they are perceived. Feel free to create a handout for clients to take home and follow. You and your team can read through the following suggestions and see if you are putting your best foot forward.

Personal Presentation Guidelines:

Hair For Staff And Attorneys:

For women: clean, well-groomed hair in an appropriate cut with no obvious roots or unnatural colors is best for the law firm environment. Hair ornaments, bands, ties and ribbons should be small, kept to a minimum and match the outfit they are accessorizing.

For men: clean, well-groomed hair in a cut appropriate for the law firm culture and not featuring unnatural colors or obvious roots is preferred. Facial hair should also be well tended.

Accessories For Staff And Attorneys:

Jewelry and other accessories should be conservative in size and few in number. Earrings should not exceed half the size of the ear. Necklaces should be limited to one or two. One or two bracelets, or two bracelets plus a watch, is appropriate. No obvious

TIP

Take a few moments to evaluate yourself in the mirror. If your look seems a little well-worn, upgrade it by purchasing a new pair of shoes, a briefcase, or even an entirely new suit. Changing your appearance in small ways can make a big difference in both your personal and professional life.

ankle bracelets. Cuff links and tie-clips should be small in size and tasteful in appearance. Tattoos or facial rings should not be on display.

Clothing For Staff And Attorneys:

Clothing should be clean, unwrinkled and of a style appropriate to the type of business the law firm conducts. Every attempt should be made to look well put together and coordinated, whatever your style. Low-cut, cleavage-revealing tops or dresses are best for after-hours and not appropriate for the law firm. Cropped tops that reveal the midriff and skirts that are too tight and too short don't look professional.

Courtroom Attire For Attorneys, Staff Members And Clients:

Err on the side of comfortable but conservative business attire. Men should wear ties and dark suits or dark sports jackets with coordinating pants. Blue suits are considered the best for enhancing credibility. Shoes should be dark, coordinated with the suit or pants, and always clean and polished. All clothing should be clean and unwrinkled. Women should wear business-like blouses, jackets and coordinating skirts or pants. Also good are pantsuits or dresses that are not low-cut or revealing. Clean, closed-toe shoes are preferred, some sandal styles may work if they don't look too informal – but forget about flip-flops.

Makeup For Staff And Attorneys:

Minimal, natural-looking makeup, devoid of glitter or other additives, should be worn. Makeup should enhance facial features and look polished, but not appear unnatural or too exaggerated. Piercings and tattoos should be covered up or minimized for both court appearances and in the law firm.

Mirror, Mirror On The Wall

With the guidelines in mind, take a long look in the mirror. If you like the way you look, great. If not, ask yourself if you need to upgrade your wardrobe or shine your shoes or buy a better briefcase. You may not be a paid performer, but every day you are onstage playing the role of someone who can be trusted to handle complex matters (and be paid handsomely). Make sure you and all the supporting players dress the part. Borrow a page from Disney's book on grooming and you may find that running a Mickey Mouse operation isn't such a bad thing after all.

To officially acquire this Asset you must first evaluate your own appearance, then that of the staff. If what you see doesn't suggest the appropriate image, take remedial action by using and enforcing grooming guidelines for the firm.

One of the biggest challenges facing attorneys in the area of marketing is time. Finding the time to make lunch appointments, follow-up with phone calls, or send thank you notes. Much of marketing requires an investment of time on the part of the attorney. Certainly some of this can be helped by using a Marketing Assistant (Asset #3), but still it may seem there are not enough hours in the day. If you relate to this, read on to learn how you can make time for marketing and still have a life.

ASSET #20

A MARKETING TIME TEMPLATE

One cannot manage too many affairs: like pumpkins in the water, one pops up while you try to hold down the other. ~ Chinese Proverb

Making The Best Of Your Time

D o you spend a consistent amount of time each week on your marketing efforts — attending at least three events a week, sending out thank you notes to referrals, cultivating your Farm Team or new business contacts — or are your efforts hit and miss? Do you attend two networking breakfasts, host a customer appreciation event and send out a newsletter all in one week — and then do nothing for months?

Common sense tells us that setting a schedule is critical to ensure successful, consistent marketing efforts. This Asset introduces an extremely helpful time management and marketing tool, the Marketing Time Template. Utilizing this tool, you'll dramatically improve the time you spend on your marketing efforts.

TIP

In addition to a long to-do list, a messy desk can add to your feeling that you aren't in control of your day. Try this: stop working 10 minutes before you leave at night and dedicate that time to straightening your desktop.

The Law Office Is Often Disruptive

Many attorneys work in a rather chaotic environment and cope with it by being relentless multitaskers. They are interrupted constantly – which leads them to juggle many different types of tasks at once. Peek into any law firm – you will likely find that the typical attorney will have several layers of open files on his or her desk, be talking to a client on the phone, signaling to a staff member waiting by the door, all the while running late for an appointment with a client sitting in the lobby.

Working amid this level of chaos invariably promotes a feeling of incompletion and anxiety as the attorney remembers at the end of the day, or in a sleepless moment at four o'clock in the morning, that their intended marketing efforts were forgotten in the rush.

Prioritize Before You Schedule

To help with this problem, the following is an excerpt from our book, *Time Management for Attorneys*, in which we discuss the problem of setting and keeping priorities: "Attorneys often find themselves overwhelmed by conflicting priorities. This sense of feeling overwhelmed is created by the barrage of new problems they face each day, and for many is triggered each morning when they look at their seemingly inexhaustible to-do list. You may be able to relate to this syndrome if you find yourself staring at your to-do list in the morning, choosing a task at random, and hoping that nothing falls through the cracks. This is a painful way to work, as most attorneys are goal-oriented individuals who strive to do everything all at once and do it well. The simple truth is this: Having too many priorities is the same as having no priorities. In the face of no clear priority, attorneys choose one seemingly urgent, important task that is easily done just to quickly check something off the list. Be aware, however, that urgency is quite often mistaken for importance.

> **TIP**
>
> Keep a copy of your professional vision or mission statement where you can easily access it as you plan your week. It will keep you focused on your big-picture goals instead of the daily crises.

It isn't always easy to tell the difference between urgent and important, and just because something is urgent does not automatically make it important. Unfortunately, urgent tasks are generally much more compelling than those that are merely important. Think of the squeaky wheels among your clients. You often feel compelled to solve their problems at the expense of more cooperative clients just because they're making noise. When you stock your practice with high-maintenance, impossible-to-satisfy clients, you have introduced a lot of urgency in your life without much long-term gain. In such a practice, it is entirely possible to spend your days responding to the latest client crisis. That leaves important work undone, and at the end of the month you find that you spent a great deal of time on non-billable activities. Your profit margin will suffer if you only attend to urgent activities and put off important ones.

To keep yourself on top of what is truly important, we recommend that you **triage your to-do list**. To accomplish this, examine all the items on your list and rank them according to their importance. How can you distinguish what is most important among the myriad tasks on the list? You begin by looking for what we call the A (or highest) priority tasks. You can identify a task as A priority if one or more of these four questions receives a "yes" answer.

• *Does this task forward your long-term goals?* Long-terms goals are those that come from your overall vision, such as buying an office building, learning a new practice area, or cultivating new Referral Sources. Read your vision statement prior to planning your week to remind yourself of what is truly important.

• *Are there pending legal deadlines associated with these files?* Block out time for these tasks on your computer or delegate them to staff. These time-sensitive issues must be handled because they are extremely important.

• *Are there client expectations attached to this file or task?* Have you made a promise to a client, for example, to complete something by the end of the week? Always calendar these promises. These are your "soft" deadlines. They are not legal deadlines, but are nonetheless very important in terms of maintaining the confidence a client has in you. Monitor yourself to make sure you aren't consistently over-promising to the client and un-

der-delivering. It is much better to under-promise and then over-deliver.

• *Are there cash flow needs that should dictate your next step?* You may interfere with your own cash flow by not focusing on production. Many attorneys are the bottleneck in their own system due to the number of files that accumulate in their offices and remain untouched.

Once you have pulled out the A priority tasks, look for the remaining tasks on your to-do list – the B and C tasks. How do you tell the difference? Here are the guidelines for those tasks:

• B priority – tasks that do not require your unique talents or abilities and can be easily delegated.

• C priority – tasks that are not worth your time and attention and should absolutely be delegated or delayed as long as possible.

Take Priority-Based Action: Delegate, Eliminate, Or Schedule

Now that you have triaged your to-do list, you have a method to plan intelligently. Delegate the B priority tasks and seek to eliminate as many of the nonessential C priority tasks as possible. Next, label the A priority tasks with a 1 (most important), 2, or 3, and take action accordingly. Let actions associated with your vision statement, legal deadlines, and client expectations drive your decisions. Though it may sound like work initially, once you are in the habit of triaging your tasks, your to-do list won't seem like one long, indistinguishable roster. It becomes more helpful because you have identified the truly important tasks. Use this approach to lift yourself out of the daily game of catch-up.

TIP

How can you tell if you are the bottleneck in your office? If you have files piled on your desk, credenza, visitor's chairs, or floor, the evidence strongly suggests it's you.

Systemize With A Marketing Time Template

To give your client development activities a higher priority on your calendar, this Asset looks at ways you can schedule specific marketing activities as permanent, standing appointments on your weekly schedule. We've found that being proactive and setting up certain blocks of time to incorporate marketing into your week is more productive and yields better results than the usual hit-and-miss approach.

In addition, seeing the time blocked out on your calendar every week makes it more difficult for you to "forget" to market yourself. This is when the real value of the time template becomes apparent. It is a visual reminder for you, and your Marketing Assistant, to think about what your marketing objectives are, and what clients you can meet with to fill those open slots.

TIP

When your marketing time blocks are pre-set and blocked in advance, it is easier for your Marketing Assistant to schedule marketing meetings and lunches since she doesn't have to constantly recheck your availability.

Two Types Of Time Blocks

To create your own time template you will need to create two different blocks of time for marketing yourself: These blocks, once scheduled, should be sacrosanct and not available to override without your express permission. You can have your secretary put them on the calendar for a year at a time so they are permanent and predictable.

Here are the two types of time blocks you'll need:

1 Block Time for the Weekly Marketing Meeting: Time to meet with your Marketing Assistant for 15 minutes to an hour, once a week

2 Block Times for Marketing Activities : Time to meet with and develop clients – 3 separate blocks of 1 to 1 ½ hours a week, for a total of 3 to 4.5 hours a week

1 The Weekly Marketing Meeting

This block of time to meet with your Marketing Assistant and other relevant firm members once a week gives you the opportunity to review and prioritize the work that goes into marketing your practice. Monday and Friday seem to be popular days for these meetings, though any day will do. Some attorneys we know have lunch at their desks once a week and specifically dedicate that time to talking about marketing with their Marketing Assistant.

These meetings can be as short as 15 minutes or as long as an hour – rarely do they go longer. The idea is to meet with your Marketing Assistant – or other team members who help with marketing – and go over your marketing goals for the week. If all you have to talk about is which Referral Sources you want to schedule for lunch in the near future, it will go quickly. If you have major projects to plan, such as launching a newsletter or hosting a Signature Event, the meeting will require more time.

Subjects To Cover In Your Weekly Marketing Meeting

To reiterate some of the ideas we talked about in Asset #3, *The Marketing Assistant,* below is a list of issues and activities typically discussed in a marketing meeting.

• planning future meetings, lunches and other activities with referral sources

• delegating tasks to your Marketing Assistant

• planning an annual meeting or Signature Event

• discussing the firm newsletter

• scheduling 'thank you' phone calls or writing notes

• buying thank you gifts to acknowledge recent referrals

• reviewing tracked marketing data — the number of new calls and intake appointments plus reviewing the success of phone book and online ads

TIP

Don't be reluctant to use your Marketing Assistant to schedule lunches with other professionals. It's a commonly accepted practice and your assistant will generally be dealing only with the other person's assistant as they schedule the lunch.

• brainstorming Public Relations goals such as:

•What firm news is worthy of a press release?

•What community sponsorship opportunities are available?

• discussing the Web site and any updating it may need

• delegating task related to social media networking sites

259

To prepare for these meetings, it is a good idea to create a **planning folder** and include the following items for use in your marketing meeting:

• the firm's annual marketing goals

• your Monthly Marketing Plan

• your Top Twenty and Farm Team Lists

2 Times For Marketing Activities

We believe that the best, most loyal and least price-sensitive clients come from Referral Sources who know you, like you and trust you. Developing this level of rapport with Referral Sources does not happen overnight. It takes time for the relationship to build. Clients may come from a new Referral Source after just one or two meetings, but most likely it will take numerous contacts for the referrer to get to know you well enough to risk their reputation to recommend you.

As you know, we recommend three substantial marketing contacts a week. Three lunches are ideal. If you block out three lunches a week and dedicate them to marketing, they will result in over 100 marketing lunches a year. This provides a lot of time to maintain rapport with existing Referral Sources as well as to cultivate new Referral Sources.

It is helpful to have your Marketing Assistant work with you to keep your lunch schedule filled well in advance. If you supply the assistant with your Top Twenty list, you can get them booked into your schedule on a regular basis. If you feed the assistants the names of new contacts you meet as you interact in the community, they can be added to the rotation. Having someone schedule these for you can be a huge help, especially if you, like many of our clients, won't take the time to make the calls and issue invitations.

An alternative to the marketing lunch idea is to have a standing Friday afternoon or Wednesday afternoon time block that is dedicated to marketing. For many of our clients who play golf or tennis, the Friday afternoon game or match is a popular marketing strategy. It allows them to invite one to three other people to join them on a weekly basis. That amounts to approximately 50 golf or tennis games over the course of a year. When multiplied by one to three people, the result is a minimum of 50 and a maximum or 150 marketing contacts yearly. Given the amount of time there is to talk when playing golf, that is a significant amount of rapport-building time with Referral Sources and important friends of your firm.

If you don't play golf or tennis, there may be another sport that you would enjoy doing on a weekly basis. A number of our clients get season tickets to ball games and use them as an opportunity to invite their Referral Sources. Many of our clients put a once- or twice-monthly evening event on their template, to which they invite Referral Sources and their spouses out to dinner or to some other function, such as a community event, a charity function, or gallery opening. You can plan marketing events that allow you to spend more time with all members of your family, which is most likely one of your personal goals. You can invite Referral Sources and their families to outings and events such as a picnic or a barbeque in the park, a pool party, a boating excursion or a sporting event. Going to a game with your son or daughter and inviting Referral Sources to bring along their kids is a great way to spend additional time with your own family. There are numerous ways to work marketing into your schedule – and they should be as enjoyable and entertaining for you as possible.

It is important for your staff and the other attorneys in your office to understand how and why you are attempting to implement a Marketing Time Template. You really need the support of other people to make your marketing efforts work. We suggest that you sit down with your staff and having an initial meeting in order to explain the concept to them. You are the first line of defense when it comes to implementing and enforcing your time management. Your staff, if they do not recognize the value and the importance of your marketing time blocks, can be the first ones to sabo-

tage it. Open by asking for the staff's support:

> **"I need your support to help me manage my time better. As you know, I end up working a lot of weekends and evenings, trying to get all my work done, and I never have time to market myself and the firm. If we don't have new clients coming through the door on a regular basis, we can't grow as a firm."**

Next, explain that the time template is a new approach to calendaring time, but it is not an actual calendar. It is a set of new calendaring rules that allows for certain activities at certain scheduled times.

By following the Marketing Time Template, there will be a standardized time blocked for client development lunches and a short weekly marketing meeting which will help you focus on client development. Close with a final request for their cooperation:

> "I would really appreciate it if you would support this Marketing Time Template. Please post this time template near the phones to remind you of when I am and am not available. I would appreciate it if you commit to following these new rules that I have set up. I think it will help me dedicate much more time for client development, which is important for all of us."

Be sure to encourage questions from the staff about the marketing time blocks, and include a discussion about when they can override them in the event of a conflict. If the staff is not aware of how important marketing is, they will book you solid with other kinds of appointments. You must have their cooperation to make this work.

Proactively Make Time For Marketing

At Atticus, we instill in our clients the idea that there must be continual Top Of Mind Awareness (TOMA) regarding word-of-mouth marketing. People must remember you. The way they remember you is by having a variety of interactions with you throughout the year. These interactions can be small: a telephone call will sometimes suffice. But usually they occur in the form of a lunch meeting or an evening event that requires time: the time it takes to schedule them and the time it takes to attend them. Use the time template idea to proactively create time for your client development efforts. If you don't claim the time, ahead of time, there will never be a good time to market yourself and your firm.

To claim this Asset you must have time for a marketing meeting blocked out on your schedule, as well as three blocks of time for weekly marketing activities such as lunch or other events. For a more complete understanding of the time template and how it can help with more than just client development, we have included a bonus chapter on time management in the Appendix that was excerpted from our book: *Time Management for Attorneys: A Lawyer's Guide to Decreasing Stress, Eliminating Interruptions and Getting Home on Time.*

The one emotion that is said to be the grandfather of all other emotions is gratitude. In the next Asset we'll talk about how you can systematically express your gratitude so no referral goes unacknowledged and no Referral Source feels unappreciated.

Sample Weekly Time Template

Here's an esample of a time template with only marketing events shown.

	MONDAY	TUESDAY	WEDNESDAY	THURSDAY	FRIDAY
9:00 a.m.					
9:30 a.m.					
10:00 a.m.					
10:30 a.m.					
11:00 a.m.					
11:30 a.m.					
12:00 p.m.	Marketing Lunch		Marketing Lunch		
12:30 p.m.					
1:00 p.m.					
1:30 p.m.					↑
2:00 p.m.					
2:30 p.m.					
3:30 p.m.					Standard Marketing Event (golf)
4:00 p.m.					
4:30 p.m.					
5:00 p.m.					
5:30 p.m.					↓

ASSET #21

A THANK YOU SYSTEM

Appreciation can make a day, even change a life. Your willingness to put it into words is all that is necessary.
~ Margaret Cousins

The Importance Of Acknowledgment

To build your relationship with all Referral Sources, never let them wonder, whether they are business professionals, fellow attorneys, your clients (present and past) or your next-door neighbor, whether or not you received their referrals. Always express your appreciation as quickly as you can — even if the client they referred did not engage your services. Even if a referring attorney receives a referral fee — a personal acknowledgment is also needed.

While sending thank you notes may seem archaic in our busy world, the concept of expressing gratitude and appreciation is ageless. And while many enlightened souls may offer unconditional referrals – not expecting any acknowledgment or response, most people welcome and appreciate recognition and acknowledgment of their efforts. Since written thank you notes are becoming so rare, a personal (dare I say handwritten?) and genuine expression of thanks will make you stand out among the daily bombardment of rushed and impersonal mass mailings, advertisements and SPAM.

You want to continually reinforce your appreciation of the fact that they thought of you, so your name is the first to come up the next time they have an opportunity to recommend an attorney. Send referrers thank you notes and take them out to lunch every so often to acknowledge their trust and confidence in you. Never take them for granted.

To make a thank you note personal and genuine, be sure to spell the client's name correctly, refer to something pertinent about them, the client they sent, or something else that will distinguish this acknowledgment from a quickly produced form letter. Always send it out in a timely manner – within the week, if possible. If you absolutely balk at sending a note, pick up the phone and express your appreciation verbally. E-mail is appropriate when you know the person extremely well and know that he or she prefers to communicate via e-mail.

Systemize for Success

Option One:
Do It Yourself

Option Two:
Use Preprinted Cards

Option Three:
Take Help from Your Team

Option Four:
Have the Team Do it All

Option One: Do It Yourself

If you want to personally take this task on, buy (or ask someone in the office to do this for you) small 3x5 or 4x6 cards and have them printed with your letterhead and logo. The cards may be of the folded or unfolded variety – both are nice – just make sure the quality of the paper is substantial. If for some reason you can't get customized cards, or you must wait awhile to have them printed, have someone in your office purchase ready-made thank you cards that have a professional look and are printed on substantial card stock. Wherever you get the notes, make sure you like the way they look and feel. If they represent you and your firm well, you are more likely to use them.

In writing the note, express your gratitude along with any other personalized information you care to add about the client – such as the client's name. These notes are not business letters and shouldn't be lengthy, just long enough to get your sentiment across. Here are some phrases you can incorporate into the text of your note:

> Thanks so much for thinking of us – we'll do our best to serve Mr. Trimble...
>
> Or,
> The highest compliment you can pay us is to send us your clients – thank you for thinking of us. We'll take good care of Mr. Warshaw...
>
> Or,
> We appreciate your thoughtfulness and thank you for sending business our way. We'll do everything we can to help Mrs. Williams resolve her situation...

TIP

While sending thank you notes may not be a habit you have cultivated in the past, it is one of those small, highly meaningful activities that can make a significant impact on your Referral Sources.

One of our clients actually keeps a sheet of phrases for reference with her box of notes. That way she doesn't have to agonize over what to say.

For maximum accessibility, store your note cards at your desk, within arm's reach. You might stash them in a drawer in your desk, a cubbyhole in your credenza or in a file folder with your other files. Just make sure they are handy. If obtaining the notes requires any extra effort on your part, you run the risk of avoiding this task. Make it as easy and fast as possible so you are most likely to do it.

When you receive a referral, simply reach over, grab a conveniently-located note card and jot down the appropriate sentiment. Then hand it to your secretary to address and mail. Then give yourself a mental pat on the back: by doing this one small thing, you've just reinforced your Referral Source's urge to send a referral the next time he or she has one. Handwritten notes leave a lasting impression.

Option Two: Use Pre-Printed Cards

Most of the steps in this approach are similar to Option One in that you, or someone you may delegate to, buys small 3x5 or 4x6 cards printed with your letterhead and logo. However, in this case you take it a step further and have the cards pre-printed with a message along the lines of the following (or make up your own):

> Thanks so much for thinking of us — we'll do our best to serve your client.
>
> Or,
>
> The highest compliment you can pay us is to send us your clients — thank you for thinking of us.
>
> Or,
>
> We appreciate your thoughtfulness and thank you for sending business our way.

Keep in mind that even though you've purchased cards with a built-in sentiment, you should still add a quick,

personal note with your signature. You might say something like:

> We'll take good care of Mrs. Smith.
>
> Or,
>
> I'll keep you posted on our progress.
>
> Or,
>
> Thanks for remembering us.
>
> Or,
>
> We really enjoy working with your clients; thank you for sending Mr. Mader our way.
>
> Or,
>
> I'll call you next week to set up a lunch date.

Once this is done, hand it off to your secretary to address and mail for you. Some attorneys find that if they don't have to fill an entire note card with text, they are more likely to do this. The finished product is slightly less personal than a fully handwritten note, but still beats an e-mail because it requires more effort. It's that little bit of extra effort that communicates that you genuinely appreciate that the Referral Source sent a client your way.

Option Three: Take Help From The Team

This approach is for the attorney who won't write out a card without additional prompting from the staff. The initial steps are the same in that you (or someone you delegate to) must purchase small cards printed with your letterhead and logo.

But in this scenario, you store the cards with one of two people: whoever is in charge of opening your files or your Marketing Assistant. Then, when a referred client file is officially opened, the file opener or your Marketing Assistant brings you a blank card and, if necessary, stands there while you fill it out. Then they address it and mail it off.

To make sure your team member remembers to do this, add this step to your "file opening" checklist. In fact, in all of the approaches, this step can and should be on your checklist. If you don't have a checklist, you should have the team make one up. It's useful for ensuring that all necessary steps are covered.

Option Four: Total Delegation

This approach, which we recommend if you know you absolutely won't take the time to write out a personal note, no matter how convenient or fast we make it, is similar to the first three in that it starts with a note card. In this case, it is stored with whomever is in charge of opening your files, or with your Marketing Assistant.

But here is where this method diverges from the other: when a referred client file is officially opened, the file opener or Marketing Assistant writes out the card instead of you. They handwrite a sentiment that is a slight variation from what we've listed before:

> Thanks so much for thinking of our firm — we really appreciate the clients you send and want you to know we'll do our best to take care of Mrs. Lee.

TIP Don't make the mistake of sending the same tired form letter when thanking Referral Sources. It makes you appear as if you don't value the efforts of your referral sources enough to send something personalized.

Thanks Again

We work with one personal injury attorney who takes his own approach to the concept of reinforcing referrals. He dislikes sending thank you notes over and over again to referrers who send him a lot of business. He feels those who send significant business deserve something more, so he's created a checklist which includes the name of the Referral Source, and which is routinely handed to him when a potential new client comes for a consultation. The checklist offers different options for expressing his appreciation to the Referral Source, such as:

• Send a handwritten thank you note.

• Send a gift basket with a favorite wine, scotch or other beverage.

• Send tickets to a sports event.

• Take Referral Source to lunch.

• Send a gift certificate for a favorite restaurant.

• Take Referral Source golfing.

• Send the referring staff a basket of chocolate cookies (sometimes referrals come from staff members of Referral Sources).

• Make a donation to an appropriate charity in the referrer's name.

Then they sign it with the name of the firm. This is not as personal as the earlier approaches since it is not even signed by the attorney, but it can still strike a somewhat personal tone. It can be presented to the attorney who looks it over before it is sent, but the attorney does not have to set pen to paper for this note to be written. Obviously, once the attorney approves it, the staff mails it out.

TIP

If you systemize your approach to sending out thank you notes and other tokens of appreciation, your team can support you in this effort. Left to memory, this kind of thing is often forgotten.

He reviews his checklist, considers who the Referral Source is, the potential value of the case, and how many referrals this person has sent. With all this in mind, he checks off his preferred way to thank his Referral Source, the team carries out his directions, and makes a note in the database for future reference. The burden of buying the gift certificate or arranging for tickets then falls on

his staff and not on him. If it were up to him alone, none of this would happen. His intentions are good, but his ability to follow through is not the best. With the checklist system, his referrers are thanked appropriately every time.

Many Referral Sources have switched attorneys because they felt they were being taken for granted. It's a smart marketer who knows that doing the little things (or delegating them) makes all the difference in marketing.

Gift Giving – A Story

This story emphasizes the value of giving small gifts that are personal to your Referral Sources.

One of my clients discovered that his best Referral Source had the interesting hobby of art collecting. However, this colleague did not collect works of art that were necessarily expensive. Instead, he preferred art that was unique. He wanted to be assured that what he had hanging on his wall would not be found on anybody else's wall. This collector of unique, unpopular art would travel on vacation and buy works from local, obscure artists, not in galleries.

Armed with this information, my client came up with the brilliant idea of framing a creative work that his daughter had painted. During the holidays he personally presented the framed original with a certificate of authenticity and note guaranteeing that additional prints will never be made.

The overall message of this gift is, "I KNOW YOU." I know your hobbies, your humor, your interests and your values. You do not need to blow big bucks to communicate that message. You just need to be personal.

To acquire this Asset you will need to have an inventory or resources (thank you cards and gifts) to acknowledge and thank your Referral Sources.

In the next section, we'll wrap up the Rainmaking program and leave you with a few important reminders.

FINAL WORDS

You now have the complete explanation of all the Assets and Habits required to market yourself successfully. As we've pointed out, the ability to develop clients exists on a continuum with "Mistmaker" at one end and "Rainmaker" at the other. We are confident that you will be able to use the components within this book to accelerate your graduation to full Rainmaker status.

Also, please remember to visit www.atticusrain-makers.com. Click on the image of this book, type in the code **RM521,** plus your e-mail address to access an audio download companion to each Asset and Habit in this book. Also, call **888.644.0022,** to order a full diagnostic work-up of your marketing strengths and weaknesses. The diagnostic includes a DISC Behavioral Profile, a Web Analysis by an independent Web expert, a client development and time management assessment, a six-month marketing roadmap, along with an hour-long coaching call with an Atticus Practice Advisor.

By clicking on "Programs," you can also participate in the Rainmakers live program, and become one of the many attorneys who finds that attending live tele-classes and being supported by a live person is just the help they need.

APPENDIX #1

Bonus Chapter

BONUS CHAPTER

PROACTIVE STRATEGY #5:

This is an excerpt from the book, *Time Management for Attorneys: A Lawyer's Guide to Decreasing Stress, Eliminating Interruptions & Getting Home on Time,* by Mark Powers and Shawn McNalis

Schedule Like Tasks Together

*C*ommon sense tells us that setting a schedule is critical to successful proactive time management. In this section, we discuss managing your time by using your calendar and grouping similar, or "like" tasks together. This includes the introduction to an extremely helpful time management tool, the time template, some tips on how to use it and how to introduce it to your staff to enlist support as well.

Why Schedule Like Tasks Together?

Time and motion studies reveal that grouping similar tasks together and doing them in the same time period results in increased efficiency. When you apply this theory to your scheduling habits, you'll dramatically improve how you manage your time. Lawyers find it especially helpful because when there is increased complexity, grouping like tasks together boosts efficiency even more. When your brain is allowed to focus on similar tasks, you can accomplish results four times faster than when you are either continually switching the types of tasks you do or being constantly interrupted.

Contrary to what is most efficient, many attorneys are relentless multi-taskers. That is, they attempt many different types of tasks at once and find that much stopping and starting ensues. It is not unusual to find the typical attorney with several layers of open files on his or her desk, talking to a client on the phone, signaling to the staff member who waits in the door, and late for an appointment with a client waiting in the lobby.

This kind of work style promotes a feeling of anxiety as the attorney wonders at the end of the day, or in a sleepless moment at four o'clock in the morning, what important details were lost in all the chaos. The risk of liability goes up as chaos reigns.

And rightfully so, given that 80% of the grievances filed against attorneys involve missed deadlines and/or disorganization.

Block And Tackle Your Office Tasks

To avoid this type of stress, let's take a look at how you might get started grouping like tasks in your office. We call the approach to grouping "the *block and tackle* method." That is, once you "block" like tasks together, they are easier to "tackle." You might think that the grouping process would be impossible, given the many different types of tasks you undertake, but we believe the nine categories of tasks we list below cover the tasks that occur in the typical attorney's day:

1. planning time (either once a week, or daily)

2. production time – producing documents, supervising technical/legal tasks, preparing for trial, where applicable

3. court time (where applicable, may alternate days with production)

4. meetings with staff members, partners (general staff meetings, daily pre-production meetings, case status review meetings, partner meetings, etc.)

5. meetings with clients

6. time to return phone calls

7. administration time

8. time for client development

9. time to systematize your practice

The multitasker tries to do these tasks at the same time. This involves accessing different parts of the brain and never allows for great efficiency in any one task due to the choppy start, stop, and restart rhythm that is inherent in multitasking. For example, the reactive time manager reaches for the ringing phone no matter what he or she is doing. In addition to losing time, the quality of all the tasks suffers when dissimilar tasks are concurrently done. If you are in the habit of multitasking, you may be surprised at how much time the block and tackle approach saves you and how it increases the quality of your work.

rate all the types of tasks that normally occur in a typical week and block time for them to be done.

For example, when there is complex legal work to be done, that is all that is being done; when it is time to meet with clients, they are the sole focus of your attention. By working on one thing at a time you are increasing your overall effectiveness and you have a visual reminder of all the critical areas of business you need to focus on.

At the end of the chapter, you will find two examples of completed time templates to give you an idea of what you will be working toward when you design your own time template. We have provided examples for attorneys who have regularly scheduled court appearances and those who have low court appearances: Regularly Scheduled Court Appearance Time Template and Low or No Court Appearance Time Template.

Use A Time Template To Help You Block And Tackle

In order to put the time blocking approach into effect, we suggest using a *time template.* A time template is a structure that enables you to sepa-

Schedule And Implement Key Time Template Blocks

Now that you have some background on the purpose and the usefulness of the time template and have seen our examples, you may want to design your own. Before you take that step, you will benefit from some guidance on how to choose the right time to schedule certain tasks, how to determine the amount of time you need, and how to get the staff on board with the idea of working with a time template. We address each of the key time template blocks to help you focus on just how you want your template to look and perform. Note: We have combined comments about court and production time since, for some of you, they may occur at the same time but on alternate days.

Key Block #1: Plan Your Week

Weekly planning is the process of taking time to map out your week, so that you are proactively making time for the achievement of both your long-term and short-term goals every day. Research tells us that one hour spent planning will increase your efficiency by a minimum of four hours. Remember this when you are tempted to just jump into your day or week – planning ahead of time doesn't set you back; it makes you more efficient. It may feel like you are wasting your time, but don't be misled by your own desire to jump in – planning where to jump in and what to focus on are very important.

Before you design your own time template, follow these ground rules to make sure you're on solid ground right from the start:

• *Choose the right time.* Find a time for your planning session that will not be bumped by court appearances or encroached upon by any other activity. Over what time slot during your week do you have the greatest amount of control? For most attorneys, Monday mornings or Friday afternoons are the best opportunities for a planning session.

• *Choose the right setting.* If your office is a place of stress, not a setting for reflection, find a more enjoyable spot where you can focus without distraction. Popular choices among our attorney clients are:

> • home office, patio or deck

> • coffee shop or breakfast place

> • the firm's library or conference room

• *Review the Big Picture.* To start your planning session, review your personal vision statement and goal grid. They will remind you of the personal life goals you have set for yourself and the strategic goals you have set as stepping stones. Why review? The answer is simple: you will forget. Client demands and everyday urgencies compete for your attention much more successfully than your life goals do.

It is a good idea to designate a *planning*

1. Open your calendar and review one month out, three weeks out, two weeks out and finally, one week out.

2. Note the client meetings, mediations, marketing opportunities, court appearances, and any other events or deadlines on your calendar.

3. Work backwards from these events and deadlines by estimating how much preparation is required for each.

4. Look at your daily blocks of production time. Note the specific files you will address on your calendar. Make an appointment with yourself to work on the "Smith" file or "Jones" file so that you complete them prior to their deadlines.

folder and include the following items:

- personal vision statement

- strategic goals

- client list

- to-do list

Finally, have your calendar either physically or virtually on your laptop or hand-held device. This is critical to your planning process.

When you actually map your own time template, after having taken the preliminary steps we have just mentioned to ensure success, you begin as follows:

Prioritize Before You Schedule

Before we move on to the other blocks on the time template, we would like to mention a critically important element in regard to creating your weekly plan. This is the element of prioritization. Attorneys often find themselves overwhelmed by conflicting priorities. This sense of being overwhelmed is created by the barrage of new problems they face each day, and for many is triggered each morning when they look at their seemingly inexhaustible to-do list.

You may be able to relate to this syndrome if you find yourself staring at your to-do list in the morning, choosing a task at random and hoping that nothing falls through the cracks. This is a painful way to work since most attorneys are goal-oriented individuals who strive to do everything all at once and do it well. The simple truth is this: having too many priorities is the same as having no priorities. In the face of no clear priority, attorneys choose one seemingly urgent, important task that is easily done just to quickly check something off the list. Be aware, however, that urgency is quite often mistaken for importance.

It isn't always easy to tell the difference between urgent and important, and just because something is urgent does not automatically make it important. Unfortunately, urgent tasks are generally much more compelling than those that are merely important. Think of the squeaky wheels among your clients. You often feel compelled to solve their problems at the expense of more cooperative clients, just because they're making noise and the good clients are not.

When you stock your practice with high maintenance, impossible to satisfy clients, you have introduced a lot of urgency in your life without much long-term gain. In such a practice, it is entirely possible to spend your days responding to the latest client crisis. That leaves important work undone and at the end of the month you find that you spent a great deal of time on non-billable activities. Your profit margin will suffer if you attend just to urgent activities and put off important ones.

Triage Your To-Do List

To keep yourself on top of what is truly important, we recommend that you *triage* your to-do list. To do this, examine all of the items on your list and then rank them according to their importance. How can you distinguish what is most important among the myriad tasks on the list? You begin by looking for what we call the "A priority tasks," or the highest priority tasks. You can identify a task as an A priority if one or more of these four questions receives a "yes" answer.

- *Does this task forward your long-term goals?*

Long-terms goal are those that come from your overall vision, such as buying an office building, learning a new practice area or cultivating new Referral Sources. Read your vision statements prior to planning your week in order to remind yourself of what is truly important.

- *Are there pending legal deadlines associated with these files?*

Block out time for these tasks on your computer or delegate them to staff. These time sensitive issues must be handled because they are extremely important.

- *Are there client expectations attached to this file or task?*

Have you made a promise to a client, for example, to complete something by the end of the week? Always calendar these promises. These are your "soft" deadlines. They are not legal deadlines, but are nonetheless very important in terms of maintaining the confidence a client has in you. Monitor yourself to make sure you aren't consistently over-promising to the client and under-delivering. It is much better to under-promise and then over-deliver with your clients.

• Are there cash flow needs that should dictate your next step?

You may interfere with your own cash flow by not focusing on production. Many attorneys are the bottleneck in their own system due to the number of files that accumulate in their office and remain untouched.

Once you have pulled out the A priority tasks, look for the remaining tasks

on your to-do list – these are the B and C tasks. How do you tell the difference? Here are the guidelines for those tasks:

• B priority – tasks that do not require your unique talents or abilities and can be easily delegated.

• C priority – tasks that are not worth your time and attention and should absolutely be delegated or delayed as long as possible.

Take Priority-Based Action: Delegate, Eliminate Or Schedule

Now that you have triaged your to-do list, you have a method to plan intelligently. Delegate the B priority tasks and seek to eliminate as many of the non-essential C priority tasks as possible. Next, label the A priority tasks with a 1 (most important), 2 or 3 and take action accordingly. Let actions associated with your vision statement, your legal deadlines and client expectations drive your decisions.

Though it may sound like work initially, once you are in the habit of triaging your tasks, your to-do list won't seem like one long, indistinguishable roster. It becomes more helpful because you have identified the truly important tasks. Use this approach to lift yourself out of the daily game of catch-up in which you may find yourself.

Key Block #2: The Three-Part Power Hour

(Meet With Staff; Focus On Production; And Return Phone Calls)

The intention behind this block is to set yourself up to focus only on production for one to three hours, at the same time every day. We have grouped three important blocks into one that we call the *Three-Part Power Hour:*

• The initial time block is spent *meeting with staff.* It allows the staff to get their batched questions answered and could take from five minutes to an hour, depending on the work load to be discussed.

• The second part, the power hour itself, involves going behind closed doors and *focusing on production.* This block of time is for you to concentrate only on production and can last from one hour to several, depending on work load.

• The third part, *returning phone calls,* happens after production time, and allows the attorney to return calls from clients.

Ideally, the power hour is scheduled in the morning before the challenges of the day set in. Fortunately, most people report that they are the freshest and most able to handle their complex work first thing in the morning.

Unfortunately, many go to court with some frequency in the mornings as well. We instruct attorneys who go to court quite often in the mornings to block out their mornings as court/production time. That way, the attorney or the person who schedules for the attorneys knows that if he or she is not scheduled for court, the attorney automatically defaults to production time and will not be available for other appointments.

For some attorneys who cannot manage to schedule production time in the morning; the late afternoon is their next best time. You can give staff members a copy of your time template for reference when scheduling your time in case you can't pre-block your calendar.

Whenever it is scheduled, it is your private time of intense, concentrated production. Plan to spend this time very wisely. schedule yourself to focus on the most important, A level, non-delegatable work you have.

An In-Depth Look At Meeting With Staff

Let's look at the first part of the three-part power hour formula:

meeting with staff. The purpose of this meeting is to answer questions and to delegate items. A key strategy here is to instruct staff to group all their questions together and for you to delegate tasks at this meeting. We call this technique *batching*. Batching refers to the theory that grouping questions together increases the efficiency of getting them answered with the fewest interruptions.

Many of the attorneys we work with meet staff members for 15 or 20 minutes in a quick "huddle" to talk about the goals for the day, to give quick direction, to answer batched questions and delegate tasks. Some attorneys make this a half-hour or an hour-long meeting because they are supervising many files that have quick turnaround times. Use your own judgment on how much time this meeting must take. In this way, you train the staff to batch their questions and save them for you in this meeting, thereby pre-empting many interruptions. The pre-empting of interruptions is one of the main benefits of scheduled staff meetings to answer batched questions. We talk more about this in the next section entitled "Manage Interruptions."

You can also batch the questions and instructions you have for your staff, which forces you to be more organized when you delegate. We talk more about this in a later section on delegation. This meeting is also an opportunity to insure that all of your staff members have plenty to do while you are focused on your production. Re-mind your staff that they can get a lot of work done while you are behind closed doors. They usually appreciate the fact that you won't be interrupting them for a short time, as well.

An In-Depth Look At Focusing On Production

Let's look at the second part of the three-part power hour formula: the time to focus on production. The purpose of this part of the power hour is to set yourself up for one to three hours of production without interruption, behind closed doors. We talk in depth, in a later section on managing interruptions, about more techniques and practices that will help you limit or eliminate interruptions during this time, but closing your office door is the most important.

Since this way of working is a new discipline for you, expect that the first few times you try to concentrate like this will be uncomfortable. Once you get used to the power hour, you will come to view it as a sacred time during your day that is to be protected as very valuable. Many of the clients we advise come to rely upon it as their island of sanity and as the space in which they can do their best work. Their production time is what they use to feel a sense of control over the chaos, especially when they've planned out what they'll work on in the beginning of the week. It is no longer a matter of using personal time to make up time that was stolen from them during the workday. For them, there is a newfound sense of control over their practice and a feeling that they can depend upon themselves.

In your production time, you focus on production that can't be delegated:

• producing documents, doing high-level research

• writing briefs, opinions, memos

• reviewing discovery and deposition information

• preparing for hearings, mediations and trials

• reviewing work that has been delegated

An In-Depth Look At Returning Phone Calls

Let's look at the third part of the three-part power hour formula: returning phone calls. The purpose of this block of time is to learn how to get work done and still maintain the illusion of accessibility.

This is an hour in which you return the phone calls that have come in while you were "in production." Your assistant or call screener should have made call appointments for you while you were behind closed doors. We suggest instructing the screeners to

make the appointments at 15-minute intervals, if possible. Your return call schedule would look something like this:

> 11:00 – Mrs. Jones
>
> 11:15 – Mr. Johnson
>
> 11:30 – Mr. Roberts
>
> 11:45 – Mr. Smith

Or it may be that only two calls came in and your hour looks like this:

> 11:00 – Mr. Lee
> (He said that he needs at least 1/2 hour)
>
> 11:30 – Mrs. Jones

It is important that callers feel like the attorney is still accessible to them, that their call is important and that they are left with a definite idea of when they will be able to talk to the attorney. Always make your callbacks faithfully and answer whatever questions your clients have. Try to never sound rushed. If, in the event something comes up and you know you won't be able to call at the scheduled appointment time, have your assistant call and apologize and make the appointment for another time.

We feel that one of the critical elements in this part of the power hour is to work with staff on screening calls properly while the attorney is behind closed doors. The first rule of course is this: they should never be told to just call the attorney back. This is very unsatisfying to the caller. If the caller is a client, it seems uncaring and you, the attorney, seem inaccessible.

One way to work with staff on screening calls is to provide them with scripts that they can use or adapt to fit your particular situation. Here are a few phrases that your secretary, assistant or call screener can use to set up the appointments. The bolded phrases are important variations and communicate caring and a sense of rapport with the client:

• "I know that Mrs. Attorney **would like to speak with you.** She will be returning calls at 11:00. Will you be available then? Great, give me the number where we can reach you. How much time do you think you'll need?"

or

• "Mr. Attorney is not available right now **but I know he'll want to speak with you as soon as he can.** To make sure that you connect, may I set up a time when he can call you back? How does ____o'clock sound? Is that convenient for you? At what number may he reach you? How much time do you think you'll need?"

or

• "Mr. Attorney is behind closed doors right now **but he'll be sorry he missed your call.** May he call you back between 11:00 and 12:00…?"

When a phone call comes in, check to

see if a Designated Hitter can help. We will talk more about the term Designated Hitter later on, but for now think of him or her as a person, preferably a paralegal, who, as mentioned before, shoulders much of the lower-level client communication burden of the attorney.

• "Mrs. Attorney is not available right now, but _____ may be able to help you. Let me put her through…"

If the Designated Hitter cannot help the caller:

• "Let me go ahead and set up a phone appointment so Mrs. Attorney does not miss you."

Key Block #3: See Clients

Another very important block in your time template is the time you reserve for seeing clients. In the reactive mode of scheduling, your time is up for grabs any time that you aren't in court. Clients can come in any time. In the proactive approach, your emphasis is on carving out time for production, then fitting your other tasks around your production time. This includes seeing clients.

For most of the attorneys we advise, the afternoon is the most popular choice for seeing clients as the attorneys are often in court or "in production" in the morning. They typically block off one to three hours a day depending on their caseload and typical new client intake rate per week. In addition to the morning being taken up by court and production time, many of them report that their energy level is a little lower in the afternoon and they prefer the stimulation of seeing and talking to people later in the day. This allows them to use their best energy for focused concentration in the mornings. If business is slow one week and they have an afternoon in which no client appointments are scheduled, they usually use it as extra production time to get caught up, for systemizing their practice, or to catch up on client development activities

At first it may seem too restrictive to offer a limited amount of time for client appointments. However, we find that when offered several afternoon appointment times, the clients will find a time that works for them without your having to offer any morning time slots. We know, however, that there is a small group of clients who have to come in the morning. In this situation, we suggest you see them in the morning and swap your morning power hour time for time in the afternoon. This way you do not lose production for that day. Some of the attorneys we advise occasionally see clients on a Saturday morning. It is okay to see clients on a Saturday morning, or even sometimes in the evenings, if they rank as a good client with a lot of potential. You might even swap time out during the week or during the day if you know you are going to be seeing somebody on a Saturday or in the evening. Just try not to do this very often. The idea is not to have you working more hours using the time template, but to maximize your efficiency for the hours you work.

As with your power hour block, it is especially important to block all interruptions when meeting with a client. Give the clients your complete attention in order to thoroughly interview them, understand their needs and assess their goals. There is nothing worse than an attorney who meets with a client and takes telephone calls at the same time. You should never be interrupted with phone calls unless they are an absolute emergency. Allowing yourself to be interrupted indicates to the client that you are not sensitive to them or that interested in their case. It is important to have the client like and trust you. Use your time with them to build rapport and determine if you can help them with their situation.

An important time saving practice is to have someone in on this first conversation, the initial meeting with a client, so that you do not have to spend a lot of time getting someone up to speed if you are behind closed doors or otherwise unavailable. We call this person your "Designated Hitter." This is a key person in making the time template work. We will refer to *Designated Hitters* in several sections of the book relating to their usefulness regarding interruptions and delegation. We have already mentioned the usefulness of the Designated Hitter as someone who is trained to take phone calls when the attorney is unavailable (see scripts for returning calls).

Let's take a minute to give a more detailed description of what we mean by this term. A Designated Hitter is, ideally, a specialized paralegal or legal assistant who is responsible for assisting the attorney on each case and who shoulders much of the lower-level client communication burden. The ideal candidate for this position is someone who is enough of a technician to handle the legal work delegated to them and enough of a "people person" to provide help to clients without disturbing the attorney.

The clients don't see this as a negative when a relationship with the Designated Hitter is established in the original meeting, and they can call him or her to get their questions answered more quickly.

Some law offices have the individual spend time with the potential clients upon their arrival. He or she can pre-interview them and get to know them before they go into the attorney's office or conference room. This is especially useful if the individual is a warm and comforting person, and the attorney is not.

Key Block #4: Case Status Review Meeting

Another very important block of time to dedicate in a new time template is something called "the *case status review* meeting." This is a systematic way for attorneys to track and follow up all the cases on their staff's workload. When done correctly, the attorney should leave with the feeling that he or she has been updated on the substantive and financial status of each case. This meeting, by the way, should not be confused with the short daily staff meetings that focus on short-term goals of that day. During this case status review meeting, individual files can be discussed and specific direction given in more detail.

If you are someone who doesn't delegate any work on your cases whatsoever, this is not a meeting that will interest you. However, most of you are delegating to one or more staff members or associates. As the confidants to many overwhelmed attorneys, we know that a lack of a system to track and follow up on delegated work is a rampant practice.

You may be someone who feels very out of touch with what is going on in your cases, which usually means feeling out of control and wondering everyday what important detail, date or deadline you are missing. It is highly uncomfortable to worry every day about what might fall through the cracks and we have already talked about the high percentage of grievances against lawyers on the basis of missing deadlines and disorganization. The potential for liability and client dissatisfaction is greatest in these situations: 1. When an attorney is either trying to do all the work himself or herself and just doesn't have the ability, or 2. When an attorney is delegating work without a system to track it and ensure it is being done correctly.

Schedule Case Status Review Meetings

To begin having a case status review meeting and tracking the financial status of each, you first block one or two hours a week or a couple of hours every other week on your time template. Choose a time in your week that won't be commonly affected by the court system or other obligations and commit to having this meeting without fail when it is scheduled. Emphasize the importance of the meeting to the staff (even if your staff is only one person) and have them see it as another opportunity to get their questions answered.

Make sure that all relevant staff has the meeting scheduled on their calendars for the entire year. Once you start holding the meetings, don't tolerate absences or excuses. This meeting is too important to let slide. If

you really desire a greater sense of control over your caseload, you must take responsibility for making the meeting happen. Don't hold it a few times, decide all is well and then abandon the idea because you get too busy. This is a system designed to support you when you are very busy. If a truly legitimate reason arises that forces you to cancel the meeting, be sure that it is rescheduled, not just dropped. This meeting, when done right, allows you to supervise a greater number of cases by improving your efficiency; thus, saves time and ensures that the needs and expectations of your clients are being met, or even exceeded.

The frequency with which you need to review your caseload depends on how many cases you have that are open and active – as well as your tolerance for long meetings. In all cases, special time and attention are spent on the A and B level clients (refer to the client scorecard in the section entitled "Select Clients Wisely") to maximize the care they receive. Here are the two most popular approaches taken by our attorney clients:

• *The Once-Per-Week Review* – This schedule is for those attorneys who don't have a high tolerance for long meetings, but have a large caseload to review. Divide the caseload, listed in alphabetical order, into quarters and review one quarter of the cases every week. At this level of frequency, it takes one month to review all the cases in your inventory.

• *The Twice-Per-Month Review* – For those attorneys who can tolerate a longer meeting, divide the caseload, listed in alphabetical order, in half and review half of the cases at each sitting. At this level of frequency, it takes two weeks to cycle through all of your caseload.

Whenever the meeting is held, all relevant staff members assemble in the attorney's office or conference room. They should have reviewed their batch of files in advance and preplanned their questions. The files are discussed one by one. In some cases the update only takes a minute or two, especially when there has not been any movement on the case. Other, more problematic or complex files will require a five, ten or fifteen minute discussion.

When problems are discussed, you may want to have the staff propose their suggestions on what is to be done. Though the supervising attorney is always the legal authority, critical thinking should be encouraged among the staff where it is appropriate. Having the staff think of and suggest solutions educates the staff to be more proactive when working the files. Often, afraid of making a mistake, staff members and even some associates are paralyzed by fear and unable to use their own judgment even within the limits of their job description. One of the solutions to this problem is the use of systematized checklists that we address in the section entitled, "Systemize Your Office." Basically, checklists help you keep track of what is happening with a file.

Many law offices spend an hour or two in the case status meeting and keep track of how much discussion time was spent per file in order to bill clients appropriately. Some don't keep track and don't bill for the time. If the discussion has been a substantive one, and the smallest increments of your billing program are not too large to apply, billing is appropriate.

Another way to approach this meeting is to meet with one staff member at a time to discuss just the files that are in that person's control. If you divide your practice among several disciplines and each staff member works a different type of file, you may just meet with that one staff person and his or her files and have a sort of successive file review. So you can either have individuals with their group of files in or you can have all of your staff involved, depending on your practice mix. To make this meeting less tedious, you can hold it on a lunch hour and bring in pizza, or some other kind of food, while you are going through the cases. Your staff will actually look forward to the meeting if you make it a little bit fun.

Some attorneys we work with combine this meeting with their weekly planning time according to the time template. The attorney will do his or her planning in the morning, then a file review afterward, so they get an overview of all the files they are working on for that week.

Include Financial Status In Case Status Meetings

The financial status of each case in your inventory is an area that is often insufficiently tracked. When this is true, it contributes further to a feeling of being out of control and may result in time and money lost. The case status review meeting is the perfect opportunity to start systematizing the tracking of the financial end of a case. If you have ever done a great deal of work on a case and not gotten paid, you are not alone. The experience of attorneys working diligently for their clients and not being paid appears to be universal. We have never worked with an attorney who hasn't been burned by non-payment, often repeatedly. On some occasions, staff spent weeks or months working on cases where no fees were ever paid. This trend is so widespread that it has almost come to be accepted as the cost of doing business as an attorney. It doesn't have to be.

One of the reasons this problem exists is that attorneys have poor accounting systems. They may have great accounting software, but they don't look at their reports until it is too late. We have found that it pays to go beyond the cursory once a month review that many attorneys give their finances. It is not difficult to do. You can incorporate a financial status review into your case status review meeting and create part of what we, at Atticus, call the "Zero-Tolerance Collections System." This method involves proper client selection, always getting a retainer, and having a replenishment clause in your fee agreement. This combination of actions substantially reduces the amount of time you give away.

Here are two easy ways you can incorporate the financial status component into your case status review meeting:

1. *Bring your accounts receivables report to the meeting.* Before the case status review meeting, have your bookkeeper print out an accounts receivables report by client. As the files are reviewed, the attorney checks the report to see the financial status of the client. If there is a problem, the attorney can, if appropriate, stop work on the file until the client's account is brought current. As the cases with outstanding balances are discussed, the attorney makes a list of clients who need to be contacted and brought current. After the meeting, the attorney and/or staff makes the calls to resolve the situation. (Note: the rules on stopping work while a case is in litigation vary from state to state; in some areas judges are sympathetic; in other areas they are not.) In any event, you should not find yourself preparing for trial or otherwise investing a lot of time in a case when you either haven't been paid, or have no guarantee of being paid after the case is resolved.

Take action early to prevent this from happening.

2. *Invite your bookkeeper to the case status review meeting.* The bookkeeper (or whoever does the billing in your office) can systematically review the outstanding balance on a per-case basis. If the bookkeeper is at the meeting, a quick discussion can be had of who should contact the client about outstanding payments and the bookkeeper leaves with an action plan. Work is stopped, or slowed when appropriate, and no one is putting time in that will never be paid. If a trial is approaching, a special "trial retainer" can be requested before work resumes (always check your local rules for compliance).

Three Side Benefits Of Case Status Meetings

Once you start scheduling your case status review meetings, you will notice several side benefits of institutionalizing this kind of meeting in your monthly or weekly schedule:

• Staff knows at all times the status of each case, making them more prepared to step in or field questions, where appropriate, without interrupting the lawyer.

• Increased ability on the part of the attorney to responsibly handle more cases. Because you are delegating a significant portion of the work, the number of cases you can handle rises, as does your profitability.

• The psychological benefit of holding this kind of meeting is the enhanced feeling of being in control of your caseload. You can forecast workloads more accurately.

As you work your way through the files in your caseload, you may notice that all have a different life cycle. This helps you in planning how much time is needed for certain types of cases.

Some cases, such as a simple will in an estate planning practice, are opened, worked on in a routine fashion, then completed. When all of the information is available, they follow a fairly predictable route.

Other cases, such as a contested divorce with custody issues in a family law practice, are highly unpredictable and will make more halting progress with much stopping and starting.

A complex case could be opened, worked on for several weeks, halted due to a change of heart, restarted and worked for several more months, then stopped, started again and almost end up in trial – only to settle at the last moment.

Some cases can drag on for years. It is important to identify the unpredictable cases, and focus on working through the predictable ones as quickly and efficiently as you can to increase your control over your inventory.

Categorize Your Files To Predict Workload

Given that all files in your caseload are not progressing at the same speed, it can be difficult to assess how much work you actually have in your pipeline. How much of your time will they take up in your weekly and monthly calendar? Glancing at your case list will give you an overview that includes all matters currently open. It may not, however, tell you which files are on hold and don't require action at this time. To help you get a true picture of the amount of work within your pipeline and how much time you need to allow, your files should be grouped into the following three categories:

Open-Active – These are the files that are currently being worked. There are no obstacles to their completion and it is appropriate for work to proceed.

Open-Suspended – This category of files includes those in a holding pattern due to an impasse, lack of cooperation on the part of clients or opposing counsel, non-payment or any other reason. These files should be discussed as to whether or not they will move from this category or stay on hold. It is useful to distinguish them from the "Open and Active" files since there is

no time being devoted to the files and they should therefore be set aside, but tracked. The decision to complete or close the file will remain pending until something occurs to dictate its course.

Open-Need Closed – These files are significantly complete and may lack one or two items before they can be officially closed. Unlike files that are open-suspended, finishing the file is dependent on actions that are within the law firm's control and not dependent on another source. Don't let a large number of these files linger on your case list, as they will just add to your sense of being overwhelmed. Better to finish up these files and move them into your longer-term storage system. If you have many of these cases, set a goal to close several a week until you get through them.

The next benefit to the case status review meeting is that it allows the staff, all of the staff, if you have them all in the meeting, to know what is going on with any file. That way, if a staff member who is not working the file takes a call regarding a specific file, they have a bit of familiarity with what is going on in the case. Not that they would answer any substantive legal questions, but they are at least informed of whatever progress is going on. They should be trained to elevate any substantive questions to the attorney and less substantive questions to the Designated Hitter.

Having the staff up to date on cases

increases the likelihood that the attorney who infrequently delegates work to his or her staff will begin to practice delegation more often. Being able to delegate to staff who are up to date can be a significant time-saving practice. This meeting also improves the efficiency of those attorneys who already delegate, but have not systematized the practice until now.

Finally, there is no benefit like peace of mind. The psychological benefit of knowing that each case has undergone a systematic review impacts everyone in the office at all levels. You have set it up so that you and your staff are spending quality, pre-scheduled time on each case as opposed to spending catch-as-catch-can moments and dreading that something is slipping through the cracks.

Use A Case Status Review Form To Organize Meetings

To ensure efficiency and continuity in your tracking process, you want to keep a succinct written record of the activity on each file. We have included a sample Case Status Review Form that accommodates the different file designations: Open-Active; Open-Suspended; and Open-Need Closed as listed above. Use our form as-is only if you have a tiny caseload. Most law offices create their own spreadsheet so that they have a couple of pages dedicated just to the Open-Active file category.

To help you in the organizational process, a sample Case Status Review Form can be found at the end of this chapter.

By having these file reviews on a regular basis and by combining this with the financial review and case-specific checklists for each file, you know each file is being touched on a regular basis and nothing is falling through the cracks.

(Note that we cover creating and using case-specific checklists in the section entitled "Practice Delegation" later in the book.) Have these meetings as frequently as you need and view them not as a tedious chore but as a tool that actually helps you manage and control the quality of a larger number of cases. We encourage you to create this worthy new tradition for yourself and your firm.

Key Block #5: Meet With Staff

At Atticus, we view meeting with staff as absolutely critical to the success of a practice. With that commitment in mind, we focus on three types of formal meetings: case status review meetings, the meeting element of the three-part power hour and general staff meetings. We have covered case status review meetings in depth because of their significance and detailed format. We provided you with some guidelines on the meeting element of the three-part power hour as well. In this next discussion, we give you some tips on general staff meetings.

In the general staff meeting, you inform the staff of your goals for the week and talk about upcoming court appearances. In turn, you discuss their goals for the week. Administrative issues may also be discussed as well. That would include systems implementation, time-keeping problems or employee benefits issues. Some firms opt to have a short general staff meeting on Mondays and then go straight into their case status review meeting.

If you are organized enough to do this on Monday, good work. It sets you up for a powerful week. If your practice is too fraught with crisis on Mondays catching up with events that have occurred with your clients over the weekend, a meeting later in the week works as well. If you hold your case status review meeting later in the week, you may be able use that meeting as a double duty case status review and general information exchange between you and staff. Keep in mind that the general staff meeting is less detailed, more an overview of the week, and may contain conversation about non-substantive issues. By contrast, the daily meeting is intended to contain the substantive issues you are dealing with that day.

However you decide to "meet with staff," let them know that you will find a time after your planning session to bring them up to date on what your goals are for the week. This is true whether your staff is one person or a team of 10. Naturally, since your goals dictate many of their goals, it is important to meet with them and give them an overview of the time-sensitive issues you will be focusing in on. You may decide to have the entire group participate in this meeting or you may decide it is more efficient to bring in one person at a time and speak with them. It all depends on how much your team is cross-utilized.

Key Block #6: Attend To Administration

Partner-level attorneys have more work of an administrative nature than non-partner associates, but every attorney has administrative work to a certain degree. For partner-level attorneys, there is timekeeping and financial reports to review, accounts receivable and accounts payable to deal with, employee evaluations to prepare and benefits package issues to consider. On your time template, this is a catch-all time block to capture all of the financial, staffing, equipment and facilities-related tasks that come up on a weekly basis. Some weeks the demand for administrative time is great-

er than others. An hour may be fine for some, and for others grossly inadequate. If you are in a partnership where the administrative responsibilities are shouldered by several partners, the burden may be less. If you have a full- or part-time bookkeeper, the financial burden is definitely lessened. Given the make-up of your firm, use your best judgment to determine how much time you must reserve for yourself in this often overlooked, but important block of time.

Key Block #7: Systemize Your Practice

At Atticus, we believe that you, whether a sole practitioner or a partner in your firm, should block time every week to work on the systems that form the infrastructure of your practice. Typical projects would be learning new practice management software or developing a new intake system or a system for screening new clients. These are projects that do not get done unless someone is dedicated to making them happen, either by doing the job themselves or delegating it. You see some specific examples of systemizing in the section entitled "Systemize Your Office."

A block of time, proactively scheduled one to three hours a week, gives you the opportunity to either do the work or review the work that goes into systemizing your practice. It is an investment in the future that allows you to save many hours on repetitive tasks. This action puts you in the pro-active camp and allows you to leave the reactive crisis mode behind. Your systems should be designed to save time and maximize profitability. It is critical to have the staff participate in the creation of any new systems (i.e., new file opening protocol) as they are usually the ones to use them.

When you choose to block this time on your time template varies. Monday and Friday seem to be popular days for these meetings, though any day will do. Some attorneys we know have lunch at their desks once a week and specifically dedicate that time to non-substantive projects. Some take themselves out to lunch and bring a project along to review at the table.

If the attorney is working on a project that involves members of their staff, they set a standing meeting for all relevant staff once a week if the need is great. Twice a month suffices if the office is fairly systemized already. We work with a couple of attorneys who work in their home office one morning a week on special systemizing projects. It provides a nice break in their week and allows them to work from home for short periods, which they really enjoy.

Clearly, many systems projects need to be worked on in the office for maximum efficiency. Wherever you

schedule yourself, find a time and a place where you are comfortable and able to concentrate. Working on the business of your practice deserves your time and attention. Don't overlook it.

Key Block #8: Develop Clients

Another very important time block in your time template should be reserved for developing clients. When we first began advising attorneys on their practices, our main focus was client development. As we worked them through the process of developing new business, one of the most common complaints we would hear was, "I don't have time to market." As legal practice advisors, we suggest that you must proactively make the time to market. Your very practice depends upon it unless you are so swamped with business that you never have to worry. If so, skip this discussion and dedicate your time to production and seeing new clients. Most attorneys, however, need to be cultivating new business even when they are busy. Troughs sometimes follow peaks in demand.

We believe that the best, most loyal and least price-sensitive clients come from Referral Sources who know you, like you and trust you. Developing this level of rapport with Referral

Sources does not happen overnight. It takes time for the relationship to build. Clients may come from a new Referral Source after just one or two meetings, but most likely it takes several or many contacts for the referrer to get to know you well enough to recommend you.

The time and repetition that client development requires makes it something of a numbers game. At Atticus, we recommend three substantial marketing contacts a week. Three lunches are ideal. If you block out three lunches a week and dedicate them to marketing, that results in over 100 marketing lunches on a yearly basis. This provides a lot of time to maintain rapport with existing Referral Sources as well as cultivate new Referral Sources.

Whatever number of lunches you decide to dedicate to marketing, you need to block them out and stick to them. Seeing them blocked out on your calendar makes it more difficult for you to "forget" to market yourself. This is when the real value of the time template becomes apparent. It is a structure of support and a visual reminder for you to think ahead about what clients or influencers you can take out to lunch to fill those slots.

It is helpful to have an assistant to work with you to keep your lunch schedule filled well in advance. You supply the assistant with a list of existing influencers you wish to see on a regular basis. You feed the assistants the cards of new contacts you meet as you interact in the community. This can be a huge help, especially if you are bad about taking the time to initiate lunches, but you are great once you get to your lunch meeting.

An alternative to the marketing lunch idea is to have a standing Friday afternoon or Wednesday afternoon time block that is dedicated to marketing. For many of our clients who play golf, the Friday afternoon golf game is a popular marketing strategy. This strategy allows them to invite one to three other people to join them in golf on a weekly basis. That amounts to 50 some-odd golf games over the course of a year. When multiplied by one to three people, the result is a minimum of 50 and a maximum or 150 marketing contacts yearly. Given the amount of time there is to talk when playing golf, there is a significant amount of rapport-building time with Referral Sources and important friends of your firm.

At Atticus, we instill our clients with the idea that there must be continual Top Of Mind Awareness (TOMA) regarding word-of-mouth marketing. People must remember you. The way they remember you is by having a variety of interactions with you throughout the year. These interactions can be small, even in the form of a telephone call. They can be a bit larger, and occur in the form of a lunch meeting or an evening event.

Many of our clients put a once or twice monthly evening event on their template, to which they invite Referral Sources and their spouses out to dinner or to some other function such as a community event, a charity function, or gallery opening.

You can plan marketing events that allow you to spend more time with all members of your family, which is most likely one of your personal goals. You can invite Referral Sources and their families to outings and events such as a picnic or barbeque in the park, a pool party, a boating excursion or a sporting event. Going to a game with your son or daughter and inviting Referral Sources to bring along their kids is a great way to spend more time with your family.

Use your time template to structure your client development efforts. It is important to institutionalize your marketing time blocks, because you will find you never have the time to market unless you take this proactive approach and carve out time very aggressively in your schedule.

Design Your Own Time Template

In the next exercise, "Designing Your Own Time Template," you are provided with some guidelines to help you focus in on the first draft of your time template. Refer to the examples you have seen earlier in this section and use the information given on the key blocks. As you continue to practice, you will soon be in control of your valuable time and not in the predicament of being a victim of reactive time management.

• Exercise: Design Your Own Time Template

Instructions: Look at the two time template examples we have provided at the end of this chapter: Regularly Scheduled Court Appearance Time Template and Low Court Appearance Time Template. Decide which one best fits your type of practice. Using the blank weekly time template provided, create time blocks for the nine key time blocks listed below:

1. plan your week

2. production – producing documents, preparing for trial and supervising technical/legal tasks (may alternate days with court)

3. court time (where applicable, may alternate days with production)

4. meet with staff in various types of meetings, (general staff meetings daily pre-production meetings, case status review meetings)

5. see clients

6. return phone calls

7. attend to administration

8. develop clients

9. systematize your practice

Plan Your Weekly Appointments With A Planning Sheet

Now that you have your time template in place, you have control of blocks of time in your week. What you don't know at this point is what appointments you need to make or what administrative duties you have to attend to, etc. We think it is valuable to make decisions regarding exactly what you will attempt in a given week with the framework of the time template in mind. To assist you in doing that, we have provided you with a blank Weekly Time Template Block Planning Sheet at the end of the chapter. Make a master copy of the blank sheet and then follow the instructions to assist you with the process. As you fulfill your commitment to your weekly planning hour and become skilled at planning week by week, you may not need a tool to help you through the process. In the beginning, it gives you added support in staying on target.

Ensuring Support For The Time Template Concept From Staff

It is important for your staff and the other attorneys in your office to un-derstand how you are attempting to implement and why you are attempting to implement a time template. You really need the support of other people to make the time template work. We suggest sitting down with your staff and having a meeting in order to explain to them the concept of the time template. We say that you are the first line of defense when it comes to implementing and enforcing your time template and your self-management. However, your staff, if they are not enrolled in the idea, if they do not recognize the value and the importance of the time template, can be the first ones to sabotage it, though they may have the best of intentions.

It is useful to have a script when you have this conversation because the time template concept is new and different. We have included a script entitled "Ensure Staff Support for the Time Template Script" in the Appendix of this book. It is helpful to use our language, or at least be guided by our language, when enlisting support for your new time management plan.

Frequent Court Appearance Time Template

The time template shown below is intended for use by the attorney who spends a lot of time in court. Use this sample template as a guide to creating a time template that works for you.

	MONDAY	TUESDAY	WEDNESDAY	THURSDAY	FRIDAY
9:00 a.m.	Plan Week	Court or Prod. Time	Court or Prod. Time	Court or Prod. Time	Court or Prod. Time
10:00 a.m.	Gen. Staff Meeting				
11:00 a.m.	Return Calls	Return Calls	Return Calls	Return Calls	Return Calls
		Meet w/Staff	Meet w/Staff	Meet w/Staff	Meet w/Staff
12:00 p.m.	Systemizing Lunch	Client Dev. Lunch	Client Dev. Lunch	Case Status Review Lunch	
1:00 p.m.	See Clients	See Clients	See Clients	See Clients	Client Dev. Event
2:00 p.m.					
3:00 p.m.					
4:00 p.m.					
5:00 p.m.	Production	Production	Production	Administration	

Low Court Appearance Time Template

The time template shown below is intended for use by the attorney who does not spend a lot of time in court. This template features three client development lunches instead of two, eliminating the Friday afternoon client development event. The template includes a three-hour case status meeting on Friday morning.

	MONDAY	TUESDAY	WEDNESDAY	THURSDAY	FRIDAY
9:00 a.m.	Plan Week	Meet w/ Staff	Meet w/ Staff	Meet w/ Staff	Case Status Review
10:00 a.m.	General Meeting	Production	Production	Production	
11:00 a.m.	Return Calls	Return Calls	Return Calls	Return Calls	
12:00 p.m.	Systemizing Lunch	Client Dev. Lunch	Client Dev. Lunch	Client Dev. Lunch	Free Lunch
1:00 p.m.	See Clients	See Clients	See Clients	See Clients	See Clients
2:00 p.m.					
3:00 p.m.					
4:00 p.m.	Return Calls	Return Calls	Return Calls	Return Calls	Return Calls
5:00 p.m.	Production	Production	Production	Production	Admin.

Sample Case Status Review Form

To ensure efficiency and continuity in your tracking process, keep a written record of the activity on each file. Use our form as-is only if you have a tiny caseload.

File Name	Tasks	By Whom	Date Asgn.	Date Due
Open-Active				
Open-Suspended				
Open-Needs-Closed				

Weekly Time Template

Use this blank weekly time template to work out your own weekly time blocks. Give each staff member a copy of this template so that he or she can keep it handy when screening your calls. Your staff can use these blanks to create their own time templates as well.

	MONDAY	TUESDAY	WEDNESDAY	THURSDAY	FRIDAY
9:00 a.m.					
9:30 a.m.					
10:00 a.m.					
10:30 a.m.					
11:00 a.m.					
11:30 a.m.					
12:00 p.m.					
12:30 p.m.					
1:00 p.m.					
1:30 p.m.					
2:00 p.m.					
2:30 p.m.					
3:30 p.m.					
4:00 p.m.					
4:30 p.m.					
5:00 p.m.					
5:30 p.m.					

Weekly Time Template Blank Planning Sheet

Instructions: Review your personal and professional vision statements, then your calendar. Work backwards from upcoming deadlines and court dates to block preparation time in advance on your calendar.

PRIORITY PRODUCTION:
What are your <u>most important</u> production goals this week?
(Set appointments for these tasks in the "Production" of your Weekly Time Template.)

_____   _____
_____   _____

PRODUCTION SUPERVISION:
List <u>the most important</u> tasks you are supervising/tracking this week.

_____   _____
_____   _____

MARKETING ACTIVITIES:
Who will you initiate contact with?

_____   _____
_____   _____

SYSTEMS/OPERATIONS:
How will you improve your systems/operations this week?

_____   _____
_____   _____

ADMINISTRATIVE GOALS:

_____   _____
_____   _____

STAFFING:
What can you do to –
Acknowledge/reward/motivate staff? _____
Train staff? _____
Hire staff? _____
Meet with your designated hitter? _____
Practice delegating more? _____

PROFITABILITY/FINANCIAL GOALS:

_____   _____
_____   _____

FAMILY/PERSONAL GOALS: **EXERCISE GOALS:**   **SPIRITUAL GOALS:**

_____   _____   _____
_____   _____   _____
_____   _____   _____

APPENDIX #2

Rainmaker Profile

21 Marketing Assets™

☐ **1. The Top Twenty List**
The top twenty refers to referral sources who send you the best files and most frequently. To qualify, your list must have <u>at least</u> twenty good referral sources to be a complete asset.

☐ **2. Contact Management Software**
This is software specifically designed to capture personal and professional information about a firm's clients and referral sources. To claim this asset, you must have the software installed, your referrals in the database, and use it daily.

☐ **3. A Marketing Assistant**
The Marketing Assistant assists the attorney in achieving their marketing goals.

☐ **4. The Laser and Elevator Talks**
These are brief, but powerful introductory statements that educate the listener as to the type of clients the attorney works with; the kind of problems the attorney solves; and the approach the attorney takes to solving those problems.

☐ **5. Storytelling**
Stories are the "stealth bomber" of marketing. You will need at least three Marketing Stories in your portfolio to complete this asset.

☐ **6. A Professional Website**
To claim as an asset, the firm's website should be brochure level, meaning informative, professional in appearance, consistent with the rest of the firm's marketing materials and easy to navigate.

☐ **7. A Public Relations Campaign**
Also known as "PR", this is the process of raising an attorney's or firm's profile through print, radio and televised media.

☐ **8. The Interview Process**
For attorneys that want to build rapport with their referral sources, the Interview process is unmatched. In order to count this asset, you must have an interview script and have completed at least 10 interviews.

☐ **9. An Accountability Partner**
This refers to a person who holds an attorney accountable for the marketing actions they have agreed to carry out.

☐ **10. An Annual Marketing Retreat and Plan**
An annual retreat in which marketing objectives are discussed and established helps a firm to focus on its most important strategies for growing the firm.

☐ **11. A Monthly Marketing Plan**
To claim as an asset, one must have specific marketing goals for each month which breaks down the often-overwhelming task of developing new clients into smaller, more achievable steps.

21 Marketing Assets ™

☐ **12. Signature Marketing Event**
Often themed around holidays, this group event can serve to announce a new office, introduce a new partner, celebrate a win, or support a charity. To claim this asset, the firm must have an annual event to gather referral sources and friends of the firm together.

☐ **13. Client Intake Matrix**
In order to screen new clients and their legal needs prior to converting them to paying clients it is important to evaluate prospective client- based criteria such as: their ability to pay, their personality, the referral source who sent them, the type of work they bring and other factors which shift according to practice area.

☐ **14. Referral Map**
To use a Referral Map an attorney identifies the different categories of referral sources who exist in the community and who intersect with the attorney's potential clients.

☐ **15. A Client "Aftercare" Program**
An aftercare program can be a service or product, fee based or free, that is provided after the primary service has been completed and adds value to the clients life.

☐ **16. TOMA Tool**
TOMA stands for "Top Of Mind Awareness". To claim as an asset, one must have a regular, at least quarterly, communication channel to their client.

☐ **17. Tracking System**
This is an automated or manual process by which new clients are asked who referred them to the law office. This information is then tracked so that the referral source is thanked appropriately for their actions.

☐ **18. A Client-Centered Office**
An office space that is designed to meet the needs of clients will convey a sense of professionalism and competence, but will also be friendly and welcoming in its appearance. To claim this asset, attorneys will want to complete the *"From the Clients Eyes"* checklist.

☐ **19. A Professional Image**
The way you present yourself to other people is often the deciding factor in how you will be perceived. It is important to be well groomed, but comfortable with yourself, authentic in your presentation and at the same time, put your best foot forward.

☐ **20. A Marketing Time Template**
Blocking out time for marketing actions such as breakfast, lunches, dinners or events is vital to ensuring that your plan is implemented. To claim this asset, the Marketing Time Template must be organized and place.

☐ **21. A "Thank You" Template**
Acknowledging referral sources for their efforts is an important part of the rainmaking process. A "Thank You" System would include having an inventory of cards and/or gifts at your disposal to send out to referral sources.

TOTAL = _____

Five Marketing Habits™

1. Three Marketing Contacts a Week Habit

In order for a contact to be considered substantial it must be long enough (20 minutes to 1 hour) to allow you to connect with your referral source and develop further rapport. Generally, lunches, dinners, longer phone calls, and face-to-face meetings fall into this category.

2. Asking for Referrals Habit

It is important to regularly let clients and referrals know, either at the conclusion of a case, or somewhere in the middle, that your practice thrives on referrals from people like them. At a minimum, asking for one referral per day would constitute a habit.

3. Sharpening the Saw Habit

Reading a marketing book, article, or attending a workshop once per quarter can keep you on top. Staying current with the latest marketing ideas by reading a marketing book once per quarter can help to keep you in action and motivated to promote your firm.

4. The Thank You Habit

Thanking your referral sources <u>every time</u> they send a referral will reinforce your referral base. Even if you don't end up working with the referred client, thanking your referral sources is vital to maintaining your referral relationship. Depending on the situation, this can be done through cards, letters, phone calls, gifts, lunches, dinners, gift certificates or site visits.

5. The Adding Names Habit

Adding new names to your contact management list will give you a great base to grow your practice. Add <u>at least</u> five new contacts each month to your list and you can claim this habit.

Your Atticus Rainmaker™ Score:

Enter the number
of marketing habits

Enter the number **X**
of marketing assets

Multiply assets times habits
to reach your overall score

RAINMAKER PROFILE	
Mist-Maker	0-10
Rainmaker	11-30
Rainmaker II	31-50
Rainmaker III	51-80
Master	81-105

INDEX